Place-names of
Greater London

JOHN FIELD

B. T. BATSFORD LTD.
London

First published 1980
© John Field 1980

All rights reserved. No part of this publication
may be reproduced, in any form or by any means,
without permission from the Publishers

ISBN 0 7134 2538 5

Printed in Great Britain
by Redwood-Burn Ltd.,
Trowbridge & Esher
for the publishers, B. T. Batsford Ltd.,
4 Fitzhardinge Street, London W1H 0AH

Typesetting by Malvern Typesetting Services

Contents

LIST OF ILLUSTRATIONS   vi

ACKNOWLEDGMENTS   vii

MAP OF GREATER LONDON   viii–ix

INTRODUCTION   1

   The development of London   2
   The pattern of naming   3
   Settlers and their languages   4
   Interpretation of place-names   8
   Some common place-name elements   8
   Street-names   13
   Arrangement of dictionary entries   14

LOCATION OF PLACES   15

   Postal Districts   16
   Tables of abbreviations:
      1. Location symbols   18
      2. General   18

PART 1. DICTIONARY OF GREATER LONDON
         PLACE-NAMES   23

PART 2. STREET-NAMES OF GREATER LONDON   105

   The oldest street-names   105
   Street-names alluding to direction and topography   107
   High Streets and High Roads   110
   Field-names and descriptive names   112
   Aeronautical and railway names   118
   Places of worship and saints' names   120
   Place-names, estates of the nobility and gentry   127
   Foreign place-names   135
   Personal names in street-names   141
   Names from literature, painting, music and history   142
   Communications and the world of learning   151
   Politicians and generals   155
   Numerical and alphabetical names   158
   Memorials to philanthropy   160
   Games and recreation   161
   Some curiosities   164

GLOSSARY OF PLACE-NAME ELEMENTS   166
BIBLIOGRAPHY   175
INDEX OF STREET-NAMES   177
GENERAL INDEX   183

List of illustrations between pages 86 and 87

1. A page from the Domesday Book (1086), with entries relating to East and West Ham and Chingford.

2. The East End of London in 1690 (from Jacques de la Feuille's map) showing open fields within a short distance of the walls of the City.

3. Remains of the chapel of Savoy Palace (from an engraving by S. Rawle, 1798).

4. Ely House, where Ely Place now is (from an eighteenth-century engraving).

5. The western boundary of Middlesex in 1672.

6. Western London in 1672 (from John Warburton's *Middlesex*).

7. The Lea valley and the Kent-Surrey border (from Rocque's map of the Environs of London, 1769).

8. The monument to George IV, which bequeathed its name when it was demolished to make way for a railway terminus—King's Cross.

9. The approximate boundaries of Greater London embodied in the London Postal District in 1857.

Acknowledgments

For permission to make use of copyright material, I offer sincere thanks to Professor Kenneth Cameron, Ph.D., F.B.A., Director of the English Place-Name Survey.

At the outset of this work, David Mills discussed with me a number of matters needing consideration, and gave me much encouraging advice, for which I thank him most warmly. I am grateful to my colleague Robin Brumby for his unfailing interest in the progress of the book. Thanks are due also to Leslie Dunkling for helpful suggestions and information, and to my sister, Christine Greenstock, who has kindly clarified a number of points of local history.

I am grateful for professional help and friendly suggestions provided by John Parfitt, Head of Library Services at Dacorum College. The invaluable assistance of other librarians and archivists is also cordially acknowledged. Thanks are due also to the Public Record Office for the facsimile of Folio cxxvii of Doomesday Book. I am also much indebted to Mr R. N. G. Rowland for helpful advice and information, and for the generous loan of his *Street-Names of Acton*, the value of which extends well beyond the area it nominally covers.

I offer my wife, Mary, my best thanks for her unstinting aid not only in checking and collating but also in providing much helpful comment, which has enabled me to avoid numerous obscurities. I am glad to acknowledge the assistance of all those named, as well as of others; if, despite their explanations and guidance, many imperfections remain, I alone must be regarded as responsible.

The illustration on the jacket and Plates 2, 5, 6, 7. and 8 have been taken from the collection of the Greater London Record Office and were reproduced by permission of the Curator.

Greater London, showing the boundaries of the London Boroughs and the City of London

Introduction

During the past fifty years, place-name studies—like other disciplines connected with language—have made great and rapid progress. Vast quantities of evidence have been collected and published; techniques of study and interpretation have been developed; and an increasing collaboration with archaeologists, historians, and historical geographers has provided the means of cross-checking data and confirming results. Consequently, not only is there now a high degree of certainty about the meanings of the names as words, but to a greater and greater extent the significance of place-names in their historical and geographical contexts has been demonstrated.

This book offers an informal survey of Greater London place-names. The comments and explanations are intended for the general reader, rather than for the specialist—who would probably have access to the county volumes of the English Place-Name Society. Greater London names are at present to be found in portions of no fewer than four of the Society's volumes (those for Essex, Hertfordshire, Middlesex, and Surrey), and the indebtedness of this work to those systematic studies will be obvious and is duly acknowledged.

In the Dictionary section of the book is to be found a comprehensive collection of the district names of the area. Greater London is unique in the English local-government system in that—unlike the present-day counties—its sub-units are not known as *Districts* but as *London Boroughs*, which are further divided into *Wards*. 'District name', therefore, means not that of an official administrative unit, but merely one of the names, in current use, of the parishes, hamlets, or other areas which have become the component parts of the conurbation. Occasionally, the names of main streets have become regarded as district names and so are included; designations of other features of considerable size also have a discoverable history and interpretation, and in the alphabetic sequence will also be found the names of railway stations, parks and other open spaces, some large public buildings, rivers, and lakes.

Discussion of street-names in general presents a less tractable problem. Within an area of about 700 square miles the number of streets is such that a mere enumeration in double column would fill a normal-sized book. Selection has therefore been necessary, and although the survey in Part 2 attempts to be comprehensive of the entire area, it can of course lay no claim to completeness. More detailed studies must be left to the dedicated local historians of London Boroughs or of their constituent parishes.

The development of London

For many centuries, the name *London* was used of the busy, densely-populated municipality still referred to as The City, and until the eighteenth century it would have referred to nothing but the historic 'Square Mile'. As surrounding villages grew and became suburbs, a kind of unity developed throughout the urban conglomeration, until in 1888 formal recognition was given to this inter-relationship by the creation of the County of London—of which, curiously, the ancient City was not part.

In some ways the growth of the urban area meant a diminution of the City itself. Its boundaries have remained unchanged for hundreds of years, but its population decreased from an estimated 185,000 in 1577 to a mere 27,000 in 1901, steadily declining to 4,600 in 1961. Many of those who left the City went to reside in what were formerly rural villages, but the emigrants still considered themselves Londoners. Paradoxically, local loyalties also persisted, and many inhabitants of the outer suburbs refused to acknowledge the existence of the County of London up to the very moment of its demise.

Greater London, as an administrative entity, came into existence in 1964, its Council taking full powers one year later. The new area comprised the entire former County of London, the greater part of Middlesex (which was abolished as a separate county), and the metropolitan fringes of Essex, Hertfordshire, Surrey, and Kent. The term *Greater London* was first used in 1882, with reference to the Metropolitan Police District, the boundaries of which now almost coincide with those of the new administrative area.

The component areas of the former County—the Metropolitan Boroughs, created in 1899—were abolished when Greater London was established; their place was taken by London Boroughs, which also replaced the various local authorities beyond the former L.C.C. boundaries. The new arrangements meant the disappearance of some names as titles of local authorities: Acton, Woolwich, Dagenham, Barnes, and Battersea were among these casualties of reorganisation. Although some old names were put to new uses, as when the Liberty of Havering-atte-Bower became a London Borough, only one name was actually devised to designate one of the new authorities—Newham, representing the combination of East Ham and West Ham. Greater London was happily spared the desperate inventions of uninstructed fantasy of the kind inflicted on some new Districts elsewhere in the country.

The pattern of naming

The key to the interpretation of place-names is the recognition of the elements of which each name is composed; without this knowledge, suggestions about meanings are no more than speculation and conjecture. A modern map, however accurately detailed, tells very little about the significance of the place-names; the provision of early spellings of the names is essential for this purpose—but it should not be forgotten that the map is an invaluable aid in interpretation.

With the assistance of the findings of place-name scholars, however, it is possible to look at the map of Greater London and observe particular facts about the area which the names reveal. The disadvantage of a dictionary is that groups of places cannot be viewed simultaneously, but this problem is overcome to some extent by cross-references. On the other hand, some names of particular interest (such as Harrow or Penge) are physically isolated and so suffer no handicap by being individually studied. The importance of Harrow is its association with Anglo-Saxon paganism, the name being a valuable pointer (meaning 'heathen temple'), and the hill-top site confirming the significance of the name. The interest of Penge lies in the Celtic origin of the name and in the special connexion of the place with the manor of Battersea, whose inhabitants drove their pigs to feed in the woodlands there.

The names of riverside places deserve special attention. Here there is a curious counterpoint of uniformity and variety. The second element is identical in Putney, Chelsea, and Stepney; Battersea and Bermondsey also have a component in common, but it is not the same as that of the Putney group. Lambeth, Erith, and Rotherhithe have the same second element as Putney, and their modern forms are considerably closer to their originals than those of the others; for these were landing places—*hithes*—whereas Battersea and Bermondsey were islands amid riverside marshes. Another name element associated with riverside settlements, Old English *hamm*, 'land in a river bend', is found in the Greater London names Fulham, Twickenham, and West Ham. In Hampton this element is compounded with Old English *tūn*, 'farm, estate', which also occurs frequently as an independent element in names all over the area, e.g., in Leyton, Merton, Edmonton, and Acton.

3

Three names in north-west London—Harlesden, Neasden, and Willesden—appear, from their modern spellings, to have similar meanings. Early forms, however, show that the second element in Harlesden is in fact *tūn*, 'farm', in Neasden, *dūn*, 'hill', as also that in Willesden. The modern spellings of all three give no real clue to their origin, but other names in *-den*, south of the river, have a similar derivation, namely Malden and Morden; yet in Hillingdon and Hendon the same element has become *-don* in present-day forms.

Settlements at river-crossings are found all over the country, and there is no shortage of names indicating fords in Greater London; Deptford, Brentford, Ilford, Stratford, and Romford bear sufficient witness to the numerous tributaries of the Thames crossed by the routes of early settlers. The heavy woodland to the north and south of the London basin is commemorated in such names as Barnet, Northolt, Northwood, Finchley, Bexley, and Bromley.

Other final elements in London names include *hām*, 'homestead, village', in Streatham, Tottenham, and Dagenham, *worð*, 'enclosure', in Wandsworth and Walworth, *wīc*, 'specialised farm', in Chiswick, and 'port, landing place', in Woolwich and Greenwich, and *ingas*, 'people', in Ealing and Barking. It is not surprising to find a representative sample of these common elements.

Nothing has so far been said of the first elements of the many names which contain two components. Often the final elements already discussed are compounded with a personal name: Isleworth, for instance, is 'Gislhere's enclosure', Ickenham is 'Ticca's village', and Edmonton, 'Ēadhelm's farm or estate'. In most cases nothing is known of the named individuals, and it is even uncertain whether these men founded the settlement or were prominent when the time came to give the place a name. There are some exceptions, but these are in later names: the Harold of Harold's Wood is almost certainly Earl Harold, killed at the Battle of Hastings, and Goodmayes probably refers to an identifiable family named Godemaye. It should also be mentioned that the meaning of a personal name is not likely to play any part in the interpretation of place-names containing it. Personal-name scholars can offer explanations of names like Tuda, Wændel, Orped, and Stybba—but it would be pointless to look in the places concerned for the characteristics implied, and our understanding of Teddington, Wandsworth, Orpington, and Stepney is not increased by knowing the meaning of the eponymous personal name.

Settlers and their languages

Names so far discussed have been mostly Old English, the legacy of

Anglo-Saxons who began to settle in England from about the fifth century A.D. The great majority of names in the Greater London area belong to this group, but mention has already been made of one Celtic name (Penge) and London itself must not be forgotten. Despite the appearance of some early forms (e.g., *Londinium, Lundinium*), this name is of British origin and is not, as is sometimes stated, in any linguistic sense a 'Roman' name. As occupiers rather than settlers, the Romans were more likely to use existing names of villages and towns than to devise new ones, and very few names in Britain have an indisputable Roman origin.

A London Borough bearing a Celtic name—Brent—does so by transfer rather than by way of continuous history; Celtic river-names are more numerous than settlement-names, and Brent is one of the former; the borough name was adopted when Willesden and Wembley were combined as a single entity within Greater London.

Middlesex, the core of Greater London, was an area of quite early Anglo-Saxon settlement, although it has been noted that it is anomalous that such a small shire should bear the name of one of the major divisions of the Saxon settlers. The territory almost certainly extended, however, well beyond the boundaries of the county as later defined. It is likely that the influence of the Middle Saxons extended into the Chilterns on the west, and into south and west Hertfordshire on the north. The name *Surrey* implies that this was the southern province of the Middle Saxons. The original kingdom must therefore have been of a size comparable with that of Essex, if not of Wessex.

In default of a separate historical record, the place names of Middlesex provide valuable witness to the early settlement of the county. A number are of a type no longer regarded as being the most archaic, but known to belong to a very early stage of settlement; these are the names terminating in *-ingas*, producing such modern forms as Ealing and Yeading. The actual meaning of such names is 'followers of Gilla' (etc) and the name was used when terms relating to place or territory were not regarded as necessary. Such tribal names need not point to a settlement-centre, but may be outposts or enclaves within other territories. Some such names have been lost in modern forms; Harrow, for instance, was originally *Gumeninga hergœ*, but nothing else is known of the tribe of the Gumenings. In the compound name Uxbridge the first syllable alludes to the people known as *Wixan*.

Only a small part of Surrey has been incorporated into Greater London—three of the historic Hundreds and part of a fourth (out of fourteen)—and so not quite so much can be said of the names which is relevant to the early history of the area. It is worth noting that the county name itself contains the archaic element $g\bar{e}$, 'province', related

5

to Modern German *Gau*. The term did not survive in Old English literary records.

The former County of London had not included any Essex territory, but the new arrangements have led to the creation of five London Boroughs east of the Lea. In Anglo-Saxon times Essex was a kingdom which, despite subjection at various periods to Kent and Mercia, maintained its identity in the historical record. But, again because of the smallness of the area of land transferred, comment on early settlement in Essex will not involve much of a contribution from Greater London names. Tribal names like Barking and Havering must be mentioned, but the river-name Roding is a back-formation of the village name found (well beyond the Greater London boundary) in the group of places collectively known as The Rodings. However early such a name might be, no conclusion can be drawn from it when transferred to a river, particularly when it appears that an early name for the stream may have been a Celtic one—*Hile*, 'trickling stream'—the first element in Ilford.

The London Borough of Barnet takes its name from a parish formerly in Hertfordshire. This was not an ancient settlement; in the earliest citations, the name refers to sections of the great forest which had been cleared by burning, and it may be that there was no population of any size in the area before the late eleventh or even early twelfth century.

Some Kentish territory had been absorbed by the former County of London; Greater London now also includes land to the east and south of this—the London Boroughs of Bexley and Bromley. It has been argued that, like certain names elsewhere in London (such as Kensington, Kenton, Alperton, and Harlington), Orpington is of fairly early formation; the nearness of Beckenham, which also bears a name suggesting early settlement, may be noted with considerable interest.

Although there can be no doubt that the London area endured much during the Danish raids and wars, there is little Scandinavian influence on any place-names in the area. The personal name in Gunnersbury is Scandinavian, but the identification of the bearer of the name with Gunhilda, niece of King Canute, is not supported by reliable evidence. The early forms of the name of the parish church of St Clement Danes indicate that the reference is indeed to Northmen (for which the special Latin term *Daci* is used in several documents), but the exact reason for the name is unknown. There may have been a small settlement of Danes in the neighbourhood, suggested also by references to the part of The Strand nearby as *vicus Dacorum*, or, in its Middle English equivalent, *Densemanestret*. A very much later Danish connexion gave rise to the street-name Copenhagen Street

N.W.1, from Copenhagen House, the residence of the ambassador of Denmark in 1665.

The influence of the Normans on English place-names was fairly extensive but rather subtle. In general, they established no new settlements and had no general policy of renaming, yet they have left their mark in various ways. One feature of their nomenclature is the formation of feudal or manorial names, in which the name of the feudal tenant is added to an existing name (e.g., *Friern* Barnet, Cowley *Peachey*). Occasionally the normal English naming-pattern is followed, the name of the feudal tenant being compounded with *bury*, which has in these names the sense 'manor' (Bloomsbury, Canbury).

Also characteristic of Norman names were complimentary terms such as *bel assis*, 'fine seat', of which Belsize Park is a well documented example. The word order in Mount Pleasant is undoubtedly French, but this name has been revived in recent centuries. Belmont, too, is a name in which a complimentary term was felt to be necessary. Even the use of *-ville* in the coining of new place-names elsewhere in England is evidence of the prestige the French language continues to have; this is borne out by the relatively recent name of Park Royal. The French definite article occurs in early forms of minor English place-names, but no trace is found in the modern names. The article is indifferently *le* or *la—La Mile Ende* 1288, *Le Milende* 1307 (Mile End), and *La Redeclyve* 1307, *Le Reedclyff* 1442 (Ratcliff).

French-speaking clerks were responsible for the completion of many documents containing English place-names; this had certain effects on the spelling of the names which often last to modern times. For instance, Coulsdon ('Cūðræd's hill') owes its present form to the frequent Norman habit of confusing *r* and *l*, and possibly to the presence of the *-th-*, which also presented problems to those for whom English was not their mother tongue.

The termination *-ville* (as in Pentonville) is usually modern; when it occurs (elsewhere in England) in medieval forms, it replaces Old English *-feld*, 'field', and does not signify 'town'.

With the Norman Conquest, most naming or renaming ceased. There are, of course, post-Conquest names in the London area as elsewhere. Poplar, for instance, is of French derivation and of late medieval origin; Richmond upon Thames has a transferred name dating from Tudor times, the original being either an actual complimentary name for the Yorkshire place or a further transfer from one of the French places so called. But these later names follow the general pattern of English naming, and it is neither desirable nor necessary to use such names as evidence of the early history of the place.

7

Interpretation of place-names

Users of many reference works tend to spend some time with them and then close the books with a sigh of despair. Very often it appears that explanations throw little if any light on the matter about which the book has been consulted. There are several ways in which a reference work may fail to satisfy a reader. Sometimes the explanation is couched in technical language, e.g., defining *metope* as 'space between two triglyphs'. That is, perhaps, not frustrating in itself, provided the new technical term is defined elsewhere in the reference work otherwise than by a circular reference to *metope*. But another means of frustrating a reader is by offering a rigorously bare definition. It is this which often causes objections to be raised to books about names. The reader feels that he needs to know more than that (to invent an example) *Scragby* means 'Scrag's village'. Unfortunately, it is too often true that there is not much more to be said, once the elements of the name have been identified. What must be stressed at once is that when a term like 'village' or 'farm' occurs in a place-name definition, the reader must be warned against reading this in an exclusively modern context.

It has been pointed out above that the early forms of names are required before any interpretation can be attempted. It is also necessary for the reader to appreciate the historical context of the name, when it was first applied to the place. Villages have developed and farming has much changed since the early Middle Ages, and the meanings of many terms associated with them have also been greatly transformed. But these changes cannot be referred to on every occasion that the term is used, and so the reader must exercise caution in referring to definitions, lest he or she be left feeling that the darkness has not been dispelled.

Rigorous definition cannot be used, however, as an excuse for declining further comment, and a work such as this which confined itself to mere definitions might indeed be regarded as unsatisfactory. Comments and explanations are very often provided from outside the place-name sphere, and the quotation marks used for definitions are a warning of this. Between those marks lies the meaning of the elements in the name, sometimes helped out by an explanatory word or two in parentheses. Comments which follow the definition are in general intended to throw light on the *name*, and not to supply information about the *place*.

Some common place-name elements

A few words have been said above about some place-name elements, but an extended explanation of some of the more frequent components of place-names in the area may usefully supplement the interpretations offered under the names in the dictionary section.

The part played by rivers in place-name composition should not be overlooked. The river-names themselves are often ancient and sometimes difficult to interpret, but they will be accompanied by descriptive terms (meaning 'stream', 'brook', 'inlet', etc) of later origin and application. Both *burna* and *brōc*, common Old English words for 'stream', occur in the names of tributaries (or sub-tributaries) of the Thames and duly pass to settlements on their banks. In many early forms *burna* is found, even though it may be replaced in later versions of the name. Edgware Brook, for instance, is referred to in a tenth-century Westminster Abbey charter as *stan burna*, 'stone stream', and Dollis Brook appears in the same document as *tatan burna*, 'Tata's stream'. The older term has survived into some modern names, e.g., Holborn, Tyburn, and Westbourne; the last example has been transferred to the stream itself from the hamlet name, meaning 'west of the stream'.

The Wandle (the modern name being a 'back-formation' from Wandsworth) was formerly *hlida burna*, 'loud stream', subsequently *Lotebourn* and then *The Bourne*; if a sixteenth-century name had survived, designating the entry point of the Wandle to the Thames, the area near the gas works at Wandsworth would now be called Bournemouth. In Walbrook, *brōc* occurs in medieval forms (*Walebroc* c.1120, *Walbroc*, *Walbrok* 13c.), and there seem to be no *burna* forms for Wealdstone Brook, its designation in 1453 being *Le Weldebrok*—a more convenient term, it might be thought, than its modern counterpart. In Beverley Brook the generic term is not original, and is indeed redundant, as Beverley is an alteration of the early *beferiþi*, the second element of which is a less common term for 'stream'—*riðig*—the diminutive of *rið*, found in Peckham Rye.

Some other riverside names have already been discussed, including those embodying *hȳþ*, 'landing place', *ēg*, 'island, dry ground amid marshes', and *ford*, 'river crossing'. Apart from London Bridge, Parr's Bridge, and Counters Bridge, few modern names including this element have a very long history. Stamford Bridge, of course, includes both *brycg* and *ford*, and its first element, *sand*, has undergone a baffling transformation.

Greenwich and Woolwich contain the versatile element *wīc*, and so do Hackney Wick and Chiswick. The Old English word was ultimately derived from Latin *vicus*, 'village', and from 'collection of dwellings or other buildings' the term came to mean 'building for a particular occupation', particularly 'dairy farm', land for this use evidently being set aside beyond the main settlement. Industrial and other non-agricultural purposes might also be indicated, as (elsewhere in England) such names as Dunwich, Ipswich, and Norwich confirm. In these, as in Greenwich and Woolwich, the term undoubtedly means 'port'.

Higher land may be referred to by such terms as *hyll*, *dūn*, and *hyrst*. The last is not frequent in Greater London, but occurs, with the meaning 'wooded hill', in Chislehurst and Bayhurst Wood. The modern spelling *hill* invariably appears in names derived from Old English *hyll*, but those from *dūn*, already briefly mentioned, appear in several guises, as can be seen from the modern forms Islington, Neasden, Brimsdown, and Hendon. The street-name Downage N.W.4 preserves the historic *Dounehegge*, 'hedge by or on the hill', dating from 1316.

Highwood Hill N.W.7 makes no secret of its elevation and also recalls how much of the fringes of Greater London was a thickly wooded area until the later Middle Ages. The element *wudu* is found also in Cricklewood, Ken Wood, and Wood Green. The more common *lēah*, 'wood, grove, woodland pasture', usually occurs as the second element in such compounds as Finchley, Bromley (two instances), Cowley, Yiewsley, and Wembley. The meaning 'meadow' is much later than those already given, and allusions to woodland are quite clear from other evidence. It also needs to be said that the name of the River Lea is not in any way connected with this element.

Other terms related to woodland include *(ge)fyrhðe*, found in Frith Manor (and hence in Frith Lane N.W.7). Thriff Wood S.E.26 survives as a street name near Mayow Park, and in some other minor names the element, meaning 'woodland', reminds us of former forests covering hundreds of acres that are now entirely urban. In Wormwood Scrubs the second element is not *wudu* but *holt*, 'plantation, small wood', which occurs also in Kensal Green and, even more heavily disguised, in Old Oak Common, formerly *Oldeholte*. Harrow Weald and Wealdstone contain the element *wald* or *weald*, the meaning of which developed from 'woodland' through 'upland forest' to 'high land, upland moor'. In the Harrow names, the association with woodland is clearly present, but the reason for the development of the meaning is fairly clear when the nature of the countryside is considered.

Elements such as *tūn*, *hām*, and *worð* refer strictly to settlements rather than to their natural environment, though this of course may be alluded to in elements prefixed to them. Often, however, the first element is a personal name (or a title, such as *king*); Harlesden, Lewisham, and Harmondsworth illustrate this usage. The word *tūn* seems to have meant originally 'fence, hedge'; this developed to 'enclosed land', a significance it may have in the compound *bere-tūn*, 'barley farm, grange', occurring in Norbiton, Surbiton. The usual interpretation offered is 'farm, estate', and the way the word was used in Old English literature leads us to understand that it normally implied a community of people, such as would be found in a hamlet or a village.

Names including *-ingtūn* have been given special attention in recent studies. Personal names combine with *tūn* in three ways: directly uniting the uninflected personal name with the second element, as in Edmonton (*Adelmeton* 1086), or, secondly, using the inflected possessive form of the personal name, as in Harlesden (*Herulvestune* 1086: 'Heoruwulf's estate'), or, thirdly, effecting the union by means of *-ing*, as in Kennington. It has been suggested that the last group are the earliest names, but that even before these there were forms ending in *-ing*, meaning simply 'place of . . .'. Evidence for this is at present sparse, but a careful scrutiny of names in this class would be most valuable. It is by no means impossible that the argument can be considerably developed when more early forms have been collected.

The root meaning of *hām* is more closely connected with human habitation than *tūn*; 'safe dwelling' is taken as the basis for development to 'village, collection of dwellings' and 'manor, estate'. The element is found in most parts of England, but is particularly frequent in the South East. In Greater London, Streatham, Clapham, and Balham are near neighbours, and so are Cheam and Mitcham. In Beckenham and Lewisham the first element is a personal name, as in Ickenham, north of the Thames. The circle is completed with Tottenham and Dagenham, also compounded with personal names.

This element, too, has been closely studied recently, and it has been concluded that *-hām* names are early. One of the difficulties in the investigation is to arrive at a clear discrimination between these names and those containing the element *hamm*, 'pasture, riverside land, land in a river bend', which certainly occurs in East Ham and West Ham. It is by no means improbable that with the transcription of more documentary sources, tentative conclusions can become completely firm ones.

A number of names in Greater London contain the element *worð*, 'enclosure'. In Isleworth, Wandsworth, Harmondsworth, and probably Hanworth, it is prefixed by a personal name. Walworth has as first element *walh*, 'Celtic-speaking foreigner, serf', the word from which *Wales* is derived. It is now accepted that some proportion of the British population did not, in fact, beat a hasty retreat before the victorious Anglo-Saxons. Pockets of independent Celts are traceable

11

in, amongst other places, the southern part of Greater London, witness such names as Wallington and Walworth, as well as the pure Celtic Penge.

The primary meaning of Old English *burh* is 'fortification, fortified place' and names containing the element often allude to ancient earthworks or encampments; evidently continuing in use throughout the Anglo-Saxon period, the element was used in the later Middle Ages to mean 'fortified house or manor', 'manor house, centre of an estate'. In this sense the element is used in such Greater London names as Edgwarebury, Bloomsbury, and Gunnersbury. In due course, the term became Modern English *borough*. Southwark, 'southern fortification'—namely, of the City of London—still has The Borough as an alternative designation. As this is not documented earlier than the seventeenth century, it is not possible to determine the precise sense of this subsidiary name, which may well be 'part of a town outside z town proper'. In view, however, of the meaning of Southwark itself, it does not seem likely that the alternative term means anything other than 'stronghold', the relationship between Southwark and The City (just across London Bridge) being analogous to that between Hertford and Hertingfordbury, 'fortified place of the men of Hertford'.

Several names contain the element *halh*, 'nook of land'. In Northolt the identity of the second component is not obvious in modern spellings, but its reference point, Southall, has returned to a form in which the second element is clearer, even though *Southold* 1578 and *Southolt* 1710 seemed to promise an exact counterpart of Northolt at the present time. The element is found in The Hale and Hale End, and it also occurs in Bethnal Green. All the places concerned must have originated as dependent hamlets, some developing to the size of their parent settlements.

Dependent settlements were sometimes named from their compass direction relative to the main village. Directional terms are clear enough in Northwood, Southall, Eastcote, and Westminster, but less obvious in Norbiton, Surbiton, Sudbury, Sutton, and Suffield Hatch. Westminster ('western monastery') began its existence with the foundation of the abbey at Thorney; it is west of the City of London, but of course has not the same relation with it as some of the other places bearing compass-point names.

The nature of the soil played its part in the choice of sites. Chalk Farm appears, from the modern form of the name, to be a good illustration of this; in fact, the name developed from *Chaldecote* in 1253, through *Chalcotes* in the sixteenth century to *Chalk* in the eighteenth, so that the original sense of 'cold cottages' was quite lost. The soil here, moreover, is clay. The modern forms of Stamford

Bridge and Stamford Hill are similarly misleading, both having originally referred to sandy, and not stony, fords. Gravel is alluded to in Erith and Chiselhurst; the element in the latter is found also in Chiswell Street E.C.1, popular etymology being responsible for the growth of the 'choice well' legend about the street name. Finsbury abounds in springs, but references to these all show that their names were spelt with -*well* at the time that Chiswell Street was *Chyselstrate* (13c.).

Allusions to stones in place-names are not limited to descriptions of the soil, but remind us that boulders or other stones were used as landmarks in boundaries or to indicate tribal meeting-places. Keston and Brixton are two instances in Greater London, each containing a personal name as first element. Stones were also used for road building, but paved roads (constructed by the Romans) were sufficiently noteworthy to the Anglo-Saxons for them to include references to such roads in place-names. Stratford, with a number of variants, occurs all over England at places where Roman roads cross rivers or streams, Greater London having its share of these. Streatham, 'village beside a Roman road', also contains the element *strǣt*, a word borrowed by the Germanic tribes while they were still on the Continent, from the Latin *via strāta*, 'paved or layered road'. This word became modern English *street*, used of thoroughfares of all kinds, whether stone-paved or not.

Street-names

A street is just as much a *place* as a village or a hamlet is, and yet although the population concerned may be greater than that of many settlements, the names of roads, streets, and lanes in great towns have not been studied in the same way as have major place-names. The reasons for this are not difficult to understand. The very large numbers to be found in big towns deter all but the most dedicated from collecting the modern names and exploring their history. Many names are of quite recent origin and linguistic techniques are often irrelevant in their interpretation. Very often, also, documents required for the elucidation of the names are more difficult of access than those normally used in place-name studies, being frequently the current or recent files of local authorities' memoranda and correspondence.

A work on the place-names of Greater London would not be complete, however, without some reference to the street-names in all parts of the area. Inclusion of more than a few of these names in the Dictionary section seemed undesirable, as the location of the street in respect to its neighbours is often important in interpretation, and the

13

frequent cross-references necessary would be unwelcome to many readers. A separate survey has therefore been made in Part 2 of this book, and these names, wherever they are discussed, are fully indexed.

Arrangement of Dictionary Entries

Place-names are entered alphabetically, each headword being followed by the postal district, if any, or (in abbreviated form) the name of the London Borough or other appropriate larger place if the name is found beyond the limits of the numbered postal districts. The name is usually followed by a brief interpretation, placed within quotation marks. Such interpretations occasionally include words within brackets. For example '(place by) stony pool' signifies that the name being interpreted means merely 'stony pool', but that in order to make a satisfactory place-name interpretation the reading 'place by stony pool' is suggested.

The interpretation may be followed by a brief comment; this occasionally explains linguistic points involved in the development of the name, but sometimes offers additional observations on geographical or historical implications. Then, within square brackets, a selection of early spellings will be found to provide supporting evidence for the derivation. Italic type is used for early spellings as well as, throughout the book, for names which are no longer in use. Some of these will be observed among the head-words in the Dictionary section, either because of occasional literary references (e.g., *Alsatia*) or on account of the light some of them (e.g., *Garratt* or *Tottenham Court*) shed on surviving street-names.

Place-name elements composing the name conclude each entry in the Dictionary; from the Glossary of Elements the reader will be able to trace other names constructed from these roots, and to see the variety of forms sometimes encountered. Occasionally, cross-references will direct the reader's attention at once to other names for comparison.

It should be remembered that interpretations and explanations apply to the particular place-name being discussed. A name spelt identically but occurring elsewhere may have an entirely different meaning; this can be arrived at only by an inspection of the early forms of the name concerned.

Many of the books listed in the Bibliography contain discussions, some in considerable detail, of the history and development of place-names and their component elements; with the help of such works, and using the information in this book as a starting-point, it is hoped that the reader will find in the names of Greater London a continuing and growing source of interest and enjoyment.

Location of Places

Two methods are used to indicate the location of places being discussed. When the place concerned is within the area of numbered postal districts, the appropriate reference is suffixed to the name. Beyond this area, location is shown by adding in brackets the abbreviated name of the London Borough within which the place lies, or the abbreviated name of a parish or other area in which the place is situated.

London was first divided into postal districts in 1856. At first there were ten districts: E.C., W.C., N., N.E., E., S.E., S., S.W., W., and N.W. The North-Eastern and Southern districts were discontinued within the first few years of the arrangement, and they were merged with neighbouring areas.

The original postal districts extended considerably further than the numbered sub-divisions which were introduced in the spring of 1917. Apart from the Central districts and certain additional head districts (e.g., Paddington) the numbering from 2 onwards is in an alphabetical sequence; there are two sequences in the S.W. district, one ending at West Brompton and the second beginning at Battersea. In the S.E. district, the series proceeds smoothly as far as Woolwich S.E.18 but then becomes rather irregular. There are individual anomalies in other districts.

Beyond this area, the names of London Boroughs and other districts used for location purposes are abbreviated in the Dictionary section of this book. The four-letter symbols used are intended to enable discrimination between similar names and to be, as far as possible, self-explanatory. For the sake of clarity, *Brent* and *Barnet* are not abbreviated.

Postal districts

CENTRAL

E.C.1	Finsbury, Smithfield
E.C.2	Bank, Guildhall, Moorgate
E.C.3	Aldgate, Fenchurch St, Leadenhall St
E.C.4	Fleet St, St Paul's, Temple
W.C.1	Bloomsbury, Gray's Inn
W.C.2	Charing Cross, Covent Garden

NORTHERN

N.1	Islington, Hoxton, King's Cross, Shoreditch
N.2	East Finchley
N.3	Finchley (Church End)
N.4	Finsbury Park
N.5	Highbury
N.6	Highgate
N.7	Holloway
N.8	Hornsey
N.9	Lower Edmonton
N.10	Muswell Hill
N.11	New Southgate
N.12	North Finchley
N.13	Palmers Green
N.14	Southgate
N.15	South Tottenham
N.16	Stoke Newington
N.17	Tottenham
N.18	Upper Edmonton
N.19	Upper Holloway
N.20	Whetstone
N.21	Winchmore Hill
N.22	Wood Green

EASTERN

E.1	Whitechapel, Shadwell, Stepney
E.2	Bethnal Green
E.3	Bow, Old Ford, Mile End
E.4	Chingford
E.5	Clapton
E.6	East Ham
E.7	Forest Gate
E.8	Hackney, Haggerston
E.9	Homerton
E.10	Leyton
E.11	Leytonstone
E.12	Manor Park
E.13	Plaistow
E.14	Poplar
E.15	Stratford
E.16	Victoria Docks, North Woolwich
E.17	Walthamstow
E.18	Woodford, South Woodford

SOUTH-EASTERN

S.E.1	Bermondsey, Southwark, Waterloo
S.E.2	Abbey Wood
S.E.3	Blackheath
S.E.4	Brockley
S.E.5	Camberwell
S.E.6	Catford
S.E.7	Charlton
S.E.8	Deptford
S.E.9	Eltham
S.E.10	Greenwich
S.E.11	Kennington
S.E.12	Lee
S.E.13	Lewisham

S.E.14	New Cross		Hyde Park, Bayswater
S.E.15	Peckham	W.3	Acton
S.E.16	Rotherhithe	W.4	Chiswick
S.E.17	Walworth	W.5	Ealing
S.E.18	Woolwich	W.6	Hammersmith
S.E.19	Norwood	W.7	Hanwell
S.E.20	Anerley	W.8	Kensington
S.E.21	Dulwich	W.9	Maida Hill
S.E.22	East Dulwich	W.10	North Kensington
S.E.23	Forest Hill	W.11	Notting Hill
S.E.24	Herne Hill	W.12	Shepherds Bush
S.E.25	South Norwood	W.13	West Ealing
S.E.26	Sydenham	W.14	West Kensington
S.E.27	West Norwood		

NORTH-WESTERN

SOUTH-WESTERN

		N.W.1	Camden Town, Euston, Regent's Park
S.W.1	Victoria, Westminster, St James's	N.W.2	Cricklewood
		N.W.3	Hampstead
S.W.2	Brixton	N.W.4	Hendon
S.W.3	Chelsea	N.W.5	Kentish Town
S.W.4	Clapham	N.W.6	Kilburn
S.W.5	Earls Court	N.W.7	Mill Hill
S.W.6	Fulham	N.W.8	St John's Wood
S.W.7	South Kensington	N.W.9	The Hyde
S.W.8	South Lambeth	N.W.10	Willesden
S.W.9	Stockwell	N.W.11	Golders Green
S.W.10	West Brompton		
S.W.11	Battersea		
S.W.12	Balham		
S.W.13	Barnes		
S.W.14	Mortlake		
S.W.15	Putney		
S.W.16	Streatham		
S.W.17	Tooting		
S.W.18	Wandsworth		
S.W.19	Wimbledon		
S.W.20	West Wimbledon		

WESTERN

W.1	Mayfair, Soho
W.2	Paddington,

Tables of abbreviations

1. LOCATION SYMBOLS

Alpt	Alperton
Bctr	Becontree
Bknm	Beckenham
Blvd	Belvedere
Brfd	Brentford
Brkg	Barking
Brom	Bromley
Bxly	Bexley
Chfd	Chingford
Chht	Chislehurst
Clsn	Coulsdon
Crdn	Croydon
Cstn	Carshalton
Dgnm	Dagenham
Edgw	Edgware
Elng	Ealing
Enfd	Enfield
Fltm	Feltham
Frnb	Farnborough
Gnfd	Greenford
Harw	Harrow
Havg	Havering
Hldn	Hillingdon
Hnch	Hornchurch
Hrfd	Harefield
Hslw	Hounslow
Ilfd	Ilford
Islw	Isleworth
Knly	Kenley
Kstn	Kingston
Mchm	Mitcham
Mrtn	Merton
Orpn	Orpington
Pinr	Pinner
Prly	Purley
Ptsm	Petersham
Rbrg	Redbridge
Rchm	Richmond
Rmfd	Romford
Rslp	Ruislip
Sdcp	Sidcup
Srbn	Surbiton
Sstd	Sanderstead
Sthl	Southall
Stmr	Stanmore
Sutn	Sutton
Tedn	Teddington
ThnH	Thornton Heath
Twic	Twickenham
Upmr	Upminster
Uxbr	Uxbridge
Wbly	Wembley
Wdfd	Woodford
WDtn	West Drayton
Wltn	Wallington
Wntn	Wennington

2. GENERAL

Ave	Avenue
B	British (language)
C	Celtic
c.	*circa* 'about' (c.1500 'about 1500')
c.	century (12c. 'twelfth century')
cf.	*confer* 'compare'
Clse	Close
Csct	Crescent
Ct	Court
e.g.	*exempli gratia* 'for example'
E.P.N.S.	English Place-Name Society
F	French
freq	frequent
Gdns	Gardens
Grd	Ground
Gve	Grove
i.e.	*id est* 'that is' (introduces an explanation)
L	Latin
Lne	Lane

ME	Middle English (language c.1100–c.1475)	Rd	Road
		riv	river
OE	Old English (language spoken and written by Anglo-Saxons)	Sq	Square
		St	Saint (before a name)
		St	Street (after a name)
OF	Old French (language before c.1200)	Tce	Terrace
		v.	*vide* 'see'
ON	Old Norse (language used by Vikings, c.700–1100)	viz	*videlicet* 'namely' (lists specific instances)
p., pp.	page(s)	W	Welsh
Pde	Parade	*	a postulated form, i.e., a word found as a place-name element but not occurring in literature
Plce	Place (in street-names)		
q.v.	*quod vide* 'which see' ('see under appropriate heading'; *plural*: qq.v.)		

Part 1

Dictionary of Greater London Place-names

Abbey Recreation Ground S.W.19, formerly land belonging to the canons of Merton Priory.

Abbey Wood (Rainham), 'woodland belonging to an abbey', referring to Barking Abbey.

Abbey Wood S.E.2, 'woodland belonging to an abbey'. This name is used now of the settlement by the wood, the latter, on the northern edge of which monastic ruins are still to be seen, being known as Lessness Abbey Wood.

Abney Park N.16, commemorating the family of Sir Thomas Abney, who held the manor of Stoke Newington in the early eighteenth century.

Acton W.3, 'farm or estate by the oak tree(s)'. In some medieval and later documents the main village is referred to as Church Acton, to distinguish it from the separate hamlet of East Acton [*Acton(e)*

1181, *Aketon* 1211, *Chirche Acton* 1347, *Estacton* 1294: OE *āc, tūn*].

Addington (Crdn), 'estate in Eadda's territory'. In recent discussion of names ending in *-ington*, it has been suggested that the termination *-tūn* was added to earlier forms consisting of a personal name to which *-ing* was suffixed to indicate 'place of . . .' or 'territory of . . .' the man concerned [*Eddintone* 1086, *Adingeton* 1203, *Addyngton* 1535: OE *-ingtūn*].

Addiscombe (Crdn), 'Eadda's enclosed land'. The rare element *camp* occurs almost exclusively in names in the Home Counties. As the two places are quite near, it is not impossible that the same individual provided the personal name in both Addington and Addiscombe [*Edescamp* 1229, *Adescomp* 1279, *Addescombe* 1416, *Addescombe* 1456: OE *camp*].

Adelphi W.C.2, '(place named in honour of) the brothers', an unusual instance of an English place-name of Greek origin. The streets in this

23

district were built in the late eighteenth century by the four brothers Adam, collectively remembered both in the name of the district (from Greek ἀδελφοί, 'brothers') and in Adam Street. *John Street*, commemorating the eldest brother was renamed John Adam Street in 1940; earlier, also in order to avoid repetition of names, *James Street* and *William Street* were united as Durham House Street, but the name of the most talented of the brothers survives in Robert Street.

Albany W.1, formerly the property of Frederick, Duke of York and Albany (second son of George III). Albany Street W.1 also commemorates the duke, as do other street names in London and elsewhere. After an inglorious career in the field, the duke was made commander-in-chief in 1795 and is now remembered in a nursery rhyme ('the grand old Duke of York').

Aldborough Hatch (Ilfd), '(place by) forest gate held by the Albourgh family'. John and Stephen Albo(u)rgh are referred to in documents of the early fourteenth century; the family possibly originated in one of the several places called Al(d)bury in Hertfordshire [*Albrorhhatchcrosse* 1456, *Aldborough Hacche* c.1488: OE *hæcc*].

Aldersbrook E.12, '(place by) alder stream', from a fairly late farm name replacing the unexplained *Nagethall, Nakethalle*, or *Naked Hall* [*Nakethalle, Nagethalle* 1383,

Nakedhall Hawe or *Alderbroke* 1531: OE *alor, brōc*].

Aldgate E.C.3, 'ale gate', an entrance to the City of London, earlier called *Æst Geat*, 'east gate' [*Alegate* 1108: OE *ealu, geat*].

Aldwych W.C.2, 'old outlying farm', an old name transferred to a new street and district built not far from the land earlier so called [*Aldewich* 1211, *Oldewiche* 1393: OE *eald, wīc*].

Alexandra Palace N.22, Alexandra Park N.22, like other Alexandra Parks in London, named in honour of the Danish princess who became Queen Alexandra when her husband came to the throne as King Edward VII. The 'Palace', a public entertainment hall, was opened in 1873, but some street-names honouring Queen Alexandra date from 1863, the year of her marriage to the then Prince of Wales.

Alperton (Wbly), 'farm or estate in Ealhbeorht's territory', taking the 1199 spelling to represent the personal name together with the suffix *-ingtūn*. The 1282 form, however, may represent a separate tradition of naming the place, and may mean 'Ealhbeorht's farm or estate'. The difference may appear to be slight, but could represent a considerable difference in area, since the original territory would have been much larger than the estate within it, represented by the historic Alperton [*Alprinton* 1199, *Alperton(e)* 1282: OE *-ingtūn/tūn*].

Alsatia, 'no man's land', a name formerly applied to a 'rogues' republic' in the Whitefriars district of the City. The term was doubtless an allusion to Alsace, the debatable land between France and Germany. The Whitefriars' right to grant sanctuary to fugitives notionally continued on the site even after the Dissolution, and it became a haunt of thieves, debtors, and vagabonds in much the same way as occurred in the Sanctuary of Westminster Abbey. The name under discussion was first used by Shadwell in 1688, in a play, *The Squire of Alsatia*.

Anerley S.E.20, 'lonely place'. Of late origin, the name is derived from that of a house belonging to William Sanderson. He is said to have offered, without charge, some land to the railway company, on condition that a station should be made bearing this name; this was done, and further development took place within a few years. In Northern English dialects, *anerly* means 'lonely'.

Angel E.C.1, the name of an Underground Railway station derived from that of a seventeenth-century inn nearby. Other inns of this name are commemorated in street-names in various parts of London.

Angell Town S.W.9, 'residential area named after a man named Angell'. This use of *Town*, meaning 'planned dwelling area' occurs also in Camden Town, Cubitt Town, Somerstown, and other districts in the London area, to which this usage of the term seems to be confined.

Aquarius Golf Course S.E.2, owned by the Metropolitan Water Board. The name here is used in its literal sense of 'water carrier' and the auspicious associations of the constellation are accidental or, at least, secondary.

Archway N.6 now refers to a graceful iron bridge over Archway Road, which originally received its name from a massive stone structure demolished in 1900. This acquired the sobriquet of 'London's Bridge of Sighs', from its occasional unhappy use as a means of committing suicide.

Arnos Grove N.14, '(place in or by) plantation owned by the Arnold family'. Margery Arnold is named in documents of 1344 [*Arnoldes Grove* 1551, *Arno's Grove* c.1865, OE *grāf*].

Arsenal N.5, named from the ground, in the vicinity, of the Arsenal Football Club. Founded in 1884, at the Royal Arsenal in Woolwich, the club moved to Highbury in 1913.

B

Baber Bridge 1593 (Hslw), 'bridge at Babba's enclosure'. The bridge carried the Bath road over the Crane just west of Hounslow; a farm called

Babbeworth was nearby, OE *worð* in this name being reduced to *-er*, as in Abinger, Surrey (earlier *Ebbingwurð*).

Baker Street W.1 and N.W.1 commemorates William Baker, who acquired the land from William Henry Portman and developed this extensive estate in the second half of the eighteenth century.

Balham S.W.12, 'riverside pasture belonging to Bealga', or 'rounded riverside pasture'. The second element of this name, *hamm*, often denotes 'land within the bend of a river'; Balham lies between the two arms of Falcon Brook. The first element may be OE *bealg*, possibly used to describe a convex conformation [*Bælgenham* 957, *Balgham* 1255, *Balam* 1472].

Bank E.C.2 refers to the *Bank of England*, the full name of which dates from 1694.

Barbican E.C.2, 'outer fortification of a city or castle', a term derived, through French, from Arabic or Persian; the London Barbican enabled a watch to be kept on routes entering the City from the north [OF *barbacane* < Pers. *barbār-khānah*, 'house on the wall'].

Barking, 'Berica's people'. Folknames, i.e., those indicating places but consisting merely of the name of the tribal group occupying the territory, include such designations as Norfolk, Suffolk, and Devon. But there are many more that follow the pattern of Barking, in which the Old English termination *-ingas*, 'people or followers of . . .' was added to a personal name. These are among the earliest names of Anglo-Saxon settlements, but are no longer considered to be the most ancient. The type is not abundant in Greater London, but Havering may be noted as another instance not far away. The medieval parish of Barking was more extensive than it later became, and Barkingside (now in the London Borough of Redbridge) actually adjoined it.

The London Borough comprises the parishes of Dagenham and Barking [*Bercingum* c.730, *on Byringum* c.1000, *Berchinges* 1086: OE *-ingas*].

Barkingside (Rdbg), '(place) beside Barking (q.v.)'. It was later in the parish of Ilford [*Barkingside* 1538: OE *sīde*].

Barnehurst (Bxly), possibly 'wood partly cleared by burning' [OE *berned, hyrst*].

Barn Elms S.W.13, 'elm trees at Barnes', earlier known as *Estberne(s)*, 'east Barnes' [*Barnes Elms* c.1540, *Bernelmes* 1580: OE *elm*]. See also Barnes.

Barnes S.W.13, 'the barn'. The earliest spellings are in the singular, plural forms not occurring until the thirteenth century, when perhaps they were felt to be more logical as the size of the place increased [*Berne*

1086, *La Berne* 1244, *Bernes* 1222, *Barnes* 1387: OE *bere-ærn*].

Barnet. See Friern Barnet, High Barnet.

Barnsbury N.1, 'manor of de Berners'. After the Conquest, *bury* (OE *burh*) was used with the sense, 'manor, manor house', and is frequently found in Middlesex names used in this way, as in the nearby Canonbury and Highbury. Some of the early forms of this name allude to its location in the parish of Islington [*Villa de Iseldon Berners* 1274, *Bernardysbury* 1475, *Barnesbury* 1543].

Barons Court W.14, of uncertain origin. The name may allude to the Margrave of Brandenburgh, husband of Lady Craven—after whom is named Margravine Gardens, the continuation of Barons Court Road; or it may be due to the proximity of Earls Court (q.v.), to which, however, it is not historically related.

Battersea S.W.11, 'Beadurīc's island', higher land surrounded by riverside marshes. A few deviant spellings seems to represent an attempt to connect the name with St Patrick; suggestions that these forms allude to Westminster Abbey have neither etymological nor historical warrant [*Batrices ege* c.1050, *Batriceseie* 1067, *Patriceseia* 1067, *Batriseye* 1366: OE *ēg*].

Battlebridge (now King's Cross) was originally *Bradfordbridge*, 'bridge at the broad ford', developing through an intermediate form *Batford Bridge* 1625. The ford and bridge were across the Holborn. Battlebridge survives now only in the name of a small thoroughfare [*Bradefordebrigge* c.1378: OE *brād, ford, brycg*].

Bayswater W.2, 'Bayard's watering place', originally the name of the place where the river Westbourne crossed the main road to Oxford; settlement was sparse here until the beginning of the nineteenth century [*Aqua vocata Bayards Watering Place* 1380, *Bayeswater* 1659].

Beaulieu S.E.19/S.E.25, 'fine place', with which must be associated **Beulah Hill**, 'slope by Beaulieu', the name usually applied to the district adjoining the road which is so called. The 1359 form means 'Beaulieu on the Roman road' [*Beulestret* 1359, *Bewle* 1456, *Bulay Hill* 1823: OF *beu, lieu*, OE *strǣt*].

Beavers Wood (Brom), either 'woodland in which beavers lived' or alluding to ownership by a man or family called Bever or Beaver (OE *beofor, wudu*].

Beckenham (Brom), 'Beohha's village'. The element *hām*, frequently used (as here) with a personal name, is now regarded as evidence of early Anglo-Saxon settlement; problems that remain include not only the identity of the named person, but also his (or her) relationship with the place—whether as leader of the first settlers or one to whom the place was assigned by charter from the king or church. The earliest spellings quoted both refer to 'boundary of Beckenham' [*Biohhahema mearc* 862, *Beohhahammes gemœru* 973, *Bacheham* 1086: OE *hām*].

Beckton E.6, named in honour of S. A. Beck, governor of the Gas, Light, and Coke Company, 1869.

Becontree (Brkg), 'Beohha's tree'. The use of trees as landmarks is evidenced in numerous place-names; many names of the ancient Hundreds indicate that the assembly place was at a particular tree, often specified by a personal name. The Essex Hundred of Becontree took its name from Becontree Heath, in the parish of Dagenham; a hamlet here developed in the nineteenth century, and the westward extension of this settlement became known simply as Becontree. There would almost certainly have been a signal beacon here, and the form *Beacon Tree Heath* 1805 suggests that this was thought to be the reason for the name [*Beuentreu* 1086, *Beghentro* 12c., *Beckingtre* 1227, *Becontre* 1594 (all referring to the Hundred); *Bekentre Hathe* 13c.: OE *trēow*, *hǣð*].

Beddington (Sut), 'farm or estate associated with Bēada'. As a result of recent work on names of this type it has been suggested that Addington, Beddington, &c strictly mean 'farm or estate at Eadding, Beading—i.e. territory associated with Eadda,

Bēada, &c'. The formula proposed above is a concise rendering of a statement which would otherwise be impossibly wordy [*Bedintone* 675, 933, 1318, *Beaddinctun* c.905, *Bedington* 1229: OE *-ingtūn*].

Bedfont. See East Bedfont.

Bedford Park W.4, named after Tubbs Bedford, a local landowner at the turn of the 17/18th centuries. The Russells, Earls of Bedford undoubtedly held land in Acton and Chiswick, but their connexion with the area ceased in the seventeenth century.

Bedford's Park (Havg) is a remnant of property held in the Middle Ages by the family of Robert de Bedeford 1285. It had previously been in the hands of Hugh d'Albini, Earl of Sussex [*Erles alias Bedfordes* c.1480].

Bedlam, Bedlem, Bethlem, 'Hospital of St Mary of Bethlehem', founded as a priory in 1247, one of its functions being to receive and entertain the bishop and canons of the Bethlehem diocese whenever they should visit London. It is referred to as a hospital for lunatics in a document of 1402, continuing as such after the Dissolution of the Monasteries, when it was granted to the City of London. From its original site in Bishopsgate, the hospital was transferred to London Wall in 1676 and to Lambeth in 1815. The building there now houses the Imperial War Museum [*Betleem* 11c., *Bedleem* 14c., *Bedlam* 1528].

Belgravia S.W.1, part of the manor of Ebury in the vicinity of Belgrave Square, so named from Belgrave, Cheshire, one of the other properties of the Dukes of Westminster, whose family own this area. See also Part 2, p.132.

Bellingham S.E.6, 'village of Beora's people'. Interchange of *l* and *r* in place-names occurred in the Norman period, the best known examples being Salisbury for earlier *Searoburg* and Salop for *Scrobbescīr*; the replacement of *r* by *l* in this name is another instance of this change [*Beringaham* 998, *Belingeham* 1198: OE *-ingas, hām*].

Belmont (Sut), 'fine hill'—a Norman name arbitrarily applied in the early nineteenth century to a place previously known as *Little Hell*, probably meaning 'little hill', but understandably objectionable to local people.

Belmont (Stmr), possibly 'fine hill'. The forms are late, and the first two leave some doubt about the exact meaning intended [*Bell Mount* 1754, *Belmount* 1822, *Belmont* 1900: OF *bel, mont*].

Belsize Park N.W.3, 'beautifully situated', *Park* referring to the grounds of the former manor house here. The complimentary Norman name is found also in Northamptonshire and Hertfordshire, and, as Bellasis, in Northumberland and in County Durham [*Belassis* 1317, *Bellasize* 1360, *Belsise* 1593: OF *bel, assis*].

Belvedere (Bxly), 'fine view' [OF *bel, vedeir*].

Benhilton (Sutt), 'farm by Benhill, i.e., hill on which beans were grown' [*Benhull* 1392, *Benehill* 15c.: OE *bēan, hyll*].

Bentley Priory (Harw), 'woodland pasture where bent grass grew'. Bents are grasses of the Agrostis genus and are not good pasture [*Benetlegh* 1243, *Bentleye* 1282: OE *beonet, lēah*].

Bermondsey S.E.1, 'Beornmund's island', the termination alluding to higher land amid marshes; in fact streams almost surrounded the original settlement [*Bermundeseye* 1086, *Bermonsey* 1450: OE *ēg*].

Berrylands (Kstn), in Surbiton, 'arable strips on or by a hill', the estate having taken its name from a farm so called [*La Bergh* 1241, *Le Berowe* 1439: OE *beorg, land*].

Berwick (Hvrg), 'barley farm', lending its name to Berwick Pond, fed by a tributary which joins the Ingrebourne near Abbey Wood in Rainham [*Berwyk* 1361, *Baruuyk* 1496: OE *bere-wīc*].

Bethnal Green E.1, 'village green at Blīþa's nook of land', the green being part of Cambridge Heath (q.v.). Originally a dependency of Stepney, Bethnal Green is now part of Tower Hamlets [*Blithehale* 13c, *Blithenhale in Stebenhethe* 1341, *Blethenalegrene* 1443: OE *hahl*].

Beverley Brook, 'beaver streamlet'. The explanatory *brook* is superfluous, as the second element in *Beverley* is *riðig*, diminutive of the Old English *rið*, 'stream'. As this term went out of use, not only was it felt necessary to explain the nature of the rivulet by means of the redundant *Brook*, but it was felt desirable also to make the ending more 'normal' by changing it to *-ley* [*Beferiþi* 693, *Beverey* 1548, *Beverley Creeke* 1668: OE *beofor*, *riðig*].

Bexley, 'wood or grove of box trees'. The box (Buxus sempervirens) used to be abundant in the south of England, as this and other place-names attest. The London Borough of Bexley comprises Belvedere, Welling, Sidcup, Crayford, Erith, and Bexley [*Bixle* c.780, *Byxlea* 814: OE *byxe*, *leah*].

Bickley (Brom), probably 'Bica's wood', but the first element may be a common noun, OE **bīc*, 'pointed one', suggesting such different interpretations as 'pointed wood' and 'wood in which wild bees were found' [*Byckeleye* 1297: OE *lēah*].

Biggin Hill (Brom), 'hill with or by a building' (ME *bigging*, OE *hyll*].

Billingsgate (City), 'wharf or watergate held by Billing'. The identity of the man who contributed his name has been the subject of conjecture, but must remain uncertain [*Bælȝesȝate* c.1205, *Bellinges-ȝate* c.1250: OE *geat*].

Birkbeck (Brom) commemorates Dr George Birkbeck (1776–1841), physician and pioneer in adult education, as well as philanthropist and philosopher. The direct connexion, however, is with the Birkbeck Bank and Birkbeck Building Society, so called because Francis Ravenscroft, one of the promoters, was an admirer of George Birkbeck's work through these financial organizations much nineteenth-century development in Greater London was made possible. Birkbeck Road and Ravenscroft Road are within a quarter of a mile from Birkbeck railway station in Beckenham.

Bishops Hall E.2, 'manor house of the bishop'. The Bishops of London were lords of the manor of Stepney. The site of the old house is now partly within Victoria Park, but the history of the area is marked by Bishop's Way and Bonner Road E.2. After Bishop Bonner (16c.), the manor passed into lay hands [*Bisshope Hall* 1495, *Bonners Hall* 1745].

Bishop's Park S.W.6 adjoins the grounds of Fulham Palace, residence of the Bishop of London.

Bishopswood N.6, 'woodland held by a bishop', part of the Bishop of London's manor in Hornsey [*Byssehopeswode* c.1387: OE *biscop*, *wudu*].

Blackfen (Bex), 'black boggy area', the colour usually resulting from peat [OE *blæc*, *fenn*].

Blackfriars E.C.4, '(site of priory of) Dominican friars', a large area beside the mouth of the River Fleet. The order settled in London in 1221, in premises outside the City near Lincoln's Inn, transferring to this site in 1279.

Blackfriars Bridge, 'bridge to Blackfriars', the present bridge alluding to the connexion by the pulpit-like structures incorporated in the design; the Dominicans' official title is Order of Preachers.

Blackheath S.E.3/S.E.10, 'black heathland', the colour being due to peat overlying the sand [*Blachehedfeld* 1166, *Blakehadfeld* 1190, *Blakeheth* 1275: OE *blæc*, *hǣð*].

Blackwall E.14, 'black (river) wall', an artificial bank constructed to enable riverside building to take place in a marshy area [*Blakewall* 1377: OE *blæc*, *wall*].

Bloomsbury W.C.1, 'manor held by de Blémund', one of a number of Middlesex names terminating in *-bury*, used in the sense '(fortified) manor house' rather than with the earlier meaning of 'fortification, fortress'. The family which gave the place its name probably came from Blémont (Vienne) [*Soca Blemund* 1242, *Manerium de Blemund* 1274, *Blemondesberi* 1291: OE *burh*].

Bond Street W.1, named in honour of Sir Thomas Bond, Comptroller of the Household to Queen Henrietta Maria (widow of Charles I). In association with Margaret Stafford and the Earl of Dover, Bond developed land formerly belonging to the Earl of Albemarle. The enterprise resulted in the building of Albemarle Street, Stafford Street, Dover Street and part of Bond Street, now known as Old Bond Street. Bond died in 1685, and the thoroughfare waited for its completion in New Bond Street in 1721. The street-name, without any prefix, is borne by the Underground Railway (Central Line) station.

Borough S.E.1, 'fortified place. This term was formerly, and occasionally still is, employed as an alternative name for Southwark (q.v.) but shown on modern maps as the area bounded by Borough High Street, St Thomas Street and Great Dover Street; at one time Borough High Street itself was known as The Borough. Possibly as the word *borough* came to have its modern sense of 'incorporated town', the term was regarded as a convenient contrast to The City (of London) across London Bridge [OE *burh*].

Bostall Heath, Bostall Woods S.E.2, 'place of refuge', from a term surviving in the dialect word *borstal*, used in Sussex and Kent of a pathway up a steep hill [OE *borg*, *stall*].

Boston Manor (Hslw), 'Bord's farm' [*Bordestun* 1377: OE *tūn*].

Botany Bay (Enfd), a name conventionally applied to a remote spot, alluding to the convict settlement in New South Wales regarded as 'the end of the earth'. The term also occurs as a street name (Botany Bay Lane) in Chislehurst.

Botwell (Hldn), possibly 'remedial spring', surviving in street-names at Wood End, Hayes. The name is recorded in a genuine charter of very early date [*Botewælle* 831, *Botewell* 1266: OE *bōt, wella*].

Bounds Green N.11, 'green place in the possession of le Bonde', the feudal tenants being the family of John le Bonde (1294).

Bow E.3, formerly Stratford-at-Bow (q.v.), from the arched bridge spanning the Lea, built during the reign of Henry I. According to an inquisition taken in 1303, 'Good Queen Maud', having been informed that the river crossing at Old Ford was dangerous, ordered the highway to be diverted to its present course, and had the bridge built to carry the road into Essex.

Bow Bridge E.3. See Bow.

Bow Creek E.14, the name given to the Lea at its junction with the Thames.

Bower Park (Hvrg), the SE corner of Havering Park, adjoining Bower House, on the site of *The Bowre*, the fifteenth-century royal residence (cf. Havering Atte Bower).

Bowes Park N.22, 'land held by the Bowes family'. The manor was formerly Bowes, *Park* being a recent addition. A lord of the manor appears in a 1274 document as John de Arcubus.

Boxers Wood (Crdn), 'woodland held by de Boxeford', the lord in 1279 being Robert de Boxeford, possibly from Boxford in Berkshire. The wood is on the Coulsdon parish boundary (cf. the 1461 form) [*Boxford* 1403, *Boxfordesmere* 1461: OE *(ge)mǣre*].

Brent, London Borough taking its name from the River Brent, 'holy one'. The Borough comprises the former Borough of Willesden, together with Wembley [(River Brent:) *Brægentan* c.974, *Brǣingte* c.955, *Breynte* 1274: B *brigantiā*].

Brent Cross N.W.4, 'cross-roads by hamlet of Brent Street', 'cross' being perhaps an oversimplification of this elaborate interlacing of the North Circular Road and Hendon Way.

Brentford (Hslw), 'ford over River Brent', the crossing-place being probably near the junction of the High Street and Commerce Road [*Bregunt ford* 705, *Brægentforda* c.1050, *Brainford* 1222: OE *ford*]. See also Brent.

Brentham W.5, 'district by River Brent', a modern name for a residential estate developed c.1910 in the north of the parish of Ealing.

Brimsdown (Enfd), 'Grim's hill'.

Uncertainty about the initial consonant persisted to the late seventeenth century, but the earliest forms have G-. Grim is here the personal name, with no mythological significance. The elevation is but slight, 'hill' being a courtesy appellation rather than an exact description [*Grymesdoun* 1420, 1441, *Brymesdowne* 1610, *Grymsdown, Brymsdown* 1686: OE *dūn*].

Brixton S.W.9, '(at) the stone of Brihtsige'. Besides the parish, the name also designated a Hundred (of Surrey), and the stone probably marked the location of the hundredal assembly [*(æt) Brixges Stane* 1062, *Brixistane* 1279: OE *stān*].

Broad Green (Crdn), 'wide village green' [*Brode Grene* 1543: OE *brād, grēne*].

Brockley S.E.4, probably 'Broca's wood or grove' [*Brocele* 1182: OE *lēah*].

Brockley Hill (Brnt), 'hill by or with badger-holes' [*Brokholes* 1277, *Le Brocholes by Eggeswere* 1354, *Brokeley Hill* 1593: OE *broc-hol, hyll*].

Bromley (Brom), 'grove or wood with broom shrubs'. This London Borough includes Beckenham, Chislehurst, Orpington, Penge, and Bromley [*Bromleag* 862: OE *brōm, lēah*].

Bromley-by-Bow E.3, 'bramble-covered grove or wood, beside Bow' [*Brœmbelege* c.1000, *Brameley* c.1145, *Bromlegh* 1274: OE *brœmel, lēah*].

Brompton S.W.3, 'broom farm', a hamlet south of Knightsbridge, the name surviving in Brompton Cemetery, Brompton Road, and West Brompton [*Brompton* 1294: OE *brōm, tūn*].

Brondesbury N.W.6, 'Brand's manor', possibly held by a canon of St Paul's mentioned in deeds of late twelfth-century date. Forms such as *Bromeswode* 1346 seem to have arisen by confusion with Brownswood in Hornsey, which was also held by St Paul's [*Bronnesburie* 1254, *Brondesbury* 1291, *Prebende de Braundes* 1341: OE *burh*].

Brook Green W.6, 'village green by a brook'. The stream (Parr's Ditch, q.v.) now runs underground here.

Broomfield Park N.13, ultimately derived from *Bromefeyld* c.1530, 'field near which broom grew', which gave its name to Broomfield House and so to the present open space.

Brownswood Park N.4, 'Brand's wood', from the name of the St Paul's manor incorporating the same personal name as Brondesbury, and possibly alluding to the same man [*Brandeswode* c.1250, *Brouneswode* 1291, *Broweneswood* 1482: OE *wudu*].

Bruce Castle N.17, alluding to the Bruce family, who held a manor in Tottenham known as *Bruses* 1353. Like their rivals the Balliols, the Bruces held land in England as well as in Scotland.

Buckingham Palace S.W.1. As *Buckingham House* the building was named after John Sheffield, Duke of Buckingham, who bought it in 1702 and whose heir sold it to George III in 1762. The site had been in royal hands as early as 1614, when James I had laid out *Mulberry Garden Field* in the hope of establishing a silk industry in London.

Bull's Cross (Enfd), possibly 'cross set up by man called Bull', but the form *Bellyscrosse* 1540 cannot be ignored. Bullsmoor Lane, nearby, also had early forms with *Bell-* (*Bellesmore Lane* 1619, *Belsmoor Lane* 1754, 1786) and without earlier spellings it is impossible to resolve the confusion. The Gilbert Bolle recorded in local documents in 1235 may be associated with one or both names.

Bunhill Fields E.C.1, almost certainly 'land by heaps of bones'— though the reference may not originally have been to human remains. St Paul's charnel house was cleared in 1549 and the bones were reinterred here [*Bonhilles* 1544: OE *bān, hyll*].

Bunker's Hill N.W.11, commemorating the battle in 1775. The American place is properly Bunker

Hill (from an early settler, George Bunker), but most English examples are in the possessive form. Other instances occur in Belvedere and North Cray.

Burnt Oak (Edgw), from the name of a field on the parish boundary, *Burnt Oak Close* 1754, so called from being near a burnt (possibly lightning-struck) oak tree serving as a landmark.

Burrage Town S.E.18, 'urban development named after de Burghersh'. The manorial name survives in a number of street-names near Woolwich Arsenal station.

Burroughs, The N.W.4, '(land on) the hill', alluding to the 'high down' which gives a name to Hendon itself. There has possibly been a confusion with 'burrows' in some form [*Le Berwestret* 1316, *Borowis in Hendon* c.1530, *Burrowes* 1574: OE *beorg*].

Bursted Wood (Bxly), meaning uncertain. The earliest spelling suggests 'wood in a stream-place', but *burna* occurs as a first element infrequently. The later forms imply a similar derivation to Burnstead (Essex), 'stronghold site'. The designation of Burr Farm, formerly nearby (the name surviving in that of a street, Burr Close) does not support a derivation from *burna* [*Burnes stede* 814, *Borstede* 1301, *Burstede* 1347: OE *burh-stede*].

Bush Hill Park (Enfd), possibly 'hill by enclosed bush-covered land'

[*Bussheyhill* 1549: OE *busc*, *(ge)hæg*, *hyll*].

Bushy Park (Tedn), either 'park by or at a bush enclosure' or 'shrubby parkland' [*Bushie Parke* 1650: OE *busc*, *(ge)hæg*].

Byron Recreation Ground (Harw), alluding to Lord Byron, who was at Harrow School and lives on as a kind of tutelary deity in the London Borough.

C

Caledonian Road N.1, named after the Caledonian Asylum, an orphanage for Scottish children established in 1815. The road, constructed about 1826, was at first called *Chalk Road*.

Camberwell S.E.5, meaning unknown. The second element is doubtless *wella*, 'spring, stream', but the first part of the word is not traceable to any known Old English or British root [*Cambrewelle* 1086, *Cambyrwell* 1154, *Camerewelle* 1199: OE *wella*].

Cambridge Heath E.1, possibly 'Cantbeorht's heathland'. Even if the first element is not a personal name, the 13c. spelling shows quite clearly that the name has nothing to do with Cambridge [*Camprichthesheth* 1275: OE *hǣð*].

Cambridge Park (Twic), named from Cambridge House, residence c.1750 of Richard Owen Cambridge.

Camden Town N.W.1 is named after Charles Pratt, Earl Camden, who came into possession of the manor of Kentish Town through his marriage to the daughter of Nicholas Jeffreys. He let part of the manor for building, and early streets bear the names of both families, and their estates of Bayham and Brecknock, as well as that of the contractor, Greenland. The London Borough of Camden includes Hampstead, Holborn, and St Pancras.

Canbury, 'manor held by canons', land in Kingston held by the canons of Merton Priory. The name survives in the designations of several streets near the railway station [*Canonbury* 1375, *Canbery Stret* 1503: ME *canoun*, OE *burh*].

Canning Town E.16, an industrial settlement named after the firm upon whose premises it was centred (cf. Silvertown).

Cannon Hill Common S.W.20, land formerly in the tenure of the canons of Merton Priory. Early forms had both *-down* and *hill*. Strictly speaking, *hill* was the superfluous element, but it is *down* which has now disappeared [*Cannondownhyll* 1536, *Cannondoune Hill* 1611: ME *canoun*, OE *dūn*, *hyll*].

Cannon Street E.C.4, 'street of the chandlers or candle-makers'. The early forms of this name are quite long, and the transition to the present two-syllable version is not entirely clear; it is possible that misreading or mispronunciation (as distinct from normal sound developments) played a part. The spelling *Kandelwiccestrete* 1241, though not justified historically, gave rise to the name of the ward—Candlewick Ward—in which the street is located [*Candelwrichstrete* c.1185, *Candelwrithestrate* c.1200, *Canyngesstrete* 1480: OE *candelwyrhta, strǣt*].

Canonbury N.1, 'manor of the canons'—namely those of St Bartholomew's, Smithfield, to whom the land was granted in 1253 by Ralph de Berners (cf. Barnsbury). The formation of manorial names by the addition of *-bury* is frequently found in Middlesex, other instances being Gunnersbury, Highbury, Barnsbury, Brondesbury, and Finsbury (qq.v.) [*Canonesbury* 1373, *Canonbury al. Canbury* 1570: ME *canoun*, OE *burh*].

Canons Park (Edgw), relating to the canons of St Bartholomew's, Smithfield, who were granted six acres of land in Little Stanmore in 1331. A later owner, the Duke of Chandos, is remembered in the names of a street and a recreation ground nearby, and the Duke's famous guest is commemorated in Handel Way [*Canons* c.1525: ME *canoun*].

Carshalton (Sutn), 'springside farm where cress grew'. The place is near the source of the Wandle, and references to the growing of cress are found as early as the thirteenth century. OE *ǣwiell-tūn* is found in three other splaces in the south of England, and the reference to cress was doubtless included in this one to avoid confusion [*Aultone* 1086, *Cresaulton* 1235, OE *cærse, ǣwiell, tūn*].

Catford S.E.6, 'ford near which wild cats were seen'. The crossing of the Ravensbourne here being in wooded country the presence of these animals would not be surprising [*Catford* 1254, *Cateforde* 1311: OE *catt, ford*].

Chadwell Heath (Dgnm), 'heath by Chadwell, i.e., cold spring'. The connexion with St Chad is imaginary, folk etymology having been at work—even to the length of causing a local church to be dedicated to the saint [*Chaudewell'* 1254, *Chadwellestrete* 1456: OE *ceald, wella, hǣð*].

Chafford Heath (Upmr), 'heath by calf enclosure'. There is some doubt about the etymology of Chefford (which is also the ancient Hundred name) as forms with *-l-*, e.g., *Chalfewurd'* 1183, are rare; however, early spellings do not support any probable alternatives [*Ceford* c.1075, *Ceffeorda*, *Ceffeworda* 1086, *Chaffewurth* c.1175, *Chalforde* 1594: OE *cealf, worð, hǣð*].

Chalk Farm N.W.3, 'cold dwellings'. As the soil here is clay, it is not surprising to find that the name is not to be taken literally but is a worn-down form of *Chalcotts* [*Chaldecote* 1253, *Caldecote* c.1400, *Chalcotts* 1531, *Chalk* 1746: OE *ceald, cot*].

Chancery Lane W.C.2, 'lane beside the chancellor's office', the name replacing Chancellor's Lane (*Chauncellereslane* 1320) in the fifteenth century. Originally *New Street* (*Nouus Vicus* 1185), the thoroughfare became *Converslane* after the construction of a house for Jewish converts to Christianity. This building was later the seat of the Chancery, bringing about further changes in the name of the street [*Chauncerylane* 1454: OF *chancellerie*, ME *laning*].

Chandos Recreation Ground (Edgw), commemorating Lord Chandos (see Cannons Park).

Chapel End E.17, 'district by a chapel', the site of one of the two chapels of the manor of Higham Bensted in Walthamstow [*Higham Chapel* 1521, *Le Chapellende* 1528: ME *chapel*, OE *ende*].

Charing Cross W.C.2, 'memorial cross at Charing, i.e., place at the bend'. The bend may have been that of the Thames near here, but is more probably the change in direction of the road from London to the west (Akeman Street), which turned from the line of Fleet Street and The Strand, north-westwards for a short distance and then southwards towards the river. The cross (a modern replica of which stands in the forecourt of the main-line railway station) commemorated Queen Eleanor, having been erected on one of the resting-places of her coffin on its journey from Harby to London [*Cyrringe* c.1000, *Cherring'* 1198, *La Charryngcros* 1360: OE *cierring, cros*].

Charlton S.E.5, 'village held by villeins' [*Cerletun* 1086: OE *ceorl, tūn*].

Charterhouse E.C.1, 'Carthusian monastery'. The regular English word for a house of this order is an adaptation of Old French *(Maison) chartrouse*, from the place-name Chatrousse, in Dauphiné, where the order originated—and not from La Grande Chartreuse (near Grenoble), which took its name from a monastery of the order, and not *vice versa*. The London Charterhouse was founded in 1365, by Walter de Manny [Le *Charthous next Smythfield* 1375, *Charterhous* 1385: OF *Charteus, Chartreus*].

Chase Cross (Rmfd), probably 'wayside cross in the forest'. No very early forms of the name are extant, but possible references to the cross occur in personal names of the area—Reginald de Cruce 1281 and Richard atte Crouch 1355.

Cheam (Sutn), probably 'village by tree-stumps'. The second element is certainly *hām*, and this termination persisted recognisably until the eighteenth century (*Cheham* 1722);

but the first element presents problems. The most likely suggestion is that this is the OE equivalent of the Scandinavian term *kage* 'stumps' [*Cegham* 967, *Ceiham* 1086, *Chaiham* 1232: OE *hām*].

Chelsea S.W.3, 'chalk landing-place', implying a wharf from which the cargo was shipped, or where it was unloaded. An alternative interpretation depends on only one of a number of early forms and does not yield a convincing explanation; 'landing place of the cup', (whatever it may mean) is suggested by the 801 form [*Celchyth* 789, *Cælichyth* 801, *Chelchee* 1214: OE *cealc, hȳð*].

Chessington (Kstn), 'Cissa's hill'. The unstressed final syllable gives rise to several variants, including *-den*, *-dene*, and *-denn*, before settling down to the unhistorical *-ton* in quite recent years [*Cisendone* 1086, *Chissendenn'* 1206, *Chessendone* 1255: OE *dūn*].

Childs Hill N.W.11 preserves the family name of Richard Child 1321.

Chingford N.4, 'shingle ford'. This interpretation is based on the earliest extant spellings. If, however (as has been suggested), *Chagingeford* 1219 represents a still earlier form, perhaps revived by the thirteenth-century writer who might possibly have been using pre-Conquest documents, the meaning may have been 'ford of the dwellers by the stumps'—and could refer to pile-dwellings discovered at various times

between 1869 and 1901. The name of the River Ching is a late back-formation from Chingford; the traditional name was *Bourne* (OE *burna*) [*Cingefort* 1086, *Chingeford* 1181, *Chyngelesford* 1272, *Chynegford* 1428: ME *chingel*, OE *ford*].

Chislehurst (Brom), 'gravel hill' [*Cyselhyrst* 973, *Chiselherst* 1159: OE *ceosel, hyrst*].

Chiswick W.4, 'cheese farm'. The versatile ending *-wīc* was applied to specialised farms and was often compounded with the name of the produce concerned, such as butter or cheese; there are several instances of Butterwick in England, and besides Chiswick Hall in Chrisall (Essex), examples of this name are found in the variants Cheswick (Northumberland) and Keswick (Cumbria, Norfolk, and Yorkshire) [*Ceswican* c.1000, *Chesewic* 1181, *Chisewich'* 1229: OE *ciese, wīc*].

Chiswick Eyot, 'small island by Chiswick', earlier *Ye Twigg Eight* 1650, alluding no doubt to twiggy brushwood occurring on the island. The term *eyot*, or *ait*, is used of several islets in the Thames [*Chiswick Ait* 1819: OE *iggoð*].

Chohole Gate (Richmond Park), 'park gate by a road furrowed by ruts'. The dialect word *chockhole* is defined as 'a deep rutty hole to be met with in many of the bye roads or occupation roads in the country' (Holland: *Cheshire Glossary*).

Church End N.3; **Church End** N.W.10, 'district near a church'—respectively in Finchley and Willesden. *End*, 'district, quarter', is frequently met with in Middlesex, Hertfordshire, and Essex [OE *cirice*, *ende*].

Clam Field Recreation Ground S.E.2, 'damp, infertile land' [OE *clǣme*].

Clapham S.W.4, 'village on or by a hillock'. The first element in this name is related to words in other Teutonic languages meaning 'lump' or 'rock', so that rising ground of something less than mountainous dimensions is intended [*Cloppaham* c.880, *Clopeham* 1086, *Clopham* 1184, *Clapham* 1503: OE *clop*, *hām*].

Clapton E.5, 'farm on a hillock'. This name contains the same first element as Clapham (q.v.); Clapton is on high ground which descends steeply to the river Lea on its eastern boundary [*Clopton* 1339, *Clapton* 1593: *clop*, *tūn*].

Claybury Farm (Ilfd), 'manor in clay-soil area', not far to the north of Clayhall (q.v.), which may be subsidiary to it [*Le Clayberye* 1270, *Cleyberye* 1566: OE *clǣg*, *burh*].

Clayhall (Ilfd), 'hall or manor-house in clay-soil area', less than a mile to the south of Claybury. Some early forms refer to the former inclusion of Ilford within Barking parish [*La Claie* 1203, *Berkyngcley* 1424,

Clayhall 1449: OE *clǣg*, *heall*].

Clerkenwell E.C.1, 'students' spring or well', alluding to students of the neighbourhood who frequented the waterside on summer evenings. *Clerk* is here used in the same sense as in Chaucer, whose Clerk of Oxenford was a university student [*Clerkenwell* c.1150, *Clerechenewella* c.1175: ME *clerc*, OE *wella*].

Clissold Park N.16, named from Augustus Clissold who married the heiress of the Crawshay family, landowners in Stoke Newington.

Clitterhouse Recreation Ground N.W.2, from Clutterhouse Farm, the name of which was derived from the name of the family of Robert de Cliderhou 1311, from Clitheroe, Lancs. Folk etymology transformed *Clyderhou's (Farm)* to *Clyderhouse* [*Clyderhous* 1445].

Cloysters Wood (Edgw), probably alluding to the canons of Canons Park (q.v.).

Cockfosters (Barnet), 'chief forester's place'. The position of this settlement on the edge of Enfield Chase confirms the suggested interpretation. A similar word-formation, *cockparker*, for 'chief ranger of a hunting park', occurs in Harrow documents, and a field-name in Stanstead (Herts), *Cock Shepherdes* 1556, indicates that principal officials in other walks of life were similarly designated [*Cokfosters* 1524: OE *cocc*, ME *forester*].

Cold Blow (Bxly), 'place exposed to cold winds'.

Coldfall Wood N.10, probably 'clearing in which charcoal was burned'. *Cold* and *col* ('charcoal') interchange in some place-names (cf. Coalbrookdale in Salop, from earlier *Caldebrok*, 'cold brook') [*Place called Colefall* 1599: OE *col*, **(ge)feall*].

Coldharbour Point, on the Thames near Great Coldharbour (q.v.).

Cole Park (Twic), probably, like *Cole's Bridge*, to be associated with the family of Agnes Coale 1607 and Jane Cole 1690.

Colham Green (Hldn), 'village green by Colham, i.e., Cola's riverside pasture' [*Colanhomm* 883, *Coleham* 1086: OE *hamm*].

Colindale N.W.9, 'Collin's valley', a settlement named after a family called Collin (on record in the sixteenth century). Although the earliest form has the termination *-dene* (OE *denu* 'valley'), this may be an error for 'deep', which occurs in spellings only a few years later, and which may allude to the *deopan fura* ('deep furrow') mentioned in King Edwy's charter granting land in north Hendon to his thegn Lyfing [*Collyndene* 1550, *Collin Deep Lane* 1584, *Collen Deep* 1675: OE *dēop*, *dæl*].

Collier Row (Rmfd), 'charcoal-burners' dwellings'. The area was still densely forested when this name was first recorded, and it was normal for the charcoal burners to live near the scene of their labours in their own 'row' or hamlet [*Colyers Rowe* 1453: ME *colier*, OE *rāw*].

Colliers Wood (Mrtn), 'land occupied by charcoal-burners', the wood being either one from which they gathered their material or one adjacent to land assigned for cultivation by the colliers. No early forms of the name are to be found, but *The Colliers Close* 1576 points to land use of the type described, and Colliers Wood in Lingfield (Surrey) similarly has a field-name counterpart, *Colliers Mead* 1845 [ME *colier*].

Colne *riv*, 'water', a river-name of British origin to be found in several parts of the country. As, for part of its course, the river was the historic boundary between Middlesex and Buckinghamshire, it is quite likely to have preserved an ancient name, even though, in local documents, no forms from earlier than the fourteenth century have survived; the termination *-ee*, *-ey* represents OE *ēa*, 'stream' [*Collee* 1301, *Colne* 1351, *Colneystreme* 1433: B *colün-*].

Colney Hatch N.12, of uncertain origin and meaning. *Hatch* means 'gateway' and refers to an entrance to Enfield Chase, but the meaning of the first part of the name remains obscure [*Colnehatche* 1492: OE *hæcc*].

40

Coombe (Kstn), 'valley' [*Cumbe* 1086: OE *cumb*].

Copenhagen Fields (Islington) named from Copenhagen House, so called because it was occupied by the Danish Ambassador in 1665. The name survives as that of the railway tunnel beneath the site and of one of the streets of the area [*Coopen Hagen* 1680].

Corbets Tey (Upmr), 'Corvyn's enclosure', alluding to the family of the thirteenth-century feudal tenant, Henry Corvyn c.1270 and Osbert Corbin 14c. [*Corbinstye* 1461, *Corbynsty* 1514: OE *tēag*].

Coulsdon (Crdn), 'Cūðræd's hill', alluding to a spur to the south of the town. The form *Curesdone*, found in early documents relating to Chertsey Abbey property, would have been transformed in Norman pronunciation to *Culesdone*, with which the forms found in Domesday Book and later may be compared [*Cudredesdone* 933, *Cuðredesdune* 1062, *Colesdone* 1086, *Coulesdon* 1346: OE *dūn*].

Counters Bridge (Fulham), 'Countess (of Oxford's) bridge', also formerly known as *Compton Bridge*, from Bishop Compton (1632–1713), Bishop of London and lord of the manor of Fulham, who probably reconstructed it. The bridge is across *Counters Creek* (or Chelsea Creek), which forms the eastern boundary of the parish of Fulham [*Countessebrugge* c.1350, *Countesbregge*

1475: ME *contesse*, OE *brycg*]. See also Earl's Court.

Covent Garden W.C.2, 'monastery garden', being the orchard belonging to Westminster Abbey. Although the term *convent* is now applied almost exclusively to communities of women, it was used earlier of religious houses and communities generally. A connexion between the development of a produce market (now at Nine Elms) and the sale of surplus vegetables and fruit by the monastery is entirely conjectural [*Covent Gardyn* 1491: ME *couvent*, *gardin*].

Cowley (Hldn), 'Cofa's wood'. The personal name occurs in Cowley in Buckinghamshire and in Coventry. It cannot be too often emphasised that this does not mean that the places are associated with the same individual [*Cofenlea* 959, *Covelie* 1086, *Cowelee* 1294: OE *lēah*].

Cowley Peachey (Hldn), 'property in Cowley held by Pecche'. Bartholomew Pecche was granted land in Cowley and Ickenham in 1252 [*Couele Peche* 1358, *Cowleypechey* 1560]. See also Cowley.

Crane *riv*, a back-formation from Cranford (q.v.). The river was first called *Fiscesburna* 704, 'fish's stream'; it later became simple *Le Borne* 1375, 'stream'. There is no record of the modern name before the nineteenth century [*Cran Brook* 1825].

Cranford (Hslw), 'ford frequented by cranes or herons'. The name occurs in other counties, but of course Mrs Gaskell's *Cranford* is about none of these, being really Knutsford in Cheshire. It is not surprising that a bird as large as the crane should be remembered in a wide range of names [*Cranforde* 1086: OE *cran, ford*].

Cranham (Upmr), 'crows' ridge'. An alternative name, Ockendon Episcopi, or Bishop Ockendon, was in use for several centuries and alludes to tenure by the Bishop of London. Forms in *-ham* seem to develop from earlier spellings such as *Crawenho* 1201, and arguments that these referred to two different places are unconvincing [(1) *Craohu* 1086, *Craunhoo* 1323, *Crawenham* 1397, *Cran(e)ham* c.1490; (2) *Wocheduna* 1086, *Wokindon Episcopi* 1254–5, *Bishopp Wokyndon* 1343: OE *crāwe*, *hōh*, (*hām*)]. See also North Ockendon.

Cray *riv*, 'clean, pure'. Settlements in the valley of the river include Foots Cray, North Cray, St Mary Cray, and St Paul's Ray (qq.v.), as well as Crayford, 'ford across river Cray' [(1) *Cræges æuuelma* 798 ('source of Cray'), *Craie* c.1200, (2) *Crainford* 1322: OW *crai*, OE *ford*].

Creekmouth (Brkg), 'estuary of a stream', perhaps a tautologous name in view of the normal British usage of *creek*, with the sense 'inlet' [*Fletesmouthe de Berkingge* 1323: OE *mūða, flēot*, ME *creke*].

Cricklewood N.W.2, 'deckle-edged wood', the first element being probably derived from the dialect word *crickle*, 'to bend, give way', which presumably describes the uneven outline of the wood [*Le Crikeldwode* 1294, *Crykyll Wood* 1509: OE *wudu*].

Croham Hurst (Crdn), 'hillock by Croham, i.e., farm frequented by crows'. Early spellings indicate that the first element of this name is not the same as that of Croydon (q.v.). [*Craweham* 1225, *Crouham* 1282, *Cromehurst* 1605: OE *crāwe*, *hām*, *hyrst*].

Crouch End N.8, 'district by a cross'. Wayside crucifixes were frequently erected at crossroads in the Middle Ages, and the names of settlements established at such road-junctions often commemorate this pious practice, though the crosses themselves seldom survive [*Crouchend* 1465, *Crutche Ende* 1553: ME *crouche*, OE *ende*].

Croydon, 'saffron valley'. This herb was grown for dyeing and pharmaceutical purposes in ancient times, but its cultivation in this country seems to have ceased for several centuries and was reintroduced by the Crusaders. The plant is *Crocus sativus* (not to be confused with autumn crocus, which is *Colchicum autumnale*). The unstressed final element in this name suffered a quite early change to *-don(e)*, 'hill', suggesting that by the thirteenth-century the difference between *-don* and *-den* was not fully appreciated [*Crogedene* 809, *Croindene* 1086, *Croydone* c.1240: OE *croh, denu*].

Crystal Palace S.E.19 refers to the building, originally erected in Hyde Park for the Great Exhibition of 1851, transferred to Penge as an exhibition building and concert hall, and destroyed by fire in 1936. The large proportion of glass in the structure led to its present name being first popularly applied and later adopted as the official designation of both the building and its immediate neighbourhood.

Cubitt Town E.14, commemorating the Victorian builder, William Cubitt, who laid out the district c.1850. This name exemplifies the special use of *town* in London to denote a specially planned and laid-out urban unit, especially on land not previously built upon. The term is usually combined with the name of the land-owner, developer, or builder. See also Somers Town, Camden Town.

Cudham (Brom), 'Cuda's village' [*Codeham* 1086, *Cudeham* 1278: OE *hām*].

D

Dagenham (Brkg), 'Dæcca's village', a type of name which recent research has put forward as belonging to the earliest period of settlement. The riverside site confirms this, sup-

ported by the possibility that in the fourth or fifth century Dagenham was higher above river-level than at present [*Dæccenham* 695, *Dakenham* 1261, *Dagnam* 1499: OE *hām*].

Dalston E.8, 'Dēorlāf's farm'. The personal name occurs also in Darlaston (Staffs) and Darliston (Shropshire), but of course there is no suggestion that these names refer to the same individual [*Derleston* 1294, *Darleston* 1581: OE *tūn*].

Dartmouth Park N.6, commemorates the Earls of Dartmouth. The second Earl acquired in 1755 the estate which was developed more than a century later by the fifth Earl.

Dawley (Hldn), 'wood share' [*Dallega* 1086, *Daulee* 1199: OE *dal, lēah*].

Deans Brook *riv* (earlier *Heybourne*, possibly 'yew stream'), a re-naming of the stream, associated in some way with Deans Lane, Edgware [*Yburnan* c.975, *Heybourne* 1574: OE *īw, burna*].

De Beauvoir Town E.8, estate developed by a member of the de Beauvoir family, owners of the land since 1687. Before this Guernsey family acquired the manor, it had been known as *Bammes* or *Baumes*—possibly derived from the surname *Bamme*, found in London documents in the 14th and 15th centuries.

Denmark Hill S.E.5, named from

the hunting lodge of Prince George of Denmark, husband of Queen Ann.

Dollis Brook *riv*, the upper part of the river Brent, named from Dollis (Farm) in Hendon, 'shared land', probably unconnected with Dollis Hill (q.v.).

Dollis Hill N.W.2, probably from a surname Dolley or Dawley.

Dormers Wells (Sthl), 'Dēormod's spring' [*Dermondeswell* 1235, *Dormandeswell* 1571: OE *wella*].

Down S.W.18, 'hill', the name of a former manor, surviving in Down Lodge. See also *Dunsford*.

Downe (Orpn), 'hill' [*Doune* 1316: OE *dūn*].

Drayton Green W.13, 'village green by a portage'. The place lies in a large bend in the river Brent [*Drayton* 1387, *Dreyton* 1494: OE *dræg*, *tūn*, *grene*]. See also West Drayton.

Dudden Hill N.W.10, 'Dodda's hill' [*Dodynghill* 1544: OE *-ing*, *hyll*].

Duke of Northumberland's River, a watercourse constructed to bring water to the corn-mill at Syon Abbey from the River Crane. The land was owned, in the early seventeenth century, by the Earls of Northumberland.

Duke's Meadows W.4, so called

because formerly owned by the Duke of Devonshire.

Dulwich S.E.21, 'marshy land on which dill grew'. This plant, *Anethum graveolens*, was cultivated as a therapeutic herb from very early times. The second element, the rather rare *wisce*, suggests the low-lying, well-watered nature cf part at least of Dulwich [*Dilwihs* 967, *Dilwiche* 1127, *Dilewysshe* 1277, *Dulwyche* 1555: OE *dile*, *wisce*].

Dunsford S.W.18, 'ford in a valley', alluding to a crossing of the Wandle. This name (surviving only in Dounesforth Gardens S.W.18 and Durnsford Avenue and Road S.W.19) seems to have been affected by *Down* not far away, or by *Duntshill*, 'hill of the manor of Down' [1. *Deneford* 1178, *Donesford* 1301, 2. *Dona* c.1190, *La Doune* 1371, 3. *Duneshull* 1185, *Dunchhill* 1609: OE *denu*, *ford*, *dūn*, *hyll*].

Duntshill. See *Dunsford*.

E

Ealing W.5, '(territory of) people or followers of Gilla'. It is no longer generally held that names of this type, in which the termination *-ingas* was added to a personal name, are those of the earliest period of settlement, but they certainly belong to a time when the identity of the occupying tribal group was an important feature of recognition. The

London Borough includes the two former boroughs of Acton and Southall as well as Ealing itself [*Gillingas* c.700, *Yllinges* c.1170, *Yilling* 1294, *Elyng* 1553: OE *-ingas*].

Earls Court S.W.5, 'earl's manor-house'. The lords of the manor of Kensington until the sixteenth century were the Earls of Oxford. This hamlet grew up round their manor house, which was on the site of Barkston Gardens and Bramham Gardens [*Earles Court* 1593, *Erls Cort* 1654: ME *court*].

Earlsfield S.W.18, 'land held by an earl'. No actual field-name has been traced, but land in this area was owned by Earl Spencer. The immediate source of the name of the railway station was Earlsfield Road (not far from the station), which was itself named from Earlsfield House, a residence near Spencer Park.

Earl's Sluice *riv*, named in honour of the first Earl of Gloucester, an illegitimate son of King Henry I, who was Lord of the Manor of Camberwell and Peckham. The stream rises near Denmark Hill and enters the Thames at Deptford.

East Acton W.3, 'eastern part of Acton (q.v.)', formerly a distinct hamlet [*Estacton* 1294: OE *ēast*].

East Barnet, 'eastern part of the burnt clearing' [*Est Barnet* c.1275: OE *ēast*, *bærnet*]. See also Barnet.

East Bedfont (Fltm), '(place) east of spring in a hollow'. The neighbouring West Bedfont is in the part of Middlesex transferred to Surrey in 1968. The element *funta* is an Old English borrowing from British; a possible explanation of the use of this term instead of OE *wella* is that there may have been a Celtic-speaking population in the neighbourhood [*Bedefunt* 1086, *Bedefons* 12c., *Estbedefont* 1235, *Bedfunte* 1279: OE **byde*, *funta*].

Eastbury Level (Brkg), 'flat land in the eastern manor'—or, possibly '. . . east of the manor (of Barking)' [*Estberi* 1321, *Esberi* 1557: OE *ēast*, *burh*, MnE *level*].

Eastcote (Rslp), 'eastern cottage or shelter', a hamlet to the east of Ruislip, evidently having developed from a single cottage. *Westcott* also appears in eighteenth-century Ruislip records, but the name has not survived. It may be noted that in a number of places *ēast-cot* has developed to Ascot(t), but forms in *East-* are found in Wiltshire (three instances) and Bedfordshire [*Estcotte* 1248, *Estcote* 1296, *Ascote* 1356, *Eastcote* 1819: OE *ēast*, *cot*].

East End (Pinr), 'eastern part of parish' [*Esthend* 1453: OE *ēast*, *ende*].

East Finchley N.2, 'eastern part of Finchley (q.v.)'. In its present form, the name is of recent application, but *East End* (surviving in East End Road) was recorded in the sixteenth century [*Estend* 1558: OE *ēast*, *ende*].

East Ham E.6, 'eastern riverside land'. The present course of the Thames does not suggest an interpretation 'land within a river-bend', but this requirement might be satisfied if the confluence of the Roding with the Thames were to be taken as such a bend [*Hamme* 958, *Est Hammes* c.1250: OE *ēast, hamm*].

East Putney S.W.15, 'eastern part of Putney (q.v.)', a modern name, dating from the last quarter of the nineteenth century.

East Sheen S.W.14, 'eastern part of Sheen, i.e., shelters', distinguished from West Sheen (see Richmond) [*Shenes* 1232, *Est Shenes* 1247, *Estshene* 1258: OE *ēast, *scēo*].

East Wickham (Welling), 'settlement on a Romano-British site'—distinguished from West Wickham (q.v.) near Croydon. Recent research on names containing the element *wīc-hām* has resulted in a suggested interpretation 'homestead at a *vicus*', alluding to very early Anglo-Saxon settlement at or near a Romano-British village [*Wikam* 1240, *Est Wycham* 1292: OE *ēast, wīc-hām*].

Ebury, 'manor of *Eia*, or *Eye*, i.e., island', the western part of the present City of Westminster, but formerly a separate manor, stretching from the present Grosvenor Road northwards to (and including) Hyde Park. The name survives in Ebury Bridge, Ebury Square, and some other street-names. The element, *ēg*, signifying 'dry ground amid marshes', indicates the nature of the shores of the Thames before the construction of embankments permitted general riverside building [*Eia* 1086, *Eie* 1236, *Eyebury* 1323, *Ebery* 1535: OE *ēg, burh*].

Eden Park (Bknm), perhaps 'heath-covered land'. Eden Street in Kingston was formerly *Hethenstret*, i.e., 'heathen street'; it is suggested that this refers simply to heath land.

Edgware (Barnet), 'Ecgi's fishing enclosure', the location of which is described in an ancient charter as the place where the *stanburna* ('stony stream', now Edgware brook) crosses Watling Street—here known as High Street, Edgware [*Æcges Wer* c.975, *Eggeswere* 1199, *Edggeware* 1489: OE *wer*].

Edgware Road W.2, 'road to Edgware', the name given to Watling Street between Marble Arch and Maida Vale, and to various other lengths of the road (A.5) as far as Edgware itself. The underground railway station bearing the name is at the junction with Marylebone Road [*Edgware High Waie* 1574].

Edmonton N.9, 'Eadhelm's estate'. The early forms indicate that occasionally the personal name was inflected (*Edelmeston* < *Eadhelmestun*), occasionally uninflected (*Adelmetone* < *Eadhelmtun*), and occasionally combined with *-ing* (*Edelington* < *Eadhelmingtun*); these variations do not affect the interpretation offered unless further research shows that the -ing forms derive from spellings in earlier documents than are known at present [*Adelmetone* 1086, *Edelmintone* 1211, *Edelmeston* 1214: OE *tūn*, *-ingtūn*].

Eel Brook Common S.W.6, 'common land by the stream on or by a hill', as is clear from the early forms. The slight elevation here would have been conspicuous in a dead level countryside and so received the courtesy designation of 'hill'. Later generations evidently could not take this seriously and altered the name to what seemed to them to be a more plausible form [*Hillebrook* 1408, *Hillebroke* 1459, *Hellebrook* 1444, *Helbroke* 1554, *Eelbrook* 1820: OE *hyll*, *brōc*].

Eel Pie Island W.3, 'island for picnics', modern name for a Thames islet that was formerly known as *The Parish Ayte* 1608 [OE *iggoð*].

Effra *riv*, thought to be a rather clumsy modernisation of OE *efre*, 'bank'; the river, which joins the Thames at Nine Elms, has had less romantic-sounding names in the past, including The Creek, New River, Vauxhall Creek, and even The Shore (i.e., sewer).

Elephant & Castle S.E.1, cross-roads and vicinity named from an inn with this sign.

Elmers End (Bknm), 'quarter or end

of parish held by Aylmer family' [OE *ende*].

Elm Park (Hnch), self-explanatory. The street-names of the neighbourhood suggest a veritable arboretum.

Elmstead (Brom), 'place by elm trees' [*Elmsted* 1320: OE *elm*, *stede*].

Eltham S.E.9, 'Elta's village' [*Elteham* 1086: OE *hām*].

Elthorne Park W.7, modern name, transferring that of the Hundred within which Hanwell was located, but with no historical warrant for the suggestion that this was the meeting place of the Hundred. The Hundred name means 'Ella's thorn tree', but, for the reasons given, this cannot be taken as interpreting the name of the open space in Hanwell.

Enfield, 'Eana's open land'. In extensively wooded areas the fundamental sense of OE *feld*, 'area cleared of trees', is appropriate. Much of Enfield's wooded history is recorded in local names [*Enefeld* 1086, *Enfeld* 1293: OE *feld*].

Enfield Chase, 'hunting forest at Enfield' [*Enefeld Chace* 1325: ME *chace*].

Enfield Highway. See *Ermine Street*.

Enfield Lock, 'enclosure at or by Enfield' [*Norhtlok* 1355, *Enfield Lock* 1710: ME *lok*].

Enfield Wash, 'Enfield ford or

flooded place', at the place where Cuffley Brook crosses Ermine Street—here called Hertford Road [OE *(ge)wæsc*].

Erith (Bxly), 'gravelly landing place'. The first element is probably the rare OE word *ēar*, which has the general meaning of 'earth, soil', but which is related to Scandinavian words with the sense suggested. The two possibilities—'landing-place for gravel' and 'landing place with gravelly soil' are not, of course, mutually exclusive. The second part of the name is one of the several variants of the element *hȳð*, others occurring in Lambeth, Putney, Rotherhithe, and Chelsea (qq.v.) [*Earhyð* 695, *Earhið* c.960, *Erhede* 1086, *Eryth* 1610: OE *ēar*, *hȳð*].

Ermine Street, like Watling Street (q.v.), took its name from the people through whose territory it passed, the *Earningas* 'followers of Earna'. The name is no longer used, but sections of this ancient highway are known by such modern names as Bishopsgate, Norton Folgate, Shoreditch High Street, Stamford Hill and Hertford Road. Enfield High Way is so called through its being adjacent to this road (*Erningestrate* 13c.: OE *-ingas*, *strǣt*].

Euston N.W.1, transferred name from Euston, Suffolk ('Eof's estate'), the seat of the Duke of Grafton, lord of the manor of Tottenham Court when Euston Road was constructed. Euston Square was built nearly a century later, and it was from this that the station took its name.

F

Fagg's Bridge (Fltm), named from the family of George Fagg, who owned land in the area in the nineteenth century and possibly earlier. The bridge takes Fagg's Road across the Duke of Northumberland's river.

Fairdean Downs or **Farthing Downs** (Clsn), 'hill(s) on or by land called Farthing, i.e., fourth part'. Division of property gave rise to terms such as Half and Farthing, but often, as here, the identity of the original whole estate cannot be established [*Ferthyngdoune* 1322: OE *feorðung*, *dūn*].

Fairlop (Ilfd), '(place by) lopped tree near which a fair took place'. Among the numerous legends associated with this name, there are a few undoubted facts. There was a tree known as the Fairlop Oak; it was cut down in 1820. An annual fair was indeed held, during the eighteenth century and later, in the shade of this tree; this accounts for the element *fair*, which therefore need not be taken to mean 'just' or 'beautiful'. Lastly, the term *lop* was certainly used to mean 'lopped tree'.

Falconwood S.E.9, 'wood in or near which hawks or falcons were seen or were used in hunting'.

Fallow Corner N.12, 'corner of field left uncultivated' [*Follow Corner* 1680, *Fallow Corner* 1710: OE *fealg*].

Farleigh (Crdn), 'woodland clearing overgrown with bracken' [*Ferlega* 1086, *Farleg* 1215, *Farnl'* 1247, *Farnlegh* 1255, *Farlegh* 1314: OE *fearn*, *lēah*].

Farnborough (Orpn), 'hill overgrown with bracken' [*Ferenberga* 1180, *Farnberg* 1242: OE *fearn*, *beorg*].

Farringdon E.C.1, named after two aldermen of the City of London, William and Nicholas de Farndon, who held the ward (previously called Ludgate-Newgate) in succession during the thirteenth century.

Farthing Downs. See Fairdean Downs.

Farthing Street (Orpn), 'land called Farthing (fourth part) by a paved road'. *Street* in place-names often refers to a location by or near a Roman road [*Ferthyng* 1366: OE *feorðung*, *strǣt*].

Feltham (Hslw), 'village near which mullein grew', taking the first element to be an OE plant-name *felte*, rather than *feld*, 'open country' for which there is little support in early spellings [*Feltehā* 1086, *Feltesham* 1274: OE **felte*, *hām*].

Figge's Marsh (Mchm), from the surname Fige, recorded in the fourteenth century in Mitcham [*Fygmershe* c.1530: OE *mersc*].

Finchley N.3, 'grove or wood in which finches were seen' [*Finchelee* c.1208, *Finchesleg'* 1235, Finchinge-leye 1260: OE *finc*, *lēah*].

Finsbury E.C.1, 'Fin's manor', the personal name being Anglo-Scandinavian and on record as occurring in the Home Counties around the year 1000 [*Vinisbir'* 1231, *Finesbir'* 1235, *Fynnesbury* 1535: OE *burh*].

Finsbury Park N.4, open space on the site of former Hornsey Wood, designated by statute for the use of the inhabitants of the old Parliamentary borough of Finsbury, which extended to this area. The name dates from 1857.

Fleet *riv*, 'inlet, creek', originally the lower end of the River Holborn (q.v.), but later denoting the entire course of the stream [*Fleta* c.1012, *Flete* c.1200: OE *flēot*].

Foots Cray (Sdcp), 'Fot's village on river Cray' [*Fotescræi* c.1100, *Fotescraye* 1210]. See also Cray *riv*.

Forest Gate E.7, 'gate to (Epping) forest'. The gate was in Woodgrange Road and its main purpose was to prevent cattle straying from the forest into the main road.

Forest Hill S.E.23, named from extensive woodland formerly covering the area. This (Forest Wood) was part of the great Northwood, which gave its name to Norwood (q.v.).

Fortis Green N.2, meaning unknown [*Fortessegreene* 1613, *Fortes Greene* 1638].

Fortune Green N.W.6, 'green place before the village' [*Fortune Greene* 1646: OE *forð, tūn*].

Four Wants (Upmr), 'four paths, a cross-roads'. The term also occurs as a street-name in Chingford, in the form The Four Wents (OE *feower*, ME *went*].

Freelands Wood (Crdn), 'wood by or associated with land held free of service' [*Bosc. voc. Freland'* 1302 (i.e., 'wood called Freelands'): OE *frēo, land*].

Freezywater (Enfd), 'bleak place', named from a pond in this bleak and exposed situation (*Freezwater* 1768].

Friern Barnet, 'Barnet of the brethren'. This was a possession of the Knights of St John of Jerusalem, and as such was retained in Middlesex when High and East Barnet were placed in Hertfordshire. The name Barnet originally indicated a place in the great forest which had been cleared by burning [*La Bernet* 1235, *Frerennebarnethe* 1274, *Freresbarnet* 1336, *Friern Bñet* 1535: OE *bærnet*, ME *frere*].

Frith Manor N.W.7, 'woodland

estate' [*La Frithe* 1294, *Fryth in Hyndon* 1535: OE *(ge)fyrhðe*, ME *maner*].

Fryant Farm N.W.9, formerly *Freryn Court*, 'manor of the brethren', owned by the Knights of St John (cf. Friern Barnet). *Court* occurs in place-names with the meaning 'manor house' and is sometimes extended to the manor of which the house is headquarters [*Freryn Court* 1517, *Freren al. Kyngesbury* 1544, *Friarn Manor* 1593: ME *frere, court, maner*].

Fulham S.W.6, 'Fulla's riverside pasture'. The element *hamm* is here, as frequently elsewhere, applied to land in the bend of a river [*Fulanham* c.705, *Fullanhamme* c.895, *Fuleham* 1086, *Fulham* 1274: OE *hamm*].

Fulwell (Fltm), possibly 'foul or muddy spring' [*Fulwell* 1450: OE *fūl, wella*].

G

Gallions Reach (Thames), 'stretch of river near Gallions Cottages' alluding to property formerly held by the family of John and Richard Galyon (1330). A *reach* is 'that portion of a river (&c) which lies between two bends' (O.E.D.).

Gants Hill (Ilfd), named from Richard le Gant (1285) or a member of his family [*Gantesgrave* 1291, *Gauntes Hethe* 1545].

Garratt S.W.17, '(place with or by) watch tower', a virtually lost name (apart from Garratt Green and Garratt Lane) of a small neighbourhood with its own picturesque customs [*Le Garret* 1538, *Ye Garret* 1580: OF *garite*].

Gidea Park (Rmfd), 'park at Giddyhall, i.e., foolish building'. Although this name may refer to the unwisdom of a building enterprise, rather than to particular features of the hall itself, *giddy* used elsewhere seems more likely to allude to unsteadiness of construction, as in *Gydiebernes* at Canewdon (Essex), than to a building normally known as a 'folly'. No certainty seems possible, without other evidence, about the exact sense of *giddy* in Gidea Park [*La Gidiehall'* 1258, *Giddyhalle* 1376, *Gedyhall* 1478, *Guydie Hall Parke* 1668: OE *gydig*, *hall*, ME *park*].

Gipsy Hill S.E.19, 'hill frequented by gypsies'. It was favoured by these travelling people in the eighteenth and early nineteenth centuries.

Gladstone Park N.W.2, honouring W. E. Gladstone, who was a frequent visitor at the house of the Earl and Countess of Aberdeen at Dollis Hill.

Globe Town E.2, 'urban development near Globe Road'; the thoroughfare having been earlier *Theven Lane* (c.1600) the name of the district can only have been as at present from about 1700, when 'thieves' lane' was awarded the more dignified title of *Globe Lane*, possibly from an inn sign.

Gloucester Road S.W.7, named from Maria, Duchess of Gloucester, who had a house (c.1800) in the street known until the middle of the nineteenth century as Hogmoor Lane.

Goddington (Orpn), 'land held by Goddington family', the owners having doubtless come from Godinton (Kent) [*Godinton'* 1240].

Golders Green N.W.11, from the personal name Golder (or Godyere, cf. Golders Hill, *infra*). The surname does not appear in local documents. The alternative name appearing among the eighteenth-century forms has not been explained [*Golders Greene* 1612, *Groles Green* 1754, *Groles or Godders Green* 1790].

Golders Hill Park N.W.11, 'open space on Goders Hill', named from the family called God(y)ere who may also be responsible for the name of Golders Green (q.v.). There are references in Hendon documents to John le Godere (1321) and to John Godyer (1371), either or both of whom may have been members of this family.

Goldhawk Road W.12, named from the surname Goldhawk, which occurs frequently in fifteenth-century Court Rolls. Earlier, in 1222, one Goldhauek is mentioned in a Chiswick document [*Fossa Vocata*

Goldhawkesdych 1408, *Goldehawkes* c.1410].

Goodge Street W.1, named after William Goodge, who owned the site in 1746.

Goodmayes (Ilfd), from the surname of John Godemay (1319).

Gooshays (Rmfd), 'goose enclosure'. The local family whose surname was derived from this place became so prominent that they were wrongly regarded as lords of the place, the name of which took on the 'manorial' form (with final *-s*) [*Goshaye* 1334, *Gosayes* 1378, *Goseyes* c.1510: OE *gōs, (ge)hæg*].

Gordon Hill (Enfd), named from a house in the neighbourhood, which belonged to the father of Lord George Gordon, the notorious instigator of the anti-Catholic riots in 1780.

Gospel Oak N.W.5, 'tree on a boundary at which the gospel was read', alluding to the Rogationtide ceremony of beating the bounds. The oak, on the Hampstead-St Pancras boundary, was cut down during the nineteenth century.

Goulds Green (Hldn), named from the family of John Golde (1373).

Graveney *riv*, back-formation from the manorial name found in Tooting Graveney. See Tooting.

Grays Inn W.C.1, 'residence of de

Grey'. Formerly the manor of *Portpoole* (the meaning of which is obscure), the property was held by Reginald de Grey at the time of his death in 1308 [*Purtepol* 1203, *Portepole* 1240, *Portpole Maner' vocat' Grays Inn in Holborne* 1396: OE *pol, inn*].

Great Coldharbour (Wntn), 'cheerless lodging', distinguished from Little Coldharbour in Rainham. Coldharbour Point on the Thames takes its name from Great Coldharbour [*Coleherbert* c.1560, *Great Coldharbour* 1777: OE *cald, herebeorg*].

Great Portland Street W.1, named after the second Duke of Portland, who gained possession of the Cavendish properties in London through his wife; this land was built over during the eighteenth century, numerous street names in the area commemorating the history of the estate.

Great Scotland Yard S.W.1, named from the kings of Scotland, who held a piece of land between Northumberland Avenue and Whitehall Place. As the name of the headquarters of the Metropolitan Police, it has been transferred to other premises on the removal of the offices, but in the form *New Scotland Yard*. The connexion with Scotland had ceased before the date of the earliest document mentioning the land [*Parcel of Land late of the King of Scotts* 1440, *Le Scotland Ground* c.1510, *Scotland Yard* 1656: OE *geard*].

Greenford (Elng), '(place by a) green ford'. The epithet probably alludes to a river-crossing on the route of a lesser used road; two such crossings seem to have occurred in this area—one here, and the other in Perivale (or Little Greenford) [*Grenan Forda* 845, *Greneforde* 1066, *Greneforde Magna* 1254, *Grinford* 1575: OE *grēne, ford*].

Green Park S.W.1, so named (rather unimaginatively) in the eighteenth century; it was formerly part of St James's Park.

Green Street Green (Frnb), 'village green by grass-grown paved road' [*Grenstrete* 1292: OE *grēne, strǣt*].

Greenwich S.E.10, 'green harbour or port'. Like Woolwich (q.v.), this name contains OE *wīc* in one of its extended senses; other Thames-side landing places have names terminating in -*hȳþ* (e.g., Putney, Rotherhithe, Chelsea), and it may be suggested that the names in -*wīc* were somewhat more substantial ports, as this element occurs elsewhere in England in such names as Ipswich and Norwich. Greenhithe, outside Greater London and down river from Greenwich, offers a further comparison [*Grenewic* 964, *Grenviz* 1086, *East, West Grenewych* 1291: OE *grēne, wīc*].

Grim's Ditch (Pinr), 'Woden's digging', a name (occurring also in other counties of England) for an ancient defensive earthwork, formerly more extensive than now.

Grim was an alternative name for Woden; the Saxons frequently ascribed to gods such great artefacts as they found on colonising the country [*Grimesdich* 1289, *Grymesdich* 1541: OE *dīc*].

Grovelands Park N.21, modern name for land earlier known as *Cullands Grove*, which may be associated with the Culling family who were residents in Edmonton as early as the thirteenth century.

Grove Park W.4, from Grove House on the site of *The Grove* 1412 [OE *grāf*].

Gunnersbury W.3, 'Gunnhild's fortified place or manor', embodying the name of an unidentified woman. The tradition that the personal name was that of a niece of King Canute has no documentary support, but the Norse origin of the name suggests that this is a late name in -*bury*, so that the second element is more likely to imply a manor than an early fortified place [*Gounyldebury* 1334, *Gunnyldesbury* 1348, *Gonelsbury* 1487, *Gunnersbury* 1593: OE *burh*].

Gutteridge Wood (Hldn), 'wood by or with a great hedge' [*Great Headge Wood* c.1600, *Woods called Great Hedge* 1610, *Grutedge Wood* 1745: OE *grēat, hecg*].

Guy's Hospital S.E.1, named after Thomas Guy (d.1724), who built and endowed the hospital.

H

Hackbridge (Wltn), 'bridge in a hook-shaped piece of land', the area being between two arms of the Wandle [*Hakebruge* c.1235, *Hakebrygge* 1360: OE *haca, brycg*]. See also Hacton.

Hackney E.8, 'Haca's island', the term here meaning 'dry land amid marshes' [*Hakeneia* 1198, *Hakeneye* 1236, *Hackney* 1535: OE *ēg*].

Hackney Wick E.9, 'outlying farm of Hackney' [*Ferm of Wyk* 1299, *Wyke* 1399: OE *wīc*].

Hacton (Upmr), 'farm on a hook-shaped piece of land', this place being on the tongue of land formed by the junction of the Ingrebourne and a tributary (formerly called *Hakelondsbroke*, 'stream in hookland') [*Haketon* 1310, *Aketon* 1380: OE *haca, tūn*]. See also Hackbridge.

Hadley Wood (Barnet), 'wood at Hadley, i.e., heath-covered clearing' [*Hadlegh* 1248: OE *hǣð, lēah*]. See also Monken Hadley.

Haggerston N.1, possibly 'at the stone of Hærgōd', basing the interpretation on the Domesday Book form; but all other spellings from 1220 onwards indicate an original ending in -*tūn*, and so 'Hærgōd's farm' [*Hergotestane* 1086, *Hergotestune* c.1220, *Heregodeston* c.1225: OE *stān, tūn*].

Hainault (Ilfd), '(place by) wood belonging to a monastic community', the woodland itself being now (tautologically) called Hainault Forest. The community referred to is that of Barking Abbey. The present spelling, current since the seventeenth century, has developed because of a supposed connexion with Philippa of Hainault. The earliest record of this name, however, dates from more than a century before Philippa's birth [*Henehout* 1221, *Hyneholt* 1239, *Hineholt* 1323, *West Hainault* 1654: OE *higna, holt*].

Hale, The N.W.7, 'nook, corner of land', being in the north-western corner of the parish of Hendon [*Hale* 1525: OE *healh*].

Hale End E.4, 'corner of land at extremity of parish', one of the several 'ends' of Walthamstow. Proximity to Epping Forest accounts for the alternative name in the seventeenth century, Wood End [*The Hale* 1517, *Hale End* 1636, *Woodend otherwise Halesend* 1640: OE *healh, ende*].

Haling Park (Crdn), perhaps 'slope by a hall', *Park* having been added later. The earliest spelling (associated with a personal name) suggests a folk-name 'people of Healla', but this is not confirmed by later spellings [*Hallinges* 1200, *Hallink* 1229, *Haling* 1255, *Halynke* c.1320: OE *hall, hlinc*].

Ham (Rchm), 'land in a river-bend',

the great bend of the Thames at this point enclosing both Ham and the adjacent Petersham (q.v.) [*Hama* c.1150, *Hamme* 1154, *Hammes* 1235, *Ham* 1532: OE *hamm*].

Ham, East and West. See East Ham, West Ham.

Hammersmith W.6, 'hammer smithy', formerly a hamlet of Fulham and evidently originating as an outlying industrial settlement of that parish. The London Borough of Hammersmith and Fulham unites the two places [*Hamersmyth'* 1294, *Hameresmythe* 1312: OE *hamor*, *smiððe*].

Hampstead N.W.3, 'homestead, dwelling-place' [*Hemstede* 959, *Hamstede* 978, *Hamestede* 1086, *Hampstede* 1258: OE *hām-stede*].

Hampstead Heath N.W.3, 'heath-land at Hampstead (q.v.)' [*Hampstede Heth* 1543: OE *hæð*].

Hampton (Kstn), 'farm in a river-bend', alluding doubtless to the great turn in the course of the Thames, enclosing the present-day open spaces of Bushy Park and Hampton Court Park, adjoining which is the settlement of Hampton [*Hammtone* 1086, *Hantona* 1165, *Hamton* 1202: OE *hamm*, *tūn*].

Hampton Court (Kstn), 'manor house at Hampton' [*Hampton Courte* 1476: ME *court*].

Hampton Wick (Kstn), 'outlying farm dependent on Hampton (q.v.)' [*Wica* 13c., *Hamptone la Wyke* 1263, *Hamptonwicke* 1615: OE *wīc*].

Hanger Hill W.5, 'wooded slope'. There was formerly a wood here, *Hanger Wood*, of which Hanger Hill Park is a very small remnant [*Le Hangrewode* 1393, *Aungrewode* c.1410, *Hanger Hill* 1710: OE *hangra*].

Hanwell W.7, 'spring or well frequented by cocks' [*Hanewelle* 959, *Hanawella* 998, *Hanewelle* 1086, *Hanwell* 1402: OE *hana*, *wealla*].

Hanworth (Hslw), 'Hana's enclosure' [*Haneworde* 1086, *Hanworth* 1428: OE *worð*].

Harefield (Hldn), 'open land used by an army'. Cryptic though it may be, the interpretation is fairly certain; it is not known at what period the name arose or to what army it refers [*Herefelle* 1086, *Herrefeld* 1115, *Herefeld* 1206, *Harefeld* 1223: OE *here*, *feld*].

Hare Street (Rmfd), '(place by) army road', alluding to the Roman road from London to Colchester, which would have been used by the Saxons for military purposes [*Herstrate* 1344, *Hare Street* 1514: OE *here*, *strǣt*].

Haringey N.8, 'Hæring's woodland enclosure'. The interpretation is strictly that of **Hornsey** rather than that of Haringey, the London

Borough in which Hornsey is now combined with Tottenham and Wood Green. It is necessary also to consider **Harringay**, a district within the old borough of Hornsey. The starting point for the unravelling of the confusion obscuring this name is itself not entirely certain, but at least a compound consisting of a personal name (in this case Hæring) and *(ge)hæg* is quite regular. The development from *Haringesheye* by way of *Harynsey* to Hornsey is easily intelligible, and this series of names displaced forms derived from *Haringeia* by 1600. A house built in 1792 was called by its owner *Haringay House* and this set the fashion for similar names for local government purposes from the last quarter of the nineteenth century onwards. In the form Harringay the name became familiar as that of a stadium (and of a railway station nearby) in the first half of the twentieth century, and the superfluous *r* was accepted until the reform of London local government in 1963 brought about the return of Haringey as an official name—for the London Borough itself, no less— with its single *r* and *ey* ending [*Haringeie* 1201, *Harengheye* 1232, *Haringesheye* 1243, *Haryngey* 1488, *Harnesey* 1524, *Hornsey* 1564, *Haringay al. Hornesey* c.1580: OE *(ge)hæg*].

Harlesden N.W.10, 'Heoruwulf's farm', undoubtedly a *-tūn* name despite not only the modern form but also intermediate spellings in 1291, 1564, and 1606, which point to a

possibility of derivation from either *dūn*, 'hill' or (like the modern form) *denu*, 'valley'. The modern termination is in line with those of Neasden and Willesden (qq.v.), which are similarly unhistorical [*Herulvestune* 1086, *Herleston* 1195, *Herlesdon* 1291, *Harleston* 1365, *Harlesden* 1606: OE *tūn*].

Harlington (Hldn), 'farm or estate associated with Hygered' [*Hygereding tun* 831, *Herdintone* 1086, *Hardlyngton* 1475, *Harlyngton* 1521: OE *-ingtūn*].

Harmondsworth (Hldn), 'Heremod's enclosure' [*Hermodesworde* 1086, *Heremodesworthe* 1222, *Hermondesworth* 1316, *Harmesworth* 1485, *Harmondsworth* vulg. *Harmsworth* 1675: OE *worþ*].

Harold Hill (Rmfd), Harold Park (Rmfd): named from Harold Wood (q.v.).

Harold Wood (Rmfd), '(Earl) Harold's wood'. This is part of the Liberty of Havering-atte-Bower, which was held by Harold until his death in 1066 [*Horalds Wood* c.1237, *Haroldeswoode* c.1272: OE *wudu*].

Harringay N.8. See Haringey.

Harrow (Harw), 'heathen shrine or temple', evidently for the particular use of a tribe called the Gumenings, about whom nothing further is known. The isolated hill on which

Harrow now stands, rising im-
pressively above the Middlesex plain,
would have been a typical site for a
Saxon place of worship. The per-
sistent use of plural forms down to
the late 13c. is not easily explained,
and may point to multiple shrines on
the site. The full name, Harrow-on-
the-Hill, or an equivalent, has been
in use since the fourteenth century
but it is not employed as the title of
the entire London Borough
[*Gumeninga Hergae* 767, *Hearge*
825, *Hergas* 832, *Herges* 1086,
Herewes 1234, *Heregh'* 1294,
Harwys 1295, *Harwo* 1347, *Harowe*
1369, *Harowe atte Hille* 1398,
Harowe on the Hull 1400, *Harowe
on the Hill* 1426: OE *hearg, hyll*].

Harrow Lodge (Hnch), earlier
Harrow Farm 1777, but no certainty
is possible of the origin or interpretation of the name.

Harrow Weald (Harw), 'forest or
woodland near Harrow' [*Weldewode*
1282, *Harewewelde* 1388, *Harrowe
Weale* 1603: OE *weald*].

Hatcham S.E.14, 'Hæcci's estate'
[*Hacheham* 1086, *Hachham* 1319:
OE *hām*].

Hatch End (Pinr), 'district of parish,
by a gate', alluding no doubt to an
entrance to Pinner Park [*Le Hacche-
hend* 1448, *Hacheend* 1475: OE
hæcc, ende].

Hatton (Hslw), 'heath farm', lying
on the western edge of Hounslow
Heath [*Hatone* 1086, *Hattone* 1211,

Hatton next Bedefunte 1293: OE
hǣð, tūn].

Havering-atte-Bower, '(place of the)
people of Hæfer, by a (royal)
residence', a Royal Liberty created in
1465. The Liberty contained the
parishes of Havering, Romford, and
Hornchurch and was thus virtually
identical with the present London
Borough of Havering [*Haueringas*
1086, *Haveringes* 1166, *Hauering
atte Bower* 1272: OE *-ingas, būr*].

Haverstock Hill N.W.3, perhaps
from the name of a landowner in the
area, belonging to a family originally
from Stock (Essex), *Haverstocke* in
1627.

Hawk Wood E.4, 'wood in an angle
of land', the first element here being
probably ME *halke*, diminutive of
OE *healh*, a rare term found in a few
other names in Essex, Cambridge-
shire, and one or two Midland
counties [*Gingefordeshalk* 1323—
'angle of land in Chingford', *Hauke*
1498: ME *halke*].

Haydon Hall (Pinr), named from
the family of John Heydon, mentioned in local records in 1382.

Hayes (Brom), **Hayes** (Hldn),
'brushwood', settlements in open
land overgrown with shrubs and
rough bushes [1. *Hesa* 1177, *Hese*
1254, *Heys* 1610. 2. *linga hæse* 793,
Hesa 1086, *Hese* 1232, *Heys* 1498,
Hayes al. Hese 1648: OE **hæse*].

Haynes Park (Hnch), from the

family name of William Haynes, referred to in local records in 1497.

Headstone (Harw), of uncertain origin and meaning. The second element is probably OE *tūn*, 'farm', compounded with a personal name which it is not possible to identify from the inconsistent forms of relatively late dates [*Hegeton* 1348, *Heggestone* 1367, *Hedgestone* c.1530, *Hedstone* 1754, *Headstone* 1819].

Heathrow (Hslw), 'row of houses on or by a heath', located on the western edge of Hounslow Heath [*La Hetherewe* c.1410, *Hetherowfeyld* c.1530: OE *hǣð, rǣw*].

Hendon N.W.4, '(place) on a high hill', the settlement having developed around St Mary's church, the site of which is on a prominent hill. The first element appears as *Hen-* rather than *High-* as it is derived from the oblique case *hēan*, after a preposition *on* or *æt* [*Hendun* 959, *oþ heandunes gemære* ('unto the boundary of Hendon') c.975, *Handone* 1086, *Heendon* 1305: OE *hēah, dūn*].

Herne Hill S.E.24, 'hill by a nook of land', probably alluding to a field called *Le Herne* c.1490 in Brixton [*Herne Hill* 1798: OE *hyrne, hyll*].

Heston (Hslw), 'farm among brushwood', about four miles from Hayes (q.v.) [*Hestone* c.1125, *Heyston* c.1495: OE *hǣs, tūn*].

Higham Hill E.17, 'hill by the high village' [*Hecham* 1086, *Hegham* 1264, *Heigham* 1333, *Heigham Hill* 1501: OE *hēah, hām, hyll*].

Highams Park E.4, 'park by Higham, i.e., high village'. See Higham Hill.

High Barnet, 'high settlement in Barnet, i.e., burnt place', one of several villages in a burnt clearing of the great wood that covered Middlesex and Hertfordshire. There is no mention of any of the Barnets in Domesday Book, and it is possible that permanent settlements were not established until the late eleventh or early twelfth century. When the county boundary was originally determined, High Barnet and East Barnet were included in Hertfordshire as they were possessions of St Albans Abbey. This association was completely severed, of course, on the creation of Greater London. High Barnet is also called **Chipping Barnet**, 'Barnet with a market', and is referred to as West Barnet in some early records [*Barneto* c.1070, *La Barnette* 1248, *Chepyng Barnet* 1329, *Westbarnet* 1449, *Chipping Barnet al. High Barnet* 1628: OE *bærnet, cieping, hēah, west*].

Highbury N.5, 'high manor', so called from its standing on higher ground than either Canonbury or Barnsbury (qq.v.). Highbury was probably at one time part of Stoke Newington, and early forms refer to it as *Newington Barrow*, from the family name of an early lord,

Thomas de Barewe 1271 [*Neweton Barrewe* 1274, *Newenton Barwe* 1294, *Heybury* c.1375, *Newington Barowe al. the manor of Highbury* 1548: OE *hēah, burh*]. See also Stoke Newington.

Highgate N.6, 'high (toll) gate', at 426 feet above sea level, one of the highest places in the former county of Middlesex. This early toll gate was set up on the Great North Road by the Bishop of London, lord of the manor of Hornsey [*Le Heighgate* 1354, *Heghegate* 1377, *Highgate* 1440: OE *hēah, geat*].

Highwood Hill N.W.7, 'hill by or with a high wood', high above Hendon towards the former Middlesex-Hertfordshire border [*in alto bosco* 1321, *Highwode* 1523, *Highwodhyll* 1543: OE *hēah, wudu, hyll*].

Hillend (Hrfd), **Hillend** S.E.10, 'hill district' in the respective parish [OE *hyll, ende*].

Hillingdon, 'Hilda's hill', alluding, by a pet form of the personal name, to a man named Hildrīc, Hildwulf, &c. The altitude here is modest, but amid much low-lying land the title *dūn* is well merited [*Hildendune* c.1080, *Hillendone* 1086, *Hylingdon* 1274: OE *dūn*].

Holborn *riv*, 'stream in the hollow', strictly, the whole of the river now referred to as the Fleet (q.v.), but latterly the uppermost reaches of that river were designated by the name Holborn; the 'hollow' referred to is still traceable along the course of Faringdon Road [*Holeburne* 959, *Oldborne* 1603: OE *holh, burna*].

Holborn W.C.1, W.C.2, '(place by) stream in the hollow', the former Metropolitan Borough (now part of the London Borough of Camden) adjacent to the City of London. The use of the same name for stream and parish seems not to have been confusing. The pronunciation of the name by 'real' Londoners is 'Ho-born', going back to the sixteenth century or earlier and interestingly confirmed by the evidence of a French-speaking clerk in the early eighteenth century [*Holeburne* 1086, *Howeborne* 1551, *Hautborne* 1703, *Holbourne by London* 1567: OE *holh, burna*].

Holders Hill N.W.4, embodying the surname of Roger le Holdere, mentioned in local records in 1294 [*Oldershyll* 1584, *Holears Hill* 1680, *Holders Hill* 1750: OE *hyll*].

Holland Park W.8, named from Holland House, home of the earls of Holland. Henry Rich, 1st Earl, whose wife inherited the property in 1621, established the family here [*The Earle of Hollands House* 1658, *Holland House* 1664].

Holloway N.7, 'road in a hollow', the name later being applied to the district through which the road passed [*Le Holeweye in Iseldon* 1307, *Holway* 1473, *Holowaye al. Netherholowaye* 1553: OE *holh, weg*].

Holwood Park (Frnb), 'wood in a hollow' [OE *holh, wudu*].

Homerton E.8, 'Hūnburh's farm or estate', the personal name being that of a woman [*Humburton* 1343, *Hummerton* 1581: OE *tūn*].

Honor Oak S.E.23, 'place by Oak of Honor Hill', the latter being a wooded hill in which was an oak serving as a boundary mark between Camberwell (in Surrey) and Lewisham (in Kent). This might be a sufficient explanation for the 'honour' accorded the tree, and anecdotes about Queen Elizabeth I may be treated with reserve; historical though the visits may have been, the attentions of the Virgin Queen did not necessarily convey a title to the already famous tree [*Oke of Honor* 1609, *Oak of Honour Wood* 1763].

Hook (Kstn), 'hook-shaped hill or spur of land' [*Hoke* 1227, *Houke* 1312, *Hook* 1680: OE *hōc*].

Hooley (Clsn), 'wood or grove in a hollow' [*Holegh* 1235, *Howly* 1445, *Hooley* 1789: OE *holh, lēah*].

Hoppershatch Shaw (Biggin Hill), 'wood by Hopper's gate'—alluding either to a gate, to farm premises, or to an enclosed wood. The surname was found in various places in Kent from the sixteenth century onwards [OE *hæcc, sceaga*].

Hornchurch (Rmfd), probably '(place with) church embellished with horns'—alluding to a decorative feature on the church in the thirteenth century or earlier, not now identifiable. A bull's head with horns was later affixed to the eastern gable of the church; this eighteenth-century ornament was probably derived from a similar figure depicted on the Prior's seal of 1384, which might have been simply emblematic of the name, rather than a representation of an actual feature on or about the church [*Ecclesia de Haweringis* 1163, *Monasterium Cornutum* 1222, *Hornechurch* 1233: OE *horn, cirice*].

Hornsey. See Haringey.

Horseleydown S.E.1, 'hill by horse island', alluding to dry pasturage among marshes, *hill* being possibly a flattering reinforcement in the name which refers to slightly higher ground in a marshy area beside the Thames. The intrusive *l* is probably due to the name Horsley in Surrey or to a surname derived from that place being associated with the area in some way [*Horseidune* c.1175, *Horseyedoune* 1255, *Horsadown* c.1450, *Horslydown* c.1580: OE *hors, ēg, dūn*].

Horsenden Hill (Gnfd), possibly 'Horsa's hill', the personal name being more likely to produce forms with -*n*- than would OE *hors*, 'horse' [*Horsendun* 1203, *Horsindon* 1302, *Horsington Hill* 1819: OE *dūn*].

Hounslow, 'Hund's mound or tumulus', the mound being possibly the place of burial of the named man. At the 1963 reorganization, the former local authorities of Brentford and Chiswick, Heston and Isleworth, and Feltham merged to form the London Borough of Hounslow [*Hundeslawe* 1217, *Hundeslowe* 1275, *Houndeslowe* 1341: OE *hlāw*].

Hoxton N.1, 'Hoc's farm or estate' [*Hochestone* 1086, *Hocston* 1221, *Hoxton* c.1250: OE *tūn*].

Hundred Acre Bridge (Mchm), 'bridge by or near a field called Hundred Acres'.

Hurlingham S.W.6, of uncertain origin and meaning. A derivation from OE *þyrelung*, 'gap, hollow', is remotely possible and might account for the uncertainty in the initial letter [*Hurlyngholefeld* 1489, *Hurlyngham-fyld*, *Furnynghamfeld* 1550, *Hurling-ham* 1626].

Hyde, The N.W.9, 'hide of land', an area of approximately 120 acres, regarded as sufficient for the support of a free family and its dependants [*La Hyde* 1281: OE *hīd*].

Hyde Park W.2, 'park established at Hyde', the area having once been a part of the manor of Ebury (q.v.) and doubtless consisting originally of a single hide of land (cf. The Hyde, *supra*); later, Hyde became a sub-manor and its area was increased. The Royal Park was created by King Henry VIII [*Hida* 1204, *La Hyde* 1257, *Hide Park* 1543: OE *hīd*, ME *park*].

Hyde Park Corner S.W.1 and W.1, 'road junction by Hyde Park', the meeting place of Park Lane and Piccadilly [*Hyde Parke Corner* 1553].

I

Ickenham (Hldn), 'Ticca's village'. In many early documents, place-names are preceded by the preposition *æt* ('at') or OE *æt þǣm* (ME *atten*), 'at the'. Occasionally, misdivision occurred and the phrase *atten Ashe*, for instance, was read as *atte Nashe*, giving rise to the place-name Nash, 'at the ash tree'. Ickenham and Oakington (q.v.) illustrate a reverse process, for in these the initial *T* of the first element has been read as the final *t* of the preposition [*Ticheham* 1086, *Tikeham* 1176, *Tikenham* 1203, *Thikenham* 1356, *Ikeham* 1203: OE *hām*].

Ilford (Rbrg), 'ford across river called Hyle'. Below Ongar, the Roding was once called *Hyle* or *Hile*, 'trickling stream' [*Ilefort* 1086, *Hilleford* 1234, *Hyleford* 1300: OE *ford*].

Isle of Dogs E.14, of uncertain meaning. The earliest reference is *Isle of Doges Ferm* 1593; previously, the area had been known as Stepney Marsh, which supports the suggestion that the present name is derogatory.

Isleworth (Hslw), 'Gīslhere's enclosure or homestead'. The history of this name demonstrates a bewildering variety of spellings; the first syllable alone has been *Gis-*, *Ist-*, *Yst-*, *Hist-*, *Yist-*, *Yhist-*, and even *Thist-*. That the modern form should be phonetically so close to the earliest record of the name demonstrates the strength of oral tradition and its ability to withstand scribal vacillation. The first form cited below comes from a forged charter, but the document is regarded as reliable in its spelling of place-names, almost certainly derived from an original deed of the purported date [*Gislheresuuyrth* 695, *Istlesworde* c.1120: OE *worð*].

Islington N.1, 'Gisla's hill'. The personal name is a familiar form of an OE name beginning *Gisl-*, such as Gislhere, as in Isleworth, but of course there is no necessary connexion between the two places on that account [*Gislandune* c.1000, *Isledone* 1086, *Isledon* 1320, *Islyngton* 1464: OE *dūn*].

K

Kenley (Crdn), 'Cœna's wood or grove', embodying the personal name found also in Kennington (q.v.), but of course not necessarily referring to the same individual [*Kenele* 1255, *Kenle* 1403: OE *lēah*].

Kennington S.E.11, 'farm or estate associated with Cœna' [*Chenintune*

1086, *Kenintone* 1229, *Kenyngton* 1263: OE *-ingtūn*].

Kensal Green N.W.10, 'the king's wood', the unstressed syllable developing as though from OE *healh*, 'nook', probably because of its size and position. Another *holt* (also disguised in its modern form) lies not far away—Wormwood Scrubs. It is not known which king is referred to in Kensal [*Kingisholte* 1253, *Kyngesholt 1367*, *Kynsale Grene* 1550, *Kensell Grene* 1658: OE *cyning, holt*].

Kensal (New) Town W.10, 'new urban development near Kensal', a planned estate of new dwellings built in the early nineteenth century on the site of a kind of shanty town in North Kensington.

Kensington W.8, 'farm or estate associated with Cynesige' [*Chenist'* 1086, *Kensintone* 1221, *Kensington* 1235: OE *-ingtūn*].

Kensington Gore S.W.7, 'wedge of land near Kensington', a triangle of land bounded by Queen's Gate, Cromwell Road (merging with Brompton Road), and Kensington Road (merging with Knightsbridge); the name Kensington Gore is now applied to the westward extension of Kensington Road, comprising only a small fragment of what was once a considerable estate, evidently royal property for a while, though it is not known which king is referred to in the early forms [*Gara* c.1130, *Kyngesgore* 1270, *The Gore* 1646, *The Kings Gore* 1657: OE *gara*].

Kentish Town N.W.5, probably 'estate held by man called Le Kentish' [*Kentisston* 1208, *Cantistun* c.1200, *La Kentishton* 1294, *Kentisshtown* 1488: OE *tūn*].

Kenton (Harw), 'farm or estate associated with Cœna', the personal name being the same as that found in Kenley and Kennington, and the etymology and meaning of this name being identical with the latter [*Keninton* 1233, *Kenygtone* 1282, *Kenyngton Next Harogh'* 1368, *Kenton al. Kynyton* 1548: OE *-ingtūn*].

Ken Wood N.W.3, of uncertain origin and meaning. Forms suggesting an association with Caen do not occur until the seventeenth century, and a derivation from the surname Kentwode is not supported by any early spellings of the place-name [*Canewood* 1543, *Caen Wood* 1640, *Ken Wood* 1741].

Keston (Brom), 'Cyssi's stone' [*Cystaninga mearc* 862 ('boundary of the Keston people'), *Chestan* 1086, *Kestan* 1205: OE *stān*].

Kew (Rchm), 'neck of land by a landing place' [*Cayho* 1327, *Kayho* 1330, *Keyhow* 1439, *Kayo* 1483, *Kaio* 1532, *Kewe* 1535: OE *hōh*, ME *kai*].

Kidbrook S.E.3, 'stream near which kites were seen', the earliest form showing the characteristic Kentish form, *cēta*, for West Saxon *cȳta* [*Ketebroc* 1202: OE *brōc*].

Kidney Wood (Richmond Park), so called from its shape.

Kilburn N.W.6, '(place by) cattle stream', the development of early spellings showing the interchange of *l* and *r* that is often found in post-Norman place-name forms. Other etymologies have been suggested, including a derivation from OE *cyln*, but these are difficult to support from extant forms [*Cuneburna* c.1130, *Kyneburna* c.1170, *Keleburne* 1181, *Kylleburne* 1229: OE *cū*, *burna*].

King Edward VII Memorial Park E.1, **King Edward VII Park** (Wembley), **King Edward VII Recreation Ground** N.W.10: public open spaces commemorating King Edward VII (1901–10).

King George V Dock E.16, one of the 'royal group' of docks on the Thames, others being the Royal Albert Dock and the Royal Victoria Dock. This name commemorates George V (1910–36).

King George V Memorial Gardens (Edgw), **King George V Playing Fields** (Enfd), commemorating King George V (1910–36), as do also **King George's Park** S.E.16, **King George's Park** S.W.18, and **King George's Field** in various parts of London.

Kingsbury N.W.9, 'the king's manor', granted by Edward the Confessor (1042–66) to Westminster Abbey [*Kynges Byrig* 1044, *Chinges-*

berie 1086, *Kingesbir'* 1199: OE *cyning, burh*].

King's Cross N.1, 'monument to a king' or 'king's cross-roads', from a memorial to King George IV (1820–30) which was erected after the king's death at the junction of Gray's Inn Road, Euston Road, and Pentonville Road. The curious stone structure was removed before the building of the railway terminus, which, however, adopted the name. Until the middle of the nineteenth century the area was known as Battlebridge (q.v.). See also *The Brill*.

Kings End (Rslp), 'district held by man called King'; the surname occurs in local records as early as 1296. Later, by coincidence, land here was owned by King's College, Cambridge.

Kingsland E.8, 'land held by the king', being part of Hackney in royal hands when the manor was held by the Bishop of London. The name survives as that of a road [*Kyngeslond* 1395: OE *cyning, land*].

Kingston-upon-Thames, 'the king's estate (beside the Thames)', royal property in Anglo-Saxon times. The London Borough includes Kingston, Malden and Coombe, and Surbiton [*Cyninges tun* 838, *Chingestune* 1086, *Kingeston* 1164, *Kyngeston super Tamisiam* 1321, *Kingestowne upon Thames* 1589: OE *cyning, tūn*].

King's Wood (Sstd), 'woodland belonging to a man named King', referring to a family named in local records in 1332 [*Kinges Woodes* 1595: OE *wudu*].

Kneller Gardens (Twic), named from Sir Godfrey Kneller, the portrait painter (1649–1743), who lived at Kneller Hall.

Knighton Wood (Wdfd), 'wood in Knighton, i.e., the estate of the knights', alluding to possessions in the area of the Knights of St John.

Knightsbridge S.W.1, 'bridge of the young men', at the place where the Great West Road crosses the Westbourne [*Cnightebricge* c.1050, *Knichtebrig'* 1235, *Knyghtesbrugg* 1364: OE *cniht, brycg*].

Knockholt (Brom), '(at the) oak wood', the name having collected not merely the *-n* of ME *atten*, 'at the', but an entirely superfluous *K* [*Ocholt* 1197, *Okholte* 1285, *Nocholt* 1353: OE *āc, holt*].

L

Ladbroke Grove W.10, W.11, part of an estate owned by Richard Ladbroke in 1624, sold by his family for building purposes in 1845.

Lambeth S.E.1, 'landing-place for lambs', one of the several Thames-side places terminating in OE *hȳþ* but showing considerable variety in their modern forms (cf. Putney,

Rotherhithe, Chelsea). The London Borough of Lambeth includes Brixton, Clapham, and Streatham; South Lambeth S.W.8 is still separately named (it was first recorded as *Sutlamehethe* in 1241) and lies partly in Wandsworth but mostly in Lambeth [*Lamhytha* 1088, *Lamhetha* 1089, *Lambhehithe* 1312, *Lamethe* 1207, *Lambetheeth* 1300: OE *lamb*, *hȳð*].

Lampton (Hslw), 'lamb farm' [*Lamptonfeld* 1376, *Lampton* 1426, *Lambton* 1611: OE *lamb*, *tūn*].

Langthorn, 'tall thorn tree', at or beside which the abbey stood at Stratford (q.v.) [*þone langan þorn* 958, *Langethorn in Hamme* 1199: OE *lang*, *þorn*].

Larkswood Park E.4, from the surname Laverk or Lark, occurring in local records in the fourteenth century (Thomas Laverk 1319).

Latimer Road W.10, built on land bequeathed by Edward Latymer in the early seventeenth century, for the support of a school which he had established.

Lea riv, 'bright one' or perhaps 'dedicated to Lugus'. Like those of many rivers, this name is of Celtic origin, and so the earliest recorded forms occur at a relatively late stage in its history, making interpretation difficult. As the Lea (occasionally spelt Lee) marked the western boundary of Essex, there are numerous references to it in medieval documents [*Lygan* 895, *Liggean* c.1000, *Luia* 1235, *Leye* 1235, *Luy* 1378, *Lye* 1390: OC **lug*].

Lee S.E.13, '(place in or near) a wood or grove'. This was a woodland hamlet dependent upon Lewisham [*Lee* 1086, *Lega* 1206: OE *lēah*].

Leg of Mutton Pond (Richmond Park), alluding to its triangular shape. Identically named ponds are to be found in Nut Wood N.W.7, in Bushy Park, and on West Heath, Hampstead.

Leicester Square W.C.2, first so named on a map of 1708, was formerly *Leicester Fields* adjoining *Leicester House*, which was built in 1631 by Robert Sidney, second Earl of Leicester.

Lessness Abbey Wood S.E.2, 'woodland belonging to Lessness Abbey'. The ruins of the abbey are on the north edge of the surviving extensive woodland. Lessness, also spelt Lesnes on some modern maps, was the 'meadow promontory' projecting into the Erith Marshes [*Lesneis* 1086: OE *lǣs*, *nǣss*].

Lessness Heath (Blvd), 'heathland by Lessness (q.v.)' [OE *hǣð*].

Levehurst, 'Leofa's wooded hill', a former manor whose name is preserved in Levehurst Way S.W.4 [*Lefhirst* 1286: OE *hyrst*].

Lewisham S.E.13, 'Leofsa's village'

[*Liofshema mearc* 862, *Liofesham* c.1060, *Levesham* 1086: OE *hām*].

Leyton E.10, 'farm on River Lea'. The name is similar in origin and meaning to Luton, and the forms for both names were identical in the eleventh and twelfth centuries. The epithet *Low* was applied to Leyton but was finally abandoned in the nineteenth century [*Lugetune* c.1050, *Lygetune* 1066, *Leintune* 1086, *Luiton* 1223, *Luton* 1224, *Lowe Leighton* 1585, *Low Leyton* 1594: OE *tūn*].

Leytonstone E.11, 'Leyton (q.v.) by the stone', alluding to the High Stone, reputed to be on the site of a Roman milestone [*Leyton atte Stone* 1370, *Leyton Stone* 1426: OE *stān*].

Limehouse E.14, '(place by) lime kilns'. The second element, OE *āst*, Modern English 'oast', passed through the stage *hurst* before being taken as *house* in the sixteenth century. A local deed records the granting of a cottage and garden here to Peter atte Hacche, a limeburner, in 1380 [*Le Lymhostes* 1367, *Les Lymehostes near London* 1387, *Lymost* 1496, *Lymehurst* 1535, *Lymehouse* 1547: OE *līm, āst*].

Lincolns Inn W.C.2, named from an earlier house occupied by the Society, previously owned by Thomas de Lincoln. On removal, the community of lawyers transferred the name to premises which had previously been the property of the Bishop of Chichester. By coin-

cidence, these premises were near the residence of Henry de Lacy, Earl of Lincoln (d.1311), a patron of the Society, and this connexion no doubt confirmed the use of the name [*Lincolnesynne* 1399: OE *inn*].

Lisson, 'Lille's estate or farm'. Lisson Grove and Street N.W.1 keep in existence the name of this ancient manor in the north-western part of Marylebone parish [*Lilestone* 1086, *Lilleston* 1198, *Lylleston Grene* 1547: OE *tūn*].

Little Roke (Prly), 'little place at the oak tree', distinguished from Great Roke (in Witley, Surrey), which has the same etymology. The name is derived from a wrong division of ME *atter oke*, 'at the oak tree' [*Le Roke* 1550: OE *āc*].

Little Stanmore. See Whitchurch.

Liverpool Street E.C.3, named in honour of Lord Liverpool, Prime Minister from 1812 to 1827.

Lloyd Park E.17, named after Edward Lloyd, whose family presented the estate to the local council in 1898. The property had been previously known as The Winns, from the surname of John Wynne 1498, whose family succeeded those of Cricklewood and Capp in the ownership of the estate in the Middle Ages [*John Kykylwoddys* 1487, *Capps Crofte* 1487, *Cricklewood sometime Hawkes Capps* 1684].

Locksbottom (Frnb), 'valley bottom in the tenure of the Lock family' [OE *botm*].

London, 'Londinos's settlement', a Celtic name formed in a conventional way from the personal name of a chief associated with the area, either as a founder or as a memorable ruler. The meaning of the personal name is not, of course, relevant to an interpretation of the place-name. In view of the Latin appearance of early forms, it may be as well to emphasise that the name did not originate with Roman invaders, who, like later settlers from the Continent, allowed existing names to remain virtually unaltered until there was some compelling reason to change them. There was an attempt in the fourth century to rename the place *Augusta*, but the term encountered resistance from elderly conservatives and, doubtless, ribaldry from youthful radicals, and so does not seem to have lasted long. It must be remembered that until quite recent times the name was applied only to the City of London; Southwark ('the Borough') and the nearest suburbs then began to be called by the name. The formation of the County of London in 1888 led to a fairly general use of *London* for the whole area, with the term *Greater London* held in reserve for certain technical and statistical purposes. Now that Greater London is the official name for the entire administrative area, however, there is not the same readiness to designate each locality within it by the name [*Londinium* 115, *Londinion* 150, *Lundinium* c.380, *Lundene* 962, *Lundres* 12c., *Lundin* 1205].

London Bridge E.C.4, S.E.1, 'bridge (across Thames) at London', the fame of which is such that (like that at Avignon) it is celebrated in a traditional song. South of the river, distances were measured from it [*Lundene Bricge* 10c.: OE *brycg*].

London Fields E.8, 'arable land on London side (of Hackney)' [*London Field* 1540: OE *feld*].

Longford (WDtn), 'long river-crossing', an oblique crossing of the river Colne. The same name occurs just outside the Greater London boundary at Sevenoaks, for a crossing of the Darent. There is, of course, no connexion with the Irish Longford (*Longphort*, 'fortress') and the name alludes to those places where an indirect crossing of a river was safer or more convenient than by the shortest route [*Longeforde* 1294, *Langeford* 1327: OE *lang*, *ford*].

Longford River, 'artificial watercourse originating at Longford', constructed in the seventeenth century to supply the lakes at Hampton Court. Alternative names are Queen's River (probably alluding to Henrietta Maria, wife of Charles I) and Cardinal's River (referring to Wolsey, builder of the palace at Hampton Court, who had in fact utilised water from Coombe Hill).

Long Pond (Clapham Common), so

called from its shape, as are **The Long Water**, at Hampton Court, and **The Long Water**, the northern section of the Serpentine (q.v.).

Lord's Cricket Ground N.W.8, named after Thomas Lord, owner of the land here, to which he removed a cricket ground previously established on the site of Dorset Square to the south.

Loxford Park (Ilfd), probably 'park at Locc's ford'. This may, however, be 'park at crossing of the Loxa', supposing this to be the British name (meaning 'winding stream') for the **Loxford Water** [*Loxford* 1319: OE *ford*].

M

Maida Vale W.9, commemorating a battle in Italy in 1806, is the stretch of Watling Street bounding the parish of Paddington. There was formerly a *Maida Hill* (now Maida Avenue), and the battle is remembered in other street-names in Chingford and Belvedere.

Malden (Kstn), 'hill marked with a cross', the area to the north and west of Worcester Park station. New Malden, a modern extension of the residential area, has its centre further north still [*Meldon* 1086, *Maldon* 1225, *Mauden* 1249, *Maulden* 1602: OE *mæl, dūn*].

Manor House N.4, 'manor house (of

Stoke Newington)', the site of which is now occupied by a church.

Manor Park (*freq*), the name of a number of public open spaces, usually remnants of land adjoining manor houses.

Mansfield Park E.4, 'common field' [*Manfeld* 1553: OE *(ge)mǣne, feld*].

Mansion House E.C.4, official residence of the Lord Mayor of London. The term is used here in the sense 'chief residence of a lord, a manor house'.

Marble Arch W.1, so called from its being built in Carrara marble, this imitation of the Arch of Constantine in Rome was erected in 1828 in front of Buckingham Palace, but was removed to its present position, near the site of Tyburn gallows, in 1851.

Marble Hill (Twic), perhaps 'hill by pool valley', the 'pool' being the Thames between the bank and Petersham Ait. Folk etymology undoubtedly brought about the present form of the name, but the building of Marble Hill House had nothing to do with the change, which dates from at least a century earlier [*Mardelhylle* 1350, *Marble Hill* 1650: OE *mere, dǣl, hyll*].

Mare Street E.8, 'boundary place by a paved road'—originally designating a hamlet on the Hackney-Bethnal Green border, but now adopted as the name for the chief street in Hackney [*Merestret* 1443: OE *(ge)mǣre, strǣt*].

Markfield Recreation Ground N.15, 'field by a boundary'. The place was by the parish and Hundred boundary [*Merkefeld* 1502: OE *mearc*].

Marks Gate (Rmfd), 'gate by (forest) boundary' [OE *mearc, geat*].

Marlborough House S.W.1, so called from its having been built (in 1709) for the Duke of Marlborough.

Maryland Point E.15, name transferred from Maryland, U.S.A. This was a hamlet, the first house in which was built by a merchant who had made his fortune in what was then a colony.

Marylebone. See St Marylebone.

Maryon Park, Maryon Wilson Park S.E.7, named from the landowners, the family of Sir Thomas Wilson, who on marrying an heiress to the Maryon estates, changed his name to Maryon-Wilson.

Maswell Park (Hslw), perhaps 'Mæssa's spring' [*Massewelle* 1485, *Maswell Stile* 1498: OE *wella*].

Mayes Brook *riv*, tributary of the Roding named after the family of Richard le May (1314). **Mayesbrook Park** (Bctr) takes its name from the stream.

Mayfair S.W.1, 'site of fair held in month of May', the exact location

being Brook Field (beside the Tyburn)—over which Brook Street is now built. The fair was suppressed in 1709, but was revived for a time, though building had begun in the area before 1704.

Merton S.W.19, 'farm or estate by a pool'. There is evidence in an old charter that the pool was in the River Wandle by the south-west corner of Mitcham. The London Borough of Merton comprises Mitcham, Morden, Wimbledon, and Merton [*Mertone* 967, *Meretone* 1086, *Meritone* c.1130, *Mirton al. Marten* 1679: OE *mere, tūn*].

Mile End E.1, '(place) one mile away'—from Aldgate. To the medieval traveller, the first mile undoubtedly counted—if only because it might occasion a halt to water the horses [*La Mile Ende* 1288, *La Milende* 1383, *Mylle End Gren* 1554: OE *mīl, ende*].

Mill Hill N.W.7, 'hill on which a windmill stood' [*Myllehill* 1547: OE *myln, hyll*].

Millwall E.4 '(river-) wall on which mills were built'. The wall was formerly called *Marsh Wall*; the mills stood on the wall in the eighteenth century.

Minories E.C.3, '(abbey of) Franciscan nuns or Minoresses'. At the Dissolution the convent premises were granted to the Bishop of Bath and Wells (and was temporarily known as *Bathe Place*) but in the time of Queen Elizabeth I the property passed back to the Crown and was used by the Ordnance Department. The street adjoining the convent, now known as Minories, was formerly *Minorie Street* 1624 [*The Minoresses without Alegate* 1341, *Le Myneris* 1548: L *minor*].

Mitcham (Mrtn), 'large village', possibly by contrast with Streatham ('*hām* by paved road') nearby, or with the several small places with *hām* names in Croydon, within the same Hundred [*Michelham* 1086, *Micham* c.1150: OE *micel, hām*].

Mitchley Wood (Sstd), 'big wood or grove' [OE *micel, leāh*].

Monken Frith (Barnet). See Oak Hill Park.

Monken Hadley (Barnet), 'grove or wood in heathland, held by monks'. The manor was granted to the monks of Walden Abbey, Essex [*Hadlegh* 1248, *Hadele* 1349, *Hadley Monachorum* 1485, *Monken Hadley* 1489: OE *munuc, hǣꝺ, lēah*].

Monkhams (Wdfd), altered from *Monkenebukhurst*, 'monks' holding in Buckhurst, i.e. 'beech-wood hill', and now surviving only in street-names [*Monekenebukhurst* 1286, *Buchurst alias Munkehill* c.1535, *Monnekenhyll* 1547, *Munckombe* 1630, *Monkhams* 1843: OE *munuc*].

Moorgate E.C.2, 'gate (of city) opening on to marshland' [OE *mōr, geat*].

Morden (Mrtn), 'hill by marshland', a slight elevation between the valleys of Beverley Brook and the Wandle [*Mordune* 969, *Mordone* 1086, *Moreden* 1204: OE *mōr, dūn*].

Mornington Crescent N.W.1, named after the Earl of Mornington, related (by marriage) to the Fitzroy family, owners of the estate.

Mortlake S.W.14, possibly 'Morta's stream'—alluding to Beverley Brook, which enters the Thames here [*Mortelage* 1086, *Morteslak* 1227, *Mourtlake* 1465: OE *lacu*].

Moselle *riv*, stream-name adapted from Muswell Hill, through which area the little river runs to join the Lea at Tottenham. It was earlier the *Campsborne* 1608 (cf. *Campisborne Closse* 1495, a field-name).

Mossford Green (Ilfd), perhaps 'mossy place at the foot of a hill' [*Mossfoot Green* 1777: OE *mos, fōt*].

Motspur Park (Mrtn), 'Mot's gorse-scrub'. Henry Mot's name appears in fourteenth-century records; the farm may have been held by the family at an earlier date. Another variant of the name appears to have been applied to all or part of the estate from the mid-eighteenth century— *Notcurse Farm* 1765 and *Nutcars* 1789—but these forms are explicable if a great deal of the information about the names happened to be transmitted orally [*Furse Farm* 1623, *Motes Firs Ferm* 1627, *Motspur* 1827: OE *fyrs*].

Mottingham S.E.9, 'village of the followers or family of Moda' [*Modingeham* 1044, *Motingham* 1610: OE *-ingas*, *hām*].

Mount Pleasant W.C.1, possibly ironic use of this frequent complimentary name. In the metropolitan area, the term was often applied to heaps of cinders or refuse. This interpretation may not be the right one for Mount Pleasant, Southall, but detailed local investigation might produce interesting conclusions about the name, here and elsewhere.

Muswell Hill N.10, 'hill by a mossy spring'. An alternative name for the hill itself, without reference to the spring, was *Pinnesnoll Hill* 1610, 'Pin's hillock', but the present name came into general use in the 17–18c. [*Mosewella* c.1155, *Muswell* 1535, *Muscle Hill* 1746; *Pinnesknoll* 1288, *Pinnesnoll Hill al. Muswell Hill* 1610, *Muswell Hill al. Pinchnoll Hill* 1617: OE *mēos*, *wella*, *cnoll*].

Mutton Brook *riv*, possibly 'Mordin's brook'. The probability of a surname as first element is supported by a reference to *Mordins Pyghtell* (field-name) in the sixteenth-century survey from which comes the earliest form of the name of the stream [*Mordins Brooke* 1574, *Mutton Brook* 1819: OE *brōc*].

N

Nash (Frnb), '(place) at the ash tree', a fairly common name, formed by erroneous division of ME *atten ashe*, the first word signifying 'at the' [OE *æt þǣm ǣsce*].

Neasden N.W.2, 'nose-shaped hill', probably a fairly late name embodying (it has been suggested) a Middle English, rather than Old English first element [*Neosdune* c.1000, *Nesedon* 1320: ME *nese*, OE *dūn*].

Neckinger *riv*, 'noose'. The stream enters the Thames near Neckinger Wharf, where pirates are said to have been hanged; alternatively, the name may be derived from the looping course of the tributary in Bermondsey. *Devil's Neckercher* was the cant term for the hangman's rope. The Neckinger crossed the road to Canterbury at the spot known to Chaucer as *St Thomas's Watering*.

Nelson's Fields S.W.19, commemorating the residence here of Lord Nelson, for a few years before his death. A group of street-names not far away celebrate both Nelson and Lady Hamilton, as well as Hardy, H.M.S. *Victory*, and Trafalgar.

Newbury Park (Ilfd), 'park at the new manor', first recorded in the mid-fourteenth century [*Newbury* 1348: OE *nīwe*, *burh*].

New Cross S.E.14, alluding probably to the junction of the Old Kent Road with the road to Dartford.

Newham, London Borough comprising the western part of Barking, East Ham, West Ham, and North Woolwich (qq.v.).

Newington S.E.17, 'at the new farm', *-ing* representing the case-ending of OE *nīwe* in the phrase *æt þǣm nīwan tūne* [*Neuton* c.1200, *Niwentone* 13c., *Neuwyngton juxta Suthwerk* 1325: OE *nīwe, tūn*].

New River, the artificial watercourse constructed 1609–13 by Sir Hugh Myddleton from Amwell (Herts) to Finsbury, where the terminal point, New River Head, subsequently became the headquarters of the Metropolitan Water Board [*Flumen vocatum the Newe River* 1625].

New River Playing Fields N.22, an open space lying a few hundred yards to the east of the New River (q.v.) in Wood Green.

Newyears Green (Uxbr) unexplained. The name appears to have originated c.1754.

Nine Elms S.W.8, named from *ix elmes farme* 1646, doubtless from a clump of trees constituting a landmark nearby. Cf. Seven Sisters.

Noke Hill (Rmfd), 'hill by the oak tree', initial *N-* being from mis-division of ME *atten oke* [OE *āc, hyll*].

Norbiton (Kstn), 'northern grange or outlying farm', in relation to Surbiton (q.v.), both places being

granges of the royal manor o Kingston [*Nortberton* 1205, *Nor binton* 1219: OE *norð, bere-tūn*].

Norbury (Thornton Heath), 'nor thern fortification'. It lies north o Croydon [*Northbury* 1359: OE *norð burh*].

Normand Park W.14, an open spac taking its name from *Nomans Land* 'land in disputed ownership [*Noemansland* 1492: OE *nān-mann land*].

Normanshire Farm (Chfd), probabl from *Nomans Land*, 'land i disputed ownership', with a lat alteration of the ending to *-shire* used occasionally in Essex of liberty or independent estate. Th name survives only in the street name, Normanshire Drive E. [*Normansland* 1519: OE *nān-man land, scīr*].

North Acton W.3. See Acton.

North End, *freq*, referring to northern quarter of the parish North End, Finchley, on record i 1485, is distinguished from East En (*Estend* 1558). North End, Hamp stead, documented in the mid eighteenth century onwards, seem to be later than West End (*L. Westende* 1535). North End Fulham, was originally a hamlet a the north side of the parish [OE *norð, ende*].

Northfields W.5, a name applied to new residential district, reviving th field-names *Northfeld* 1455, *Le Nether Northfeld* 1459, *Le Over Northfeld* 1459 [OE *norð, feld*].

North Harrow. See Harrow.

North Hyde (Hslw), 'northern hide of land', formerly a hamlet on the northern edge of Heston parish [*Northyde* 1243: OE *norð, hīd*].

North Mill Fields E.5, 'land north of the water-mill', now separated from South Mill Fields by Lea Bridge Road [*Mellefeld juxta Mellelane* 1443, *North-, Southmyllefeld* 1547: OE *myln, feld, norð, sūð*].

North Ockendon (Upmr), '(village) north of Wocca's hill'. Initial *W-* was lost early (*Okkendune* c.1125), but restored in some later documents; a similar uncertainty is found in other names, e.g., Offham (Sussex) and Odell or Woodhill (Beds). The occurrence of this (or a similar) personal name in place-names elsewhere (Woking, Wokingham) does not, of course, mean that the reference is to the same individual [*Wokendune* c.1070, *Wokingdon* 1301, *Southwokyngton* 1407, *Okyngton* c.1450: OE *sūð, dūn*].

Northolt (Elng), 'northern nooks', by contrast with Southall, the modern spelling of which remains close to the early forms (despite the occasional intrusion of *-hold(e)* and *-holt* spellings 16–18c.) [*æt norðhealum* 960, *Northala* 1086, *Northold* 1593: OE *norð, healh*].

Northumberland Heath (Bxly), 'rough open ground by (brook called) North Humber'. The stream name may be of Celtic origin ('good river') and occurs in a number of other places in England [*Northumbre* 1292, *Northumberlond Hethe* 1529: OW *humyr*, OE *norð, land*].

North Wembley. See Wembley.

Northwick Park, named from the Northwick family, lords of the manor of Harrow in the eighteenth century. The park, the station, and some streets also named after the family, are now in the London Borough of Brent.

Northwood (Rslp), 'northern wood', being to the north of Ruislip. The construction of the Metropolitan Railway in 1880 led to extensive development here, and what had once been a hamlet by a wood soon became a thriving suburb [*Northwode* 1435: OE *norð, wudu*].

Northwood Hills (Pinner), 'upland above Northwood (q.v.)'.

North Woolwich E.16, 'part of Woolwich north of the Thames'. The old Metropolitan Borough of Woolwich was the only local authority to have territory on both sides of the river. The district is now part of Newham.

Norton Folgate E.1, 'north farm in the tenure of Foliot'. This was a hamlet just north of the City boundary and anciently a manor of St Paul's, of which a Richard Foliot was a canon in 1241. The final *-yot, -iot* of the surname became confused with *yet*, 'gate', and in course of time this dialect form was replaced by Standard English *gate* [*Terra Nortune* c.1110, *Nortonfolyot* 1433, *Norton Folgate otherwise Norton Folyott* 1568: OE *norð, tūn*].

Norwood S.E.19, 'north wood', formerly a large wood to the north of Croydon, not entirely cut down until the nineteenth century [*Norwude* 1176, *Northewode* 1272: OE *norð, wudu*].

Norwood Green (Sthl), 'village green by the north wood'. There are, of course, several parishes to the south, but it is not known of which place Norwood was perhaps the northern wood-pasture [*Northuuda* 832, *Northwude* 1235, *Norwode* 1235: OE *norð, wudu*].

Notting Hill W.11, probably 'hill occupied by Knotting family', the surname being derived from the place in Bedfordshire. Other suggestions have been made, including a derivation from a supposed OE **cnott*, 'hill', but some of the early spellings are difficult to explain except by postulating a surname as the source [*Knottynghull'* 1356, *Notynghyll* 1550: OE *hyll*].

Notting Hill Gate W.11, 'turnpike gate by Notting Hill', situated in fact very near the site of the Underground Railway station. Earlier, the district was known as The Gravel Pits [*The Gravilpits* 1654, *Kinsington Grauill Pittes* 1675].

Nunhead S.E.15, said to have been named from an inn, *The Nun's Head* [*Nunhead* 1680, *None Head* c.1745, *Nonehead Hill* 1789].

O

Oak Hill Park (Barnet), self-explanatory name replacing *Monken Frith*, 'the monks' woodland'. The manor was formerly owned by St Albans Abbey [*Le Monkefrith* 1273, *Monkynfrythe* 1536, *Oak hill heretofore called Moncken Frieth or Monkham Frieth* 1790: OE *munuc, (ge)fyrhð*].

Oakington (Wbly), 'farm or estate associated with Toca', with loss of initial *T-* as in Ickenham (q.v.). An old spelling has been revived in Tokyngton Recreation Ground, near the river Brent [*Tokint'* 1194, *Toketon* 1235, *Tokyngton* 1508, *Okington* 1594: OE *-ingtūn*].

Oakleigh Park N.20, a name dating from the end of the nineteenth century, possibly suggested by Oak Hill Park (q.v.), not far away in East Barnet.

Oak of Honor Hill. See Honor Oak.

Oakwood Park N.14, self-explanatory name for a public park, incorporating a small fragment of land that was once in Enfield Chase.

Ockendon. See North Ockendon.

Old Bailey E.C.4, 'outer defence-work (of the City)', originally called The Bailey (cf. The Bailey, Worcester). Some early documents refer to the defence-work, but others relate to the street built along the Bailey and to a branch-street known as Little Bailey. *Old* was probably prefixed to make the distinction clearer [*Bali* c.1166, *Le Baille* 1311, *Old Baily* 1444: ME *bailey*].

Old Ford E.3, 'old river-crossing', possibly in use earlier than the ford at Stratford. The earliest form refers to a water-mill by the ford [*Eldefordmelne* 1230, *Oldeforde* 1313: OE *eald, ford*].

Old Jewry E.C.2, 'district formerly occupied by Jews'. London, like other medieval cities, assigned a restricted area to its Jewish population. Until the expulsion in 1290, the district was referred to as *The Jewry*; the reason for the change of name after this is obvious [*La Oldeiuwerie* 1327, *The Olde Jury* 1552: OE *eald*, ME *juerie*].

Old Oak Common W.3, 'old wood', the modern forms being altered from the earlier name *Old Holt*; the change probably came about in an effort to avoid the similarity in sound between the original words [*Eldeholt* 1380, *Oldeholte* c.1415, *Old Oake Lande* 1650, *Common*

called *Old Oake* 1650: OE *eald, holt*]. See also Wormwood Scrubs.

Old Street E.C.1, 'ancient paved road'; as an important artery to and from the City, the street is referred to as ancient in early records [*Ealdestrate* c.1200, *Eldestrete* 1275, *Le Oldestrete* 1373: OE *eald, strǣt*].

Old Town S.W.4, 'old town or village', the central area of Clapham until the eighteenth century.

Olympia W.14, arbitrary name for an exhibition building constructed in the 1880s and enlarged 40 years later. The appellation is grandiose and doubtless evocative, but its relevance to the purpose of the building is not clear.

One Tree Hill (Alpt), **One Tree Hill** S.E.23: self-explanatory descriptive name, possibly accurate at the time of application.

Orpington (Brom), 'farm or estate associated with Orped' [*Orpedingtun* 1042, *Orpinton* 1086, *Orpington'* 1207: OE *-ingtūn*].

Osterley Park (Islw), 'park at Osterley, i.e., wood by a sheepfold' [*Osterle* 1274, *Oysterley* 1342, *Osterley Parke House* 1576: OE *eowestre, lēah*, ME *park*].

Oval, The S.E.11, a cricket ground named from its shape. A reference to elliptical shape is found also in *Oval Plantation*, Bushy Park.

Oxford Circus W.1, at the junction of Oxford Street and Regent Street; its former name, *Regent Circus*, associated the area more closely with the grand design associated with the name of the Prince Regent.

Oxgate N.W.2, 'gate through which cattle were driven', a hamlet of Willesden beside Watling Street, just south of the Brent [*Oxegate* c.1250: OE *oxa, geat*].

P

Paddington W.2, 'farm or estate associated with Padda' [*Padington* c.1045, *Padintone* c.1110: OE *-ingtūn*].

Padnall Corner (Rmfd), 'Pada's nook of land', *Corner* having been added when the significance of the second element (OE *healh*, 'nook, corner') was no longer understood. The place was formerly at the extreme edge of Ilford parish [*Padenhale* 1303, *Padnale* 1456, *Padnalles Corner* 1609: OE *healh*].

Page Green N.15, named from a local family [*Pagisgrene* 1467: OE *grēne*].

Palewell Common S.W.14, 'common land enclosed by a fence' [*The Pale* 1560, *Palewell Common* 1802: ME *pale*].

Palmers Green N.13, named from the family of Matthew le Palmere 1341 [*Palmeresfeld* 1205].

Park Royal N.W.10, alluding to the Royal Agricultural Society, which attempted to establish a permanent showground here in the early years of the twentieth century.

Parliament Hill N.6, despite numerous speculations and some obviously fanciful suggestions, still completely unexplained.

Parr's Ditch *riv,* possibly 'pear tree stream'. The watercourse formed the boundary between Fulham and Hammersmith. The first element of the name may allude to a family as yet unidentified [*Le Perre* 1270, *Perredich* 1407, *Pardyche* 1587: ME *perie*, OE *dīc*].

Parsloes Park (Dgnm), '(lands) of Passelewe family'. Hugh Passelewe is mentioned in a document of 1250. This Norman surname is derived from OF *passelewe*, 'cross the water'; the Essex family may be related to the tenants of Drayton Parslow (Bucks), whose ancestor, Ralph, is recorded in Domesday Book as Radulphus Passaquam, but surnames of this 'nickname' type could, of course, occur in unrelated families [*Passelewesmede* 1390, *Passhlewes* 1456, *Parslowes* 1609].

Parsons Green S.W.6, 'village green by parson's premises', a hamlet which grew up round the parsonage of the parish of Fulham [*Personesgrene* 1391, *Personagegrene* 1457: ME *persoun*, OE *grēne*].

Peckham S.E.15, 'village by a hill',

referring to the position of the old village, a little to the west of what is now known as Telegraph Hill [*Pecheham* 1086, *Pecham* 1178, *Peckham* 1241: OE *pēac*, *hām*].

Peckham Rye S.E.15, 'district of Peckham by a stream'. The watercourse is now covered over [*Peckham Rye* 1512, *Peckham Rithe* 1520: OE *riθ*].

Penge S.E.20, 'head or chief wood' or '(place at) the head or end of the wood'. Penge was originally a woodland pasture 'seven miles, seven furlongs and seven feet in circumference' belonging to the manor and parish of Battersea until 1888. The adoption of this Celtic name by English-speaking colonists points to the survival of a considerable British population in the area at the time of the Anglo-Saxon settlement [*Penceat* 1067, *Pange* 1204, *Pengewode* 1472: B *penno-*, *cēd*].

Pentonville N.1, from Henry Penton, landowner in the area c.1775. The termination -*ville* came into use in the eighteenth century for names of newly developed places.

Perivale (Gnfd), 'pear-tree valley', a fairly late name for the former Little Greenford [*Greneforde Parva* 1254, *Pyryvale* 1508, *Peryvale* 1524, *Parva Greneford al. Peryvale* 1545: ME *perie*, *vale*].

Perry Hill S.E.6, **Perry Vale** S.E.23, adjacent places with late names, both doubtless alluding to pear trees [ME *perie*].

Petersham (Rchm), 'Peohtric's riverside land'. Both Petersham and Ham (q.v.) lie within a great bend of the Thames; the element *hamm* frequently occurs in names of places in such locations [*Piterichesham* 675, *Patricesham* 1086, *Petrechesham* 1276, *Petrisham* 1416, *Petersham* 1553: OE *hamm*].

Phipps Bridge (Mrtn), 'bridge over a conduit', crossing an arm of the Wandle (possibly artificially diverted) and the main stream of the river [*Pypesbrige* 1535, *Pippebridge* 1548: OE *pīpe*, *brycg*].

Piccadilly Circus W.1. 'rounded road-junction by Piccadilly'. By a strange coincidence the crossroads partially covers a circular field known as *The Round Ringill* 1585 or *The Round Rundell* 1650. It is unlikely that this fact had anything to do with the use of the term *circus*, however, as this is used of a number of other road-junctions in London, e.g., St George's Circus, Cambridge Circus, Oxford Circus, and St Giles's Circus. The street-name, Piccadilly, is probably derived from *piccadil*, 'border of cut-work inserted on the edge of an article of dress', either from the fact that the manufacture of *piccadils* was carried on here (as one historian affirms) or because houses built here were on the outskirts of the developed area of that time.

Pield Heath (Uxbr), 'rough ground bare of herbage' [*Peeled Heath* 1592: MnE *pealed*].

Pimlico (Biggin Hill), probably in imitation of Pimlico S.W.1 (q.v.).

Pimlico S.W.1, of obscure origin and meaning. Ben Pimlico, innkeeper of Hoxton, is alluded to in documents of the late sixteenth century, and his name seems to have been transferred to his hostelry. As early as 1630 the name was used of the district in Westminster, which remained almost uninhabited until the nineteenth century, but the reason why this was done has not been explained [*Pimplico* 1630, *Pimlico* c.1743].

Pinn *riv*, back-formation from Pinner (q.v.). In 1206 the river was called *Burn of Ikeham*, 'Ickenham stream', and in 1446, *Le Broke*, 'the brook'.

Pinner (Harw), 'pin-shaped river bank', alluding to the humped ridge traversing Pinner Park [*Pinnora* 1232, *Pinnere* 1332, *Pynnor* 1483: OE *pinn*, *ōra*].

Pitshanger Park W.5, 'wooded slope frequented by kites' [*Putleshangre* 1222, *Pittleshangre* 1294, *Pyteshangre* 1493: OE *pyttel hangra*].

Plaistow (Brom), 'place of recreation', an open space used for meetings (not always recreational ones) of the village community, around which a hamlet grew—eventually becoming a separate community [*Pleystowe* 1278: OE *pleg-stōw*].

Plaistow E.13, 'place of recreation', as Plaistow (Bromley). In West Ham there was also a *Playfeld* c.1530, in the neighbourhood of Plaistow [*Playstowe* 1414: OE *pleg-stōw*].

Plashet E.7, 'hedged enclosure' [*Placet* 1578: OF *plaissiet*].

Ponders End (Enfd), 'section of parish occupied by Ponder family'. John Ponder of Enfield is mentioned in a document of 1373; the surname probably originated in a keeper of the pond, possibly a relative of Luc de la Ponde, mentioned c.1200 [*Ponders Ende* 1593: OE *ende*].

Pool, The (or **Pool of London**), the Thames just below London Bridge, indicates a deep and still place in the river [*La Pole in aqua Tamisie juxta Turrim London'* 1258 ('The Pool in the river Thames beside the Tower of London'): OE *pōl*].

Poplar E.14, '(place) at the poplar tree'. As Poplar was not an independent parish until 1817, it is not surprising to note that this place, as a dependent settlement, should bear a name of post-Conquest origin. The tree-name itself is not on record actually until after the earliest spelling of this place-name [*Popler* 1327, *Le Popler* 1351: ME *popler*].

Pratt's Bottom (Frnb), 'valley bottom occupied by the Pratt family'. Stephen Prat is mentioned in a local document of 1322; the same surname occurs in Pratt's Grove, in the wood adjoining the

Sevenoaks boundary [OE *botm*, *grāf*].

Preston (Harw), 'farm or estate in the tenure of the priest(s)'. There is a reference in Domesday Book to a priest who holds land in Harrow [*Preston* 1194: OE *prēost*, *tūn*].

Priests Bridge S.W.14/S.W.15, possibly alluding to the monks of Sheen Priory. The bridge crosses Beverley Brook, which here separates Mortlake from Putney [*Prestbrig* 1479, *Prists Bridge* 1525: OE *prēost*, *brycg*].

Primrose Hill N.W.3, 'hill on which primroses grew' [*Prymrose Hill* 1586: ME *primerose*, OE *hyll*].

Purley (Crdn), 'wood with or by pear-trees'. In a wooded area it is not surprising that such names as Purley Beeches, Purley Oaks occur, referring to particular species of trees [*Pirlee* 1200, *Purle* 1220: OE *pyrige*, *lēah*].

Purley Downs 'hill(s) by Purley (q.v.)' [*Pyrlesdon* 1255: OE *dūn*].

Putney S.W.15, 'Putta's quay or landing place'. The second element is found in a number of Thames-side names, in forms as various as Rotherhithe, Chelsea, Erith, and Lambeth. The Domesday Book spelling of Putney exhibits a number of Norman peculiarities, including the confusion of *l* and *n*, and an insensitivity to certain other consonant sounds [*Putelei* 1086, *Put-*tenhuthe* 1279, *Putneth* 1474, *Putney al. Puttenheath* 1639: OE *hȳð*].

Pymmes Brook *riv*, derived from the surname of a family mentioned in early fourteenth-century records. Earlier the stream was known as *Medeseye* c.1200, 'slow-moving meadow stream' [OE *mǣd*, **sǣge*].

Pymmes Park N.18, watered by Pymmes Brook (q.v.), from which it derives its name.

Pyrgo Park/Pyrgo Wood (Havg), probably 'wood in pear-tree gore of land', though the variety and lateness of spellings make firm interpretation impossible [*Purgore* 1490, *Portegoo* c.1535, *Portgore Pergore Park* 1544, *Pirgo* 1594: OE *pyrige*, *gara*].

Q

Quaggy River, self-explanatory name for a slow-moving stream which flows into the Ravensbourne near Lewisham station.

Queen Elizabeth's Hunting Lodge E.4, alluding to Queen Elizabeth I. The building, of late 15c. date, was used by the queen for viewing the hunting in Waltham Forest (*The Great Lodg* 1588].

Queen's Bridge (Islw), referring to an unidentified queen, but possibly Isabella, wife of Edward II [*Quenebryg'* 1450: OE *cwēn*, *brycg*].

Queensbury N.W.9, a modern name originally bestowed on the Underground Railway station. *Queensbury* was selected to correspond with Kingsbury, the next station to the south on the Metropolitan line.

Queen's Park N.W.6, the name of an open space (honouring Queen Victoria) applied first to the local railway station and then to the residential area in the vicinity.

R

Rainham (Havg), 'village of the Roegings', embodying the name of a tribe unrecorded apart from references in this name and in Rainham, near Gillingham, in Kent. The tribal title means 'prevailing ones' [*Renaham* 1086, *Raineham* 1086, *Renham* 1205, *Reignham* 1352: OE *-ingas*, *hām*].

Rammey (Enfd), '. . . island, dry ground amid marshes', the first element being unidentifiable. The area is on low ground near the river Lea [*Ramhey* 1538, *Rammey Reach* 1610: OE *ēg*].

Ranelagh S.W.13, name imitating that of the pleasure gardens in Chelsea (now part of the grounds of the Royal Hospital), formerly owned by the Earl of Ranelagh.

Ratcliffe E.1, 'red cliff', a somewhat exaggerated term to apply to a slight rise from the bank of the Thames to level ground above. There is no obvious reason why the epithet *red* should have been used [*Le Rede Clive* 1294, *Radeclyve* 1305, *Le Reedclyff* 1442, *Ratclyffe* 1524: OE *rēad, clif*].

Ravenor Park (Gnfd), named from the family of Symon Ravener, referred to in a document of 1591.

Ravensbourne *riv*, 'raven stream' [*Ravensburn* 1575: OE *hræfn, burna*].

Ravensbury (Mchm), 'Ralph's manor', the apparent reference to ravens being due to popular etymology, at work even in the fifteenth century [*Ravensbury* c.1220, *Rasebery* 1377, *Ravenesbury* 1473, *Ravisbury al. Ravensbury* c.1580: OE *burh*].

Ravenscourt Park W.6, a fairly recent name of unknown history. Early documents refer to the place as *Palyngewyk* &c, 'Pælli's outlying farm', altered to *Pading(s)wick* in the sixteenth century—perhaps because of a supposed connexion with Paddington [*Palyngewyk* 1270, *Paningewik* 1274, *Pallyngwyk* 1307, *Pallyngeswyk* 1380, *Palenswyke otherwise Padenswyke* 1547, *Ravenscourt formerly known by the name of Paddingswick* 1765: OE *wīc*].

Rayner's Lane (Pinr), said to have been named after a shepherd called Rayner, who lived alone in the area in the late nineteenth century.

Raynes Park S.W.20, derived probably from the surname Rayne, but the man or family concerned has not been identified.

Redbridge (Ilfd), 'red bridge', referring to an old bridge across the Roding, which here constitutes the boundary between Wanstead and Ilford, which now together compose the London Borough of Redbridge.

Reedham (Clsn), named after Rev. Andrew Reed, who founded the Reedham Orphanage here in 1856.

Regents Park N.W.1, named in honour of the Prince Regent, corresponds approximately with the Marylebone Park of Tudor times [*Park of Maryborne* 1558, *Marybone Park* 1574, *The Regents Park* 1817].

Richmond (Rchm), name transferred from Richmond, Yorkshire, replacing the earlier (West) Sheen, 'shelters'. Sheen Palace, a royal residence from the time of Edward I, was destroyed by fire in 1501. It was rebuilt by Henry VII and renamed after his earldom in Yorkshire. The older name survives in the neighbouring East Sheen (q.v.) [*Sceon* c.950, *Shenes* c.1210, *Schene* 1272, *Westshenes* 1253, *Shene otherwise called Richemount* 1502, *Richmond al. Shene* c.1522: OE *scēo*].

Riddles Down (Clsn), 'hill by cleared wood' [*Ridelesdoune* 1331, *Redele* 1338, *Riddles Downs* 1765: OE *(ge)ryd*, *lēah*, *dūn*].

Rippleside (Brkg), 'beside the strip of land', a narrow stretch of higher ground north of Dagenham marshes [*Ripple* 1271, *Ryppylmershe* 1536, *Rypleside* 1609: OE *rippel*, *side*].

Risebridge (Rmfd), probably 'causeway made of brushwood'. Places similarly named occur in Nottinghamshire (Roy's Bridge) and Sussex (Rice Bridge), as well as at Great Waltham in Essex (Rice Bridge and Risbridge). Rise Park, nearby, bears a more recent name adapted from Risebridge [*Risebregge* c.1275, *Rysebrugge* 1323, *Risbridge* 1448: OE *hrīs*, *brycg*].

Rise Park (Rmfd). See Risebridge.

Robin Hood Gate (Richmond Park), celebrating Robin Hood, but not suggesting any local connexion with the popular hero [*Robynhood Walke* c.1530, *Robin Hoods Gate* 1785].

Roe Green N.W.9, 'green place in or by a secluded corner', embodying ME *wro*, found only rarely south of the Midlands [*Wrolandes* c.1405, *Le Wroo* 1422, *Wrogrene* 1574, *Rowe Green* 1680: ME *wro*, OE *grēne*].

Roehampton S.W.15, 'farmstead frequented by rooks', at first called simply *Hampton* or *East Hampton;* ME *roke* was later added, probably to distinguish the name from that of Hampton (across the Thames from Kingston) not far away [*Est Hampton* 1318, *Hampton* 1332, *Rokehampton* 1350, *Rowhampton* 1553: ME *roke*, OE *hām-tūn*].

Romford (Havg), '(place by) wide ford'. The river-name, Rom, is a back-formation [*Romfort* 1177, *Rumford* 1199, *Roumford* 1399, *Rompford* 1535: OE *rūm, ford*].

Roselane Gate (Rmfd), 'gate (to Hainault Forest) in Rose Lane'— the lane itself having been named from Richard Rose, referred to in fourteenth-century local documents [*Roseland Gate* 1777].

Rotherhithe S.E.16, 'landing-place for cattle'. The alternative form Redriff occurred regularly down to the eighteenth century [*Rederheia* c.1105, *Retherhith* 1127, *Rutherheth* 1255, *Rotherhethe* 1301: OE *hrīðer, hȳð*]. See also Putney.

Round Pond (Kensington Gardens), named from its shape, a frequent way of designating ponds and lakes.

Rowdown Wood (Crdn), 'wood by the rough hill' [*La Rughedune* 1263, *Rowedoune* 1279: OE *rūh, dūn, wudu*].

Roxborough (Harw), 'rook's hill' [*Rokisborw* 1334, *Rokesbergh* 1446, *Roxbourgh* 1462: ME *roke*, OE *beorg*].

Roxeth (Harw), 'pit or hollow of a man named Hrōc'. This refers to the depression in which are springs giving rise to the river Crane. In only the earliest form is the name in the plural [*Et Hroces Seaðum* 845, *Roxhe* 1235, *Roxeth* 1280: OE *seáð*].

Royal Oak W.2, named from an old inn (now demolished) near the site of the Great Western Railway station.

Ruislip (Hldn), 'rushy leap', a crossing-place of the River Pin restricted to agile travellers. It is difficult to accept an interpretation taking the second element to be OE *slǣpe*, 'slippery place', in the absence of medieval spellings with *a* [*Rislepe* 1086, *Ruslep* 1227, *Risselepe* 1241, *Ruysshlep* 1341, *Ryselypp* 1530, *Ruislipp* 1597: OE *rysc, hlȳp*].

Rush Green (Rmfd), 'green place where rushes grew' [*Rush Green* 1777: OE *rysc, grēne*].

Russell Hill (Prly), named from the Russell family, recorded locally from 1541.

Ruxley (Orpn), 'grove or wood frequented by rooks' [*Rochelei* 1086, *Rokeslea* 1175: OE *hrōc*, OE *lēah*].

S

Sadler's Wells W.C.1, 'mineral springs belonging to Sadler', referring to the happy discovery of chalybeate springs in the garden of a 'music house' owned by Sadler, c.1683. Other mineral springs in the area are commemorated in names such as Spa Fields (q.v.) and Spa Cottages (on the site of Islington Spa).

St Chad's Park (Brkg), erroneously associated with the saint through the name Chadwell, in Chadwell Heath (q.v.).

St Clement Danes W.C.2, 'parish of St Clement associated with Danes'. According to Stow, the name is due to the fact of 'Harold a Danish king and other Danes' being buried here, but this explanation cannot be substantiated. Some early forms include the term *Dacus* (see Field, *PN of Dacorum District*) [*Par. Sci Clementis Ecclesie Dacorum* c.1120, *Parochia Sci Clementis* 1204, *Denscheman Parosch* 1266, *Parochia Sci Clementis le Daneys Extra Lond'* 1274, *Seynt Clement Danes* 1500].

St George's Fields S.E.1, land adjacent to St George's Church. According to Stow, in the year 1122 'Thomas Arden gave the monks of Bermondsey the church of St George, in Southward, and five shillings rent by the year, out of the land pertaining to London Bridge'.

St Giles in the Fields W.C.2, so called from the derivation of the parish-name from that of the hospital of St Egidius (OF *Giles*). The village was originally isolated in the fields to the west of London [*Hospitali Sancti Egidii extra Londonium* c.1120, *Seintgilespitel* 1374, *Seynt Gyles in the ffield* 1563].

St James's Palace S.W.1, **St James's Park** S.W.1: named from the leper hospital dedicated to St James [*Hospital Leprosis Puellis de Scī Jacobi extra London justa (sic) Westm̄* 1204, *Hospital of St James by Charyng* 1386, *Seynt James Newe Parke* 1555].

St James's Park E.17, from the dedication of the church in St James's Street, not far away.

St John's Wood N.W.8, 'wood held by the Knights of St John'. The land was originally granted to the Templars, but this connexion does not seem to be reflected in early forms; the name alludes to the Knights Hospitallers of St John, to whom it was transferred on the suppression of the Knights Templars [*Boscum Prioris Sci Johannis* 1294, *Seynt Johns Woode* 1524].

St Katharine Docks E.1, named from the former Hospital of St Catherine (founded in 1148) [*Katerines Dokke* 1422: ME *dok*].

St Margaret's (Twic), named after the house (in Isleworth) owned by the first Marquess of Ailsa, who also owned land here and who is commemorated (as Earl of Cassilis) by a street-name—Cassilis Road—as well as by Ailsa Road and Ailsa Avenue. The area (formerly part of the Twickenham Park estate) was developed as a residential suburb in the mid-nineteenth century.

St Martin in the Fields W.C.2, so called because the church stood in the fields adjoining the royal mews.

St Mary Cray (Orpn), '(place with)

church dedicated to St Mary, on river Cray (q.v.)' [*Creye Sancte Marie* 1257].

St Marylebone N.W.1, '(place by) St Mary's stream', the river-name having been originally Tyburn, which also came to denote the famous place of execution. The settlement doubtless disliked its former name because of its association with the gallows; the meaningless -le- was introduced in the seventeenth century—possibly by analogy with St Mary le Bow—and still finds no place in the name as spoken by native Londoners [*Tiburne* 1086, *Maryburne* 1453, *Tyborne otherwise called Maryborne* 1490: OE *burna*]. See also Tyburn.

St Pancras N.W.1, '(place with) church dedicated to St Pancras'. Pancras was a Christian martyr in Rome at the time of Diocletian. Some early spellings indicate a development towards *Pancridge*, paralleled by Mrs Gamp's pronunciation of *Jonas* as 'Jonadge', but the name was doubtless brought back to its original form by awareness of its origin in the dedication— unlike *Dilewise*, which became (and remains) Dulwich (q.v.) [*Sanctum Pancratiū* 1086, *Parochia Sancti Pancrassi* 1353, *Pancrich* 1575, *Pankeridge al. St Pancras* 1588].

St Paul's E.C.4, 'church dedicated to St Paul', the cathedral of the diocese of London, lending its name to its immediate neighbourhood [*Ecclesia Sancti Pauli Apostoli* c.730, *Sancte Paules Kirke* c.950].

St Paul's Cray (Orpn), '(place with) church dedicated to St Paulinus, on river Cray (q.v.)' [*Creypaulin* 1291].

Sanderstead (Crdn), 'sandy place', the first element having been originally an adjective *sanden*, corresponding to *silvern*, *oaken*, or *wooden*, but modified by Norman influence to *sander-* [*Sondenstede* c.880, *Sandestede* 1086, *Sanderstede* 1221: OE **sanden, stede*].

Sands End S.W.6, 'edge of parish characterised by sandy soil', a riverside area near the mouth of Chelsea Creek [*Atte Sonde* 1408, *Sand End in Fulham* 1655: OE *sand, ende*].

Savoy, The W.C.2, 'manor originally held by Peter of Savoy', alluding to the uncle of Henry III, who was granted land on which he built a palace [*Le Sauveye* 1324, *Manor of Savoie* 1348].

Scadbury Park (Chht), '(old) fortification used by thieves' [*Scadebir'* 1254, *Scadbery* 1300: OE *sceaða, burh*].

Scratchwood N.W.7, perhaps 'wood fenced with hurdles' [ME *cracche*, OE *wudu*].

Seething Wells (Srbn), 'bubbling springs' (OE *wella*).

Selhurst (Crdn), 'willow wood' [*Selherst* 1229: OE *sealh, hyrst*].

Selsdon (Crdn), 'Seli's hill' [*Selesdune* c.880, *Selysdon* 1247: OE *dūn*].

Seven Dials W.C.2, 'seven aspects', alluding to the junction of seven roads marked by a Doric pillar from which (according to John Evelyn) the streets formed a star. The site was originally a field known as *Marshland* [*Les Seven Dials* 1707].

Seven Kings (Ilfd), perhaps '(place of) Seofeca's people', being then a name of the same type as Barking (q.v.), not far away. The tradition that this was the meeting place of seven Saxon kings lacks documentary support (*Sevekyngg(es)* 1285: OE -*ingas*].

Seven Sisters N.15, named from seven elm trees which formerly stood at the corner of Seven Sisters Road, near Page Green. They are first mentioned on Rocque's *Topographical Map of Middlesex* (1754) as *7 Sesters*.

Shacklewell N.16, probably 'spring at or near which animals were tethered'. There is uncertainty not in the identity or meaning of the elements, but in the exact significance of *sceacol*, 'shackle, tether', in place-names [*Shekelwell* 1491, *Shakylwell* 1509: OE *sceacol*, *wella*].

Shadwell E.1, 'shallow spring' [*Schadewelle* 1222: OE **sceald*, *wella*].

Shepherd's Bush W.12, descriptive name alluding either to an individual named Shepherd, Sheppard, &c, or to shepherds who may have resorted there [*Sheppards Bush Green* 1635].

Shirley (Crdn), 'bright wood', probably in the sense of 'thinly grown'. The position of the place not far from the former Surrey/Kent county boundary has been noted, but as the name is not uncommon elsewhere it is unlikely that OE *scīr*, 'shire', played a part in its history [*Shirleye* 1314: OE *scīr*[1], *lēah*].

Shooters Hill S.E.18, 'slope frequented by archers', the second element being *helde* rather than *hill* in some early forms; the precise activity of the 'shooters' is not recorded, but it is more likely to have been hunting rather than archery practice [*Shetereshelde* 1292, *Shetersselde* 1374: ME *schetere*, OE *helde*].

Shootup Hill N.W.2, 'sharp rise' [*Shottuppe Hill* 1566].

Shoreditch N.1, '(place by) ditch draining a slope or bank'. Numerous other interpretations have been offered for this difficult name, the main problem being not so much the meaning of the elements as the identification of the features they refer to. It is very unlikely that the shore of the Thames is involved, as the City of London lies between Shoreditch and the river [*Soredich* c.1148, *Schoresdiche* 1214, *Shordige* 1274: OE **scora*, *dīc*].

Sidcup (Bxly), 'flat-topped hill', the

top of such a hill being a 'seat' rather than a 'peak'. A hill-top site of this kind would have the advantage of commanding a wide view, and the slopes on all sides would make it difficult of access for attackers [*Cetecopp'* 1254, *Setecoppe* 1301, *Sedecoppe* 1332: OE **set-copp*].

Silvertown E.16, named after the firm of S. W. Silver and Co, explosives manufacturers here. **Canning Town**, nearby, is of similar origin.

Sipson (Hldn), 'Sibwine's farm' [*Sibwineston* c.1215, *Sibbeston* 1318, *Sybeston* c.1410: OE *tūn*].

Slade Green (Erith), 'green place in low-lying meadow', a slade being rather boggy grassland usually beside a stream [OE *slæd, grēne*].

Smitham Bottom (Clsn), 'bottom of the smooth valley'. In the modern spelling (dating from the early eighteenth century), the second element is unrecognisable, but *den(e)* had persisted for nearly five hundred years [*Smetheden* 1331, *Smithdenbottom* 1536: OE *smēðe, denu, botm*].

Snaresbrook E.11, '(place by) brook in or near which traps were set' [OE *sneare, brōc*].

Soho W.1, recalling the hunting cry that was evidently heard in the area before the open fields were built over. Hunting is known to have taken place here in the sixteenth century [*So Ho* 1632, *Soe-Hoe in St Martins in the Fields* 1681].

Somerset House W.C.2, named from the former palace built by the Protector Somerset in the reign of Edward VI. An alternative name for the building was Denmark House, from its having been given by James I to his Queen, Anne of Denmark [*Somerset Place* 1555, *Denmark House al. Somerset House al. Stronde House* 1672].

Somers Town N.1, 'urban development on estate of Lord Somers', *Town* in a number of London names having this significance. This estate included the *Brill* ('park or wood stocked with beasts of the chase'), the last remnant of which was destroyed on the building of the Midland Railway [*The Bruel* 1741, *The Bruil* 1788: OF *broile*].

Southall (Elng), 'southern nook of land', by contrast with Northolt (q.v.) [*Suhaull'* 1198, *Sudhale* 1204, *Suhall* 1246, *Southhalle* 1345: OE *sūð, healh*].

Southborough (Srbn), possibly 'southern hill' [OE *sūþ, beorg*].

Southbury (Enfd), 'southern manor' or possibly 'land south of the manor' [*Southberyfeld* 1420, *Southburyfeld* 1610: OE *sūð, burh*].

South Ealing. See Ealing.

Southend S.E.6, 'southern district',

formerly a hamlet dependent upon Lewisham [OE *sūð, ende*].

Southfields S.W.18, 'southern arable lands (of Wandsworth)'. The corresponding *Northfield* survived as late as 1865 and is now a street name, a recent revival [*Suthfeld* 1247: OE *sūð, feld*].

Southgate N.14, '(place by) southern gate', naming the hamlet which grew up by this entrance to Enfield Chase [*Suthgate* 1370, *Le South Gate* 1608: OE *sūð, geat*].

South Harrow, South Kensington, South Kenton, South Lambeth, South Ruislip. See Harrow, Kensington, Kenton, Lambeth, Ruislip.

Southwark S.E.1, 'southern defensive work'. It is across the river from the City and must have been regarded in early days as its southern outpost. Forms in use in the tenth and eleventh centuries meant 'fort of the men of Surrey'. The London Borough of Southwark comprises Bermondsey and Camberwell as well as Southwark itself [*Suthringa Geweorche* 10c., *Sudwerca* 1086: OE *sūð, (ge)weorc*].

South Wimbledon, South Woodford. See Wimbledon, Woodford.

Spa Fields W.C.1, commemorating the London Spa, which exploited several of the mineral springs which abound in the area (cf. Sadler's Wells) [*London Spaw* 1746, *Spa Fields* c.1820].

Spitalfields E.1, 'land belonging to a hospital', being the property of the priory of St Mary Spital, founded in 1197 [*Seintmariespitel in Shordich* 1394, *Spitellond* 1399, *Spyttlefeildes* 1561, *Spittel Feild* 1588: ME *spitel*, OE *feld*].

Squirrels Heath (Hnch), 'heathland held by member of the Squirrel family'. The family is named in local records several centuries before the earliest record of the place-name [*Sqyrells Called the Heth Cok* 1525: OE *hǣþ*].

Stamford Bridge S.W.6, 'bridge by the sandy ford'. The bridge, as in similar locations elsewhere, superseded the ford (while taking its name from it). The development of the name to its present form can be seen in the series of spellings [*Sandford* 1236, *Saunford* 1341, *Samfordesbregge* 1444, *Sampfordbregge* 1449, *Stamfordbregge* 1456: OE *sand, ford, brycg*].

Stamford Brook *riv*, 'brook with a stony ford', probably alluding to the crossing of the main Great West Road [*Staunford* 1274, *Stamford Brooke* 1650: OE *stān, ford, brōc*].

Stamford Hill N.16, 'hill by a sandy ford', showing the same change from *Sandford* as Stamford Bridge, *supra* [*Sanford* 1225, *Saundfordhull* 1294, *Sampfordehill* 1410, *Stamford Hill* 1675: OE *sand, ford, hull*].

Stanmore (Harw), '(place by) stony pool', possibly alluding to one of the ponds which still exist in the gravelly outcrops on the clay soil. The change from *-mere* to *-more*, not unknown in other names, was probably assisted by the occasional addition of *The More* (to distinguish this parish from Whitchurch or Little Stanmore) [*Stanmere* 1086, *Greate Sanmare* 1392, *Stanmar the More* 1563, *Stanmore the Great* 1574: OE *stān, mere*].

Staple Inn W.C.1, 'pillared dwelling or lodging' [*Le Stapledhalle* 1333, *Stapelhyne in Holbourne* 1436, *Staple Inne* c.1440: OE *stapol, inn*].

Staples Corner N.W.2, named from the Staples bedding factory nearby.

Starveall Bridge (Yiewsley), named from an adjacent field called *Starveall*. This derogatory term is frequently used of infertile land. The bridge takes Stockley Road over the Grand Junction Canal.

Stepney E.1, 'Stybba's landing place', one of the several Thamesside names in *-hȳþ*, the modern forms of which show such considerable variation. By contrast with Chelsea and Rotherhithe, however, Stepney has an exact counterpart in Putney both in its modern termination and in its first element being a personal name [*Stybbanhype* c.1000, *Stibenhede* 1086, *Stibbeneie al. Stebenuthe* 1274, *Stebenheth al. Stepney* 1542: OE *hȳþ*].

The Steyne W.3, 'stony place', a small triangular green by the main

Uxbridge road. The name formerly occurred also in Isleworth (*Stene* 1498) and, as a road name, in Drayton (*Via voc. le Stene in Drayton* 1455) [OE *stǣne*].

Stockwell S.E.9, '(place near) well or spring by a stump' [*Stokewell* 1197, *Stockewell* 1294: OE *stocc, wella*].

Stoke Newington N.16, 'new farm by the tree-stumps', the prefix distinguishing it from Highbury, formerly the manor of Newton Barrow [*Neutone* 1086, *Newinthon* 1255, *Neweton Stoken* 1274, *Stokneweton* 1274: OE *nīwe, stocc, tūn*].

Stonebridge Park N.W.10, named from its position adjoining the bridge over the Brent. Stonebridge Farm was on the site before the area was built over.

Stoop Bridge (Ilfd), 'bridge by a boundary-post', *stoop* being an Essex word for a short post fixed in the earth as a boundary-mark [*The Stoup* 1794].

Strand W.C.2, 'bank, shore'— namely, of the Thames, which before embankment was considerably broader than it is today. During the Middle Ages, sections of the street bore different names; the part near St Clement Danes was *Vicus Dacorum* or *Densemanestret* ('Danes' Street') and that near St Mary le Strand was known as *Vicus Innocentium* ('Innocents' Street'), from the earlier dedication of the

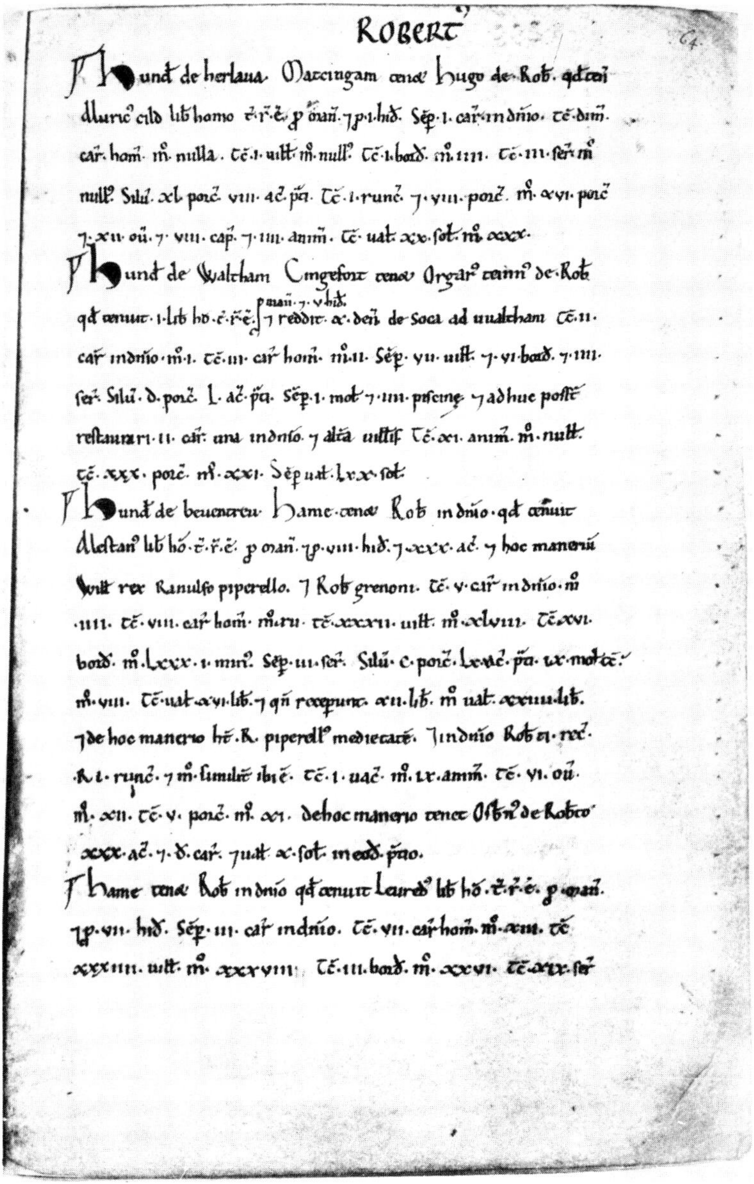

1. A page from Domesday Book (1086), with entries relating to East and West Ham and Chingford. The first paragraph refers to Matching, in the Hundred of Harlow (Essex). Next comes the Chingford entry; the manor of Earl's Chingford was held at that time by Orgar the thegn. The following entry relates to West Ham, the mill mentioned in the fifth line being almost certainly the predecessor of Temple Mills. The final entry refers to East Ham.

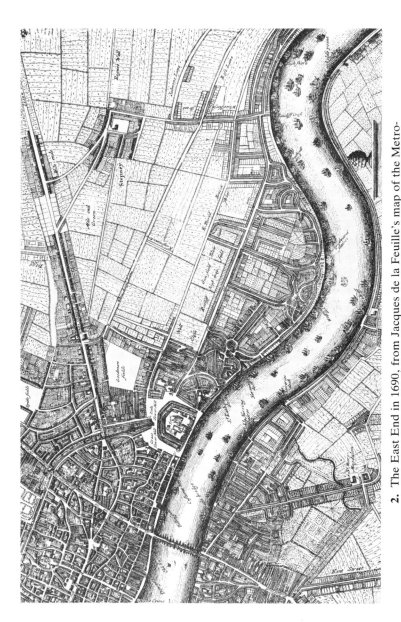

2. The East End in 1690, from Jacques de la Feuille's map of the Metropolis, published in Amsterdam. The rural nature of the Tower Hamlets at that time is clearly shown, and there were open fields within a short

3. Remains of the chapel of Savoy Palace, from an engraving by S. Rawle, 1798.

4. Ely House, where Ely Palace now is, from an eighteenth-century engraving.

5. The western boundary of Middlesex in 1672. The western edge of the present-day Greater London coincides with this border. The area around Staines was not incorporated into the new metropolitan area, but has become Surrey territory north of the Thames.

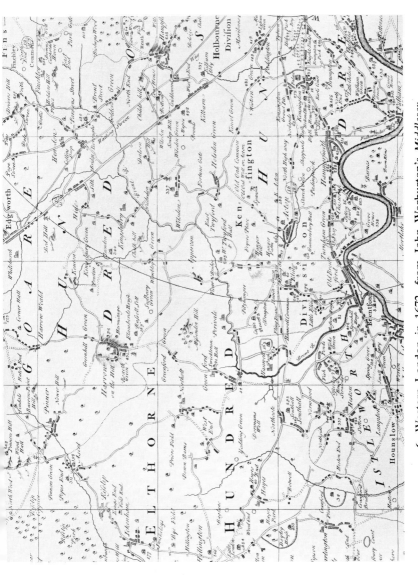

6. Western London in 1672, from John Warburton's *Middlesex*.

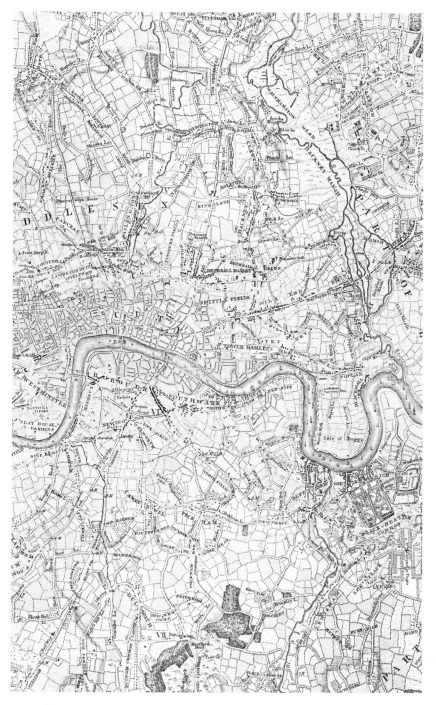

7. The Lea valley and the Kent-Surrey border, from Rocque's map of the Environs of London, 1769.

8. Land-mark into place-name, illustrated by the short-lived monument to George IV, erected at Battlebridge in 1830. It was demolished when a railway terminus was built there, but bequeathed its name to the station—King's Cross.

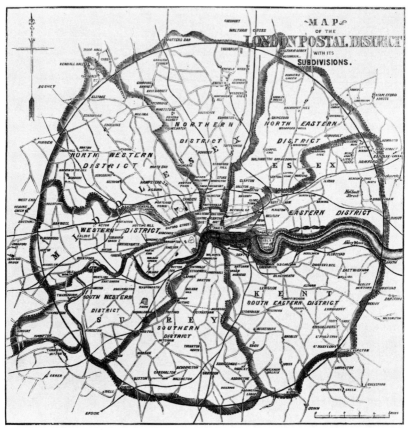

9. The approximate boundaries of Greater London embodied in the London Postal District in 1857. The subdivisions (apart from the Southern and North Eastern) form the basis of the districts in the London area today.

church to the Holy Innocents [*Stronde* 1185, *In Vico Strand'* 1222: OE *strand*].

Strand on the Green W.4, 'bank or shore beside a green place', formerly a Thames-side hamlet of Chiswick [*Stronde* 1353, *Stronde in Parochia de Cheswyk* 1412, *Strand Green* 1710, *Strand under Green* 1760, *Strand on Green* 1795: OE *strand*, *grēne*].

Stratford E.15, 'ford on a Roman road', namely the means by which the road from London to Colchester crosses the Lea. Various additions to the medieval forms of this name distinguish it from Stratford-at-Bow (q.v.), on the other side of the river; some suffixes allude to its location in West Ham, and others to its being held by the monks of Stratford Langthorne Abbey [*Stratforde* 1066, *Strætforda* 1067, *Estratford* 1291, *Stratforde Hamme* 1312, *Stratford Monachorum* 1325, *Stratford atte Thorne* 1338, *Abbei Stratford* 1389, *Stratford Longthorn* 1450: OE *strēt*, *ford*]. See also *Langthorn*.

Stratford-at-Bow, 'ford on a Roman road, by an arched bridge'. The place is now called Bow (q.v.), the old addition serving to distinguish it from the Essex Stratford, across the Lea [*Stratford* 1177, *Stratford atte Bowe* 1279, *Stratford ate Boghe* 1303, *Stratford at the Bowe* 1494: OE *strēt*, *ford*, *boga*].

Stratford Bridge (Hldn), 'bridge by a ford on a Roman road'. The main London-Bath road crosses the river Pinn at this place [OE *strēt*, *ford*, *brycg*].

Strawberry Hill (Twic), from the name chosen by Horace Walpole for the house which he bought in 1748. The property had previously belonged to a retired coachman, who may or may not have given the place its older name, *Chopped Straw Hall*. Walpole's choice was suggested by a local field-name, *Strawberry Hill Shot*.

Streatham S.W.16, 'village by a Roman road'. Streatham High Road closely follows the course of its ancient predecessor [*Estreham* 1086, *Stratham* 1175, *Streteham* 1247, *Streetham* 1422, *Streatham* 1510: OE *strēt*, *hām*].

Stroud Green (Crdn), **Stroud Green** N.4: 'marshy land overgrown with brushwood' [(1) *La Strode* 1279, *Le Strod* 1296, (2) *Strode near Hyghebury* 1407, *Strowde Grene* 1546: OE *strod*].

Sudbrook Park (Ptsm), 'park with or by the south stream' [*Suthbrok* 1332: OE *sūð*, *brōc*].

Sudbury (Harw), 'southern manor', to distinguish the place from *Northbury*, possibly Harrow itself [*Suthbery* 1292, *Sudbery* 1294: OE *sūð*, *burh*].

Suffield Hatch E.4, 'forest entry by Suffield, i.e., the south field'

89

[*Suthfeld'* 1269, *Suffeild Hatch Grove* 1641: OE *sūð*, *feld*, *hæcc*].

Summerstown S.W.17, 'urban development on land owned by Sumner or Summers'. This name is of the same type as Camden Town and Somers Town (qq.v.). The family is mentioned in documents of the seventeenth and eighteenth centuries, but the place-name occurs no earlier than 1823.

Sundridge Park (Brom), 'park at Sundridge, i.e., privately-owned enclosure'. *Park* is really superfluous in the name, but the development of *edisc* to *-idge* no doubt further concealed the meaning as *edisc* itself went out of the vocabulary [*Sundrish'* 1295, *Sundresh* 1421: OE *sundor*, *edisc*].

Surbiton (Kstn), 'southerly grange or barley farm', contrasted with Norbiton, the 'north grange', which was separated from it by the hill on which Berrylands Farm was sited. Both granges were dependencies of the royal manor of Kingston [*Suberton* 1179, *Surbeton* 1263, *Surburton* 1272, *Surbiton* 1597: OE *sūð*, *bere-tūn*].

Sutton W.4, 'south farm', with reference to Acton. The manor house, Sutton Court, is commemorated in a street-name. The place evidently commanded a fine view, as the occasional alternative name testifies [*Suthtona* 1181, *Sutton Chesewyk* 1367, *Sutton al.*

Bewregarde 1456: OE *sūð*, *tūn*, OF *beau*, *regard*].

Sutton, 'south farm', with reference to Carshalton. The London Borough of Sutton includes Beddington, Cheam, and Wallington, as well as Carshalton and the parish from which the modern administrative unit takes its name [*Sudtone* 1086, *Suthtona* 1174, *Sutton juxta Kershaltone* 1325: OE *sūð*, *tūn*].

Swakeleys (Uxbr), 'estate of the Swalecliffe family', the lords having come from Swalecliffe (Kent) or Swalcliffe (Oxon) [*Swaleclyves Maner* 1466, *Swalcliff* 1486, *Swakeleys* 1593].

Swiss Cottage N.W.3, named from a building imitating a Swiss Chalet, originally the cottage of a toll collector. A tavern was built on the site in the early nineteenth century and reconstructed after the Second World War.

Sydenham S.E.26, 'Cippa's village', embodying (in barely recognisable form) the personal name occurring also in Cippenham (near Slough) and Chippenham (Wilts). The change of *-p-* to *-d-* is not, of course, a phonetic development, but almost certainly took place because of a copyist's error [*Chipeham* 1206, *Shippenham* 1315, *Sidenham* 1690: OE *hām*].

Syon House, **Syon Park** (Brfd), named from the monastery of the Holy Saviour and St Brigid, founded by Henry V in 1414, to which 'of

Zion' was added for reasons which are by no means clear, but this was early regarded as the 'official' name of the religious house, and survived the suppression of the monastery [*Istelworth Syon* 1564].

T

Tarn, The S.E.9, 'small lake'. Applied to a pond in Mottingham Park, this name must be regarded as a fanciful transfer (in modern times) of a term historically confined to the north of England [ON *tjorn*].

Teddington (Rchm), 'farm or estate associated with Tuda'. Original *Tud-* became *Ted-* in the late thirteenth century, following the phonetic tendency shown in other names, e.g., South Tedworth (Hants) and Tedfold (Sussex), in which *u* between 'point consonants' (*t* and *d*) was unrounded to *e*. Teddington in Worcestershire is derived from a different personal name—Teotta [*Tudintun* 969, *Tudington* 1274, *Tedinton* 1294: OE *-ingtūn*].

Temple, The W.C.2, 'house of the order of Knights Templars'. The term is often used as a prefix in place-names (e.g. Temple Newsam) where this order had property, and occurs in the Greater London names of Temple Fortune (Hendon) and Temple Mills (Hackney). This religious order of knights, founded in the twelfth century to safeguard the pilgrim routes in the Holy Land,

lost its English possessions to the Crown in the fourteenth century; these premises were taken over by lawyers, who eventually grouped themselves into the societies of the Outer, Inner, and Middle Temples— of which only Inner and Middle survive.

Temple Fortune N.W.11, possibly 'Templars' precinct before the village'. Instances of *Fortune* occur elsewhere in this part of Middlesex, but no forms have been found early enough for certainty of interpretation.

Temple Mills E.10, 'mills in the possession of the Templars', a group of water-mills on both sides of the River Lea. They were also known as *Craccehege* ('hurdle-fence') *Mills* [*Molendin' de Craggehege* 1274, *Cracchegge* 1394, *Tempylmylle* 1461: ME *cracche*, *temple*, OE *hecg*, *myln*]. See also The Temple.

Thames *riv*, probably 'dark water'. Although the meaning of the British root of this name is unknown, the suggested interpretation has been put forward by some scholars because of the not unlikely connexion with a Sanskrit word *tamasa-*, 'dark'. A number of other river-names are related, including Thame, Tame, Tavy, Tamar, Team, and Teme.

Thornton Heath (Crdn), 'heath-land by Thornton'. The forms are too late to be certain that Thornton is 'farm by thorn trees'; other possibilities are 'thorn hill' or even 'thorn valley'

[*Thorneton Hethe* 1511: OE *hǣð, tūn, dūn, denu*].

Thrift Wood (Crdn), 'woodland, wooded countryside', the explanatory term *Wood* being strictly unnecessary but doubtless added when the significance of the first element (*Frith* in 1849 and on some modern maps) ceased to be understood [OE *(ge)fyrhð*].

Tockyngton Recreation Ground (Wbly). See Oakington.

Tollington, 'Tolla's hill', an old manor to the north of Islington, its name being now preserved in some street-names at Finsbury Park [*Tollandune* c.1000, *Tolentone* 1086, *Tolindon* 1274: OE *dūn*].

Tolworth (Kstn), possibly 'Tala's enclosure', although the personal name is not on record. However, the compounding of *-worð* with personal names is very common and occurs in other Greater London names, e.g., Harmondsworth, Wandsworth and Isleworth. Tala would be a complimentary name, from OE *(ge)tæl*, 'swift, prompt' [*Taleorde* 1086, *Talewurtha* c.1160: OE *worð*].

Tooting S.W.17, 'people of Tota'. In the Middle Ages there were two Tooting manors: Upper Tooting (or Tooting Bec) and Lower Tooting (or Tooting Graveney); the former was held by the abbey of St Mary of Bec-Hellouin in Normandy, which lent its name also to Weedon Beck in

Northamptonshire. Lower or South Tooting was held by Richard de Gravenel in 1215; this family probably came from Graveney in Kent [*Totinge* 675, *Totinges* c.1060, *Totinge de Bek* 1255, *Thoting Gravenel* 1272: OE *-ingas*].

Tothill, 'look-out hill', doubtless an artificial mound or barrow—probably that which still existed in the eighteenth century south-west of Horseferry Road [*Tothulle* c.1190: OE **tōt-hyll*].

Tottenham N.17, 'Totta's village'. In the marshy riverside area of the parish was Tottenham Hale, 'secluded corner of Tottenham' [*Toteham* 1086, *Totenham* 1189, *le Hale* 1502: OE *hām, healh*].

Tottenham Court, 'manor-house of Totta's angle of land', bearing the same personal name as Tottenham, but not necessarily referring to the same man. The parish-name has also affected this one, which might without such influence have become Tottenhall or Totnal. The manor-house was situated not far from the site of Euston Station [*þottenheale* c.1000, *Totenhala* 1083, *Totenhalecourt* 1487: OE *healh*].

Totteridge N.20, 'Tata's ridge' [*Taderege* c.1150, *Taterige* 1230: OE *hrycg*].

Tower, The E.C.3, 'fortress'. Originally, only a single tower, The White Tower, was on the site, but the name became regularly used for the entire

92

complex surrounding the central stronghold [*þone tur* c.1100, *þam ture on Lunden* c.1122, *the Towre of London* 1503: ME *tur*].

Tower Hamlets E.1, 'hamlets adjoining the Tower of London', virtually the medieval parish of Stepney. This was a large one, which included the hamlets of Shadwell, Bethnal Green, Poplar, Mile End, Whitechapel, and Ratcliff. The history of the area has been one of separation, consolidation, and finally reunification into a single London Borough.

Trafalgar Square S.W.1, commemorating the battle off the coast of Spain in October 1805, in which the British fleet under Nelson defeated the combined Spanish and French fleets commanded by Villeneuve. Nelson was killed in the battle; a column in his honour, surmounted by his statue, stands at the centre of the square, which was constructed between 1829 and 1841.

Trent Park (Barnet), 'estate named after Trent (Tyrol)', a name transfer intended to convey (however obliquely) a compliment to the royal family of the time. The estate, formed under the Enclosure Act of Enfield Chase in 1776, was leased by George III to his favourite physician, Sir Richard Jebb. Another royal patient, the Duke of Gloucester, had recently recovered frosm a severe illness at Trent, and Jebb applied this name to his new estate.

Tufnell Park N.7, N.19, commemorating William Tufnell, lord of the manor of Barnsbury in 1753.

Tulse Hill S.W.2, named after the Tulse family, on record locally from the middle of the seventeenth century.

Turkey Street (Enfd), meaning uncertain. The form *Turkey* did not arise until the early nineteenth century; earlier forms (*Tuckey*, *Tuckhey*) suggested a compound with *-eg* ('island') or *gehæg* ('enclosure'), neither of which was impossible. However, the earliest spelling *Tokestrete* 1441 invalidates these suggestions, but, unfortunately, puts nothing in their place. Street refers to the position of the district beside a Roman road (Ermine Street) [*Tokestrete* 1441: OE *strǣt*].

Turnham Green W.4, 'green place, or village green, by Turnham, i.e., riverside pasture by a bend'. Extant forms do not allow complete certainty about the final element, which may be *hām*, 'village, homestead', or *hamm*, 'riverside pasture, land in a river bend'; if it is the latter, the first element, meaning 'circular place, land in a bend', may be seen either as reinforcement or redundancy [*Turneham* c.1235, *Turnhamgrene* 1396: OE **trun, hamm, grēne*].

Turnmill Brook, an alternative name for a length of the Fleet which provided power for a number of water-mills.

Turnpike Lane N.8, 'lane beside a toll barrier'.

Twickenham (Rchm), 'Twicca's land within a bend of a river' [*Tuican hom* 704, *Tuuiccanham* 941, *Twikeham* 1216, *Twicknem* 1651, *Twitnam* 1644, *Twittenham* 1698: OE *hamm*].

Twyford (Elng), '(place by) a double ford', two fords across the river Brent being still in use until recent times [*Tueverde* 1086, *Twiford* 1199, *Twyford al. Twyforth* 1402: OE *twī, ford*].

suggestion of height here, as in a number of other places (e.g. Upminster) merely indicating a slight elevation above surrounding marshy land [*Hupinton* 1203, *Uptoun* 1485: OE *upp, tūn*].

Uxbridge (Hldn), 'bridge in settlement of Wixan tribe', alluding to a dispersed section of the tribe settled in alien territory. There is an ancient bridge here across the river Colne [*Oxebruge* c.1145, *Wixebrug'* c.1145, *Uxebrigg* 1200, *Wuxebr'* 1235, *Woxenbrugge al. Uxbridge* 1398: OE *brycg*].

U

Upminster (Havg), 'great church on higher ground'. In a flat countryside a slight elevation often merits being recorded in a place-name (cf. Eel Brook Common). Here the church was built on slightly rising ground [*Upmynstre* 1062, *Upmunstre* 1086, *Uppeministr'* 1216, *Upmister* 1535: OE *upp, mynster*].

Upney (Brkg), 'upon an island', alluding to dry ground amid marshes [*Upney* 1539: OE *uppan, ēg*].

Upper Edmonton N.18, 'higher part of Edmonton (q.v.)', south of Pymme's Brook.

Upper Norwood S.E.19. See Norwood.

Upton E.7, 'upper estate', the

V

Valence Park (Bctr), adjoining Valence House, bears the name of early occupiers of the property. Agnes de Valencia is mentioned in a document of early fourteenth-century date.

Valentines Park (Ilfd), an open space, is named from former occupiers, the Valentine family. The name is found in a deed of 1665.

Vale of Health N.W.3, a complimentary name bestowed by the developers of what had been a marshy valley-bottom, which they had drained and prepared for building sites. This venture, in the first decade of the nineteenth century, was a prelude to the modern growth of Hampstead.

Vauxhall S.W.8, 'manor held by Falkes', granted to Falkes (or Faukes) de Bréauté. It is ironic that the name of this supporter of King John, and a ruthless oppressor in his own right, should be so consistently preserved in an abundant documentation from the thirteenth century to the present [*Faukeshale* 1279, *La Sale Faukes in the Parish of Lamhyeth* 1293, *Fauxhall* c.1600, *Vaux-Hall* 1719: OE *hall*].

Victoria S.W.1, the district centred on Victoria Station, named after the Queen and opened in 1860.

Victoria Embankment S.W.1, constructed 1864–70 and named in honour of the queen. In spite of the existence of Albert Embankment, south of the river, it is this which is referred to as *The* Embankment, and lends its name to the Underground Railway station. The designer of both embankments is honoured in Bazalgette Gardens, New Malden.

W

Waddington (Knly), 'wheat hill'. Some early spellings suggest an origin in *hwǣten* ('wheaten') rather than *hwǣte*, and the *-en* suffix of the adjective was confused with the connective *-ing*, giving rise to the modern form of the name [*Hwǣtedune* c.880, *Watedone* 1279, *Whatendon* 1206, *Whatyngdon* 1325, *Whadington* 1558: OE *hwǣte*, *dūn*].

Waddon (Crdn), 'woad hill'. The growing of woad in England ceased only on the introduction of aniline dyes [*Waddone* c.1115, *Woddon* 1279: OE *wād*, *dūn*].

Walham Green S.W.6, 'green in the manor of Wendon', the district near the Underground Railway station now called Fulham Broadway, to which the name (formerly Walham Green) was changed in 1952. The family who gave their name to the manor possibly came from Wendens (Essex); the development of the modern form can be traced in a succession of spellings [*Wendenegrene* 1386, *Wendenesgrene* 1397, *Wandenesgrene* c.1410, *Wanam Grene* 1546, *Wanham Greene* 1668, *Wallam Green* 1710, *Walham Green* 1819: OE *grēne*].

Wallington (Sutn), 'farm of the serfs or Britons', the first element being the word from which *Wales* is derived, now taken to mean 'Celtic- or Latin-speaking foreigner'. The syllable *-ing-* seems to have been introduced by accident, but was perhaps retained in order to distinguish this name from that of Walton-on-Thames, of similar origin and (until the early fourteenth century) having a succession of similar spellings [*Waletona juxta Mordon* c.1080, *Waletone* 1086, *Walton* c.1235, *Wallyngton* 1377: OE *walh*, *tūn*].

Walthamstow E.17, 'place where strangers are welcome' or, possibly, 'religious house established by

Wilcume'. The meaning of this name has been much disputed, but most of the suggested meanings are unacceptable on linguistic grounds. The contrast between the earliest and the modern spellings is considerable, but no greater than in many other names [*Wilcumestowe* c.1076, *Welcomestowe* c.1117, *Wolcumestowe* 1235, *Walcumstowe* 1398, *Walthamstowe* 1446: OE *stōw*].

Walworth S.E.17, 'enclosure of the serfs or Britons' [*Wealawyrᵇ* 1006, *Waleorde* 1086, *Wallewurd* 1196, *Walworth* 1354: OE *walh*, *worð*].

Wandle *riv*, back-formation from Wandsworth (q.v.). An early name of the river might have developed to 'Loudbourn' or something similar [*Hlidaburnan* 693, *Ledeborne* c.1230, *Ludeburne* 1255, *Lotebourn* 1337: OE *hlȳde* ('loud one'), *burna*].

Wandsworth S.W.18, 'Wændel's enclosure', with a personal name found also in Wendlebury (Oxon) and Wellingborough (Northants), but not, of course, referring to the same individual [*Wendleswurᵒe* c.1000, *Wendelesorde* 1086, *Wendleswurda* 1184, *Wanlesworth* 1203, *Wannesworth* 1393: OE *worð*].

Wanstead E.11, 'place by a lump or hillock' [*Wænstede* c.1050, *Wenstede* 1066, *Wenesteda'* 1086: OE *wænn*, *stede*].

Wapping E.1, 'Wæppa's people' [*Wapping'* c.1220, *Wappinges* 1231, *Woppin* 1650: OE *-ingas*].

Waterloo S.E.1, commemorating Wellington's victory in 1815 and originally applied to the bridge opened by the Prince Regent in 1817. The railway terminus received the name c.1850, and the designation soon spread to the immediate neighbourhood of the station.

Waterlow Park N.6, commemorating Sir Sidney Waterlow, Lord Mayor of London in 1872, who presented this part of his estate to the London County Council in 1889, for use as a public park.

Wealdstone (Harw), 'Harrow Weald boundary stone'. The stone was originally a boundary mark separating Harrow Weald (q.v.) from the rest of the parish of Harrow. The development of Wealdstone dates from the opening of the London and Birmingham Railway in 1838.

Welling (Bxly), commemorating the Welling or Willing family, who held land here in the early fourteenth century [*Wellyngs* 1362].

Welsh Harp N.W.9, popular name for the lake officially known as the Brent or Kingsbury Reservoir, formed in the eighteen-thirties by the damming of the river Brent near its confluence with the Silk stream. The name was originally that of an inn on the main road near the reservoir.

Wembley (Brent), 'Wemba's grove or wood' [*Wemba Lea* 825, *Wambeleg'* 1249, *Wembele* 1282, *Wemlee* 1387, *Wembley* 1535: OE *lēah*].

Wennington (Havg), 'farm or estate associated with Wynna' [*Winintune* 969, *Weninton* 1190, *Wenenton* 1247, *Wynnyngton* 1553: OE *-ing, tūn*].

West Acton. See Acton.

West Barnes S.W.20, 'place with or by a barn', in the western part of the parish of Merton [*Westberne* 1290: OE *west, bǣre-ǣrn*].

Westbourne Green W.9, 'green west of the stream'. This district did not take its name from that of the local rivulet, but *vice versa*, the stream being designated by the modern term because of its course through this area. The Westbourne Brook was earlier called Knightsbridge Brook or Bayswater Rivulet; it now pursues its course mostly underground, unremarked except for two noteworthy features. It crosses the platforms at Sloane Square station in a nineteenth-century iron conduit. The stream is visible above ground in only one important place, namely in Hyde Park, where it has been dammed and widened to form the Serpentine—so called (with some exaggeration) because of its sinuous course. Urban development west of the original Westbourne Green hamlet shares the name, as Westbourne Park [*Westeburne* 1222, *Westbourne* 1294, *Westborne Grene* 1548: OE *west, burna, grēne*].

West Brompton S.W.10, 'western part of Brompton'. The modern use of the name is probably due to the designation of the Underground Railway station, which lies on the boundary of Brompton (q.v.) and Earls Court.

West Drayton (Hldn), '(west) farm by portage place', 'West' distinguishing it from Drayton in Ealing (v. Drayton Green). West Drayton is by one of the branches of the Colne [*Drægtun* 939, *Draitone* 1086, *Westdrayton* 1465: OE *dræg, tūn, west*].

West End, general term for the W.1 and S.W.1 districts of London, defined in the Oxford Dictionary as 'that part of London lying westward of Charing Cross and Regent Street and including the fashionable shopping district, Mayfair, and the Parks'.

West End (*freq*), 'western district', used in a number of parishes, e.g., Harlington, Greenford, and Hampstead. See also North End.

West Finchley. See Finchley.

West Ham E.15, 'western part of the riverside pasture'. The original *Hamme*, stretching northwards from a flattened bend in the Thames between Poplar and Barking, was divided at some time before 1186, when the first reference to West Ham occurs [*Hamme* 958, *Hame* 1086, *Westhamma* 1186, *Hammes* c.1240: OE *west, hamm*]. See also East Ham, Newham. (*Illustration No 1*)

West Hampstead N.W.6, **West**

Harrow, West Kensington W.14. See Hampstead, Harrow, Kensington.

Westminster S.W.1, 'western monastery', alluding to the location of the Abbey west of London. The site was earlier known as *Thorney*, 'thorn island', being bounded by two branches of the Tyburn and the Thames [*Thorney* 969, *Westmynster* c.975, *Westminstre* 1066: OE *þorn*, *ēg*, *west*, *mynster*].

West Norwood S.E.27, *West Ruislip*. See Norwood, Ruislip.

West Wickham (Brom), 'settlement on a Romano-British site'—*West* to distinguish the place from East Wickham (q.v.). Modern West Wickham actually lies across a Roman road, and finds of pottery and roof-tiles confirm the association with a Romano-British settlement [*Wichamm* 973, *Wicheham* 1086, *Westwycham* 1284: OE *west*, *wīc-hām*].

West Wimbledon. See Wimbledon.

Whetstone N.20, '(place by) a sharpening-stone', alluding either to a single stone used for this purpose, and large enough to be a land-mark, or in a general way to the presence of such stones in the locality. The name occurs also in Leicestershire and, in the form Wheston, in Derbyshire. Stories of the whetting of weapons before the Battle of Barnet (1471) may confirm the interpretation, but do not, of course, account for the name [*Wheston* 1417, *Whete-*

stonesstret 1437, *Whetstone* 1492: OE *hwetstān*].

Whipp's Cross E.11, 'Phip's (wayside) cross', set up by a member of the family of John Phyppe, named in local records of the late fourteenth century [*Phyppys Crosse* 1517, *Fypps Chrosse* 1537, *Phippes Cross* 1572, *Whipps Cross* 1636: ME *cros*].

Whitchurch (Edgw), probably '(place with a) stone church' the characteristic colour indicating the material. The earlier name, Little Stanmore, continued in use as an alternative [*Stanmera* 1086, *Stanmere Parva* 1291, *Whyzt Church* 1538: OE *hwīt*, *cirice*].

Whitechapel E.1, '(place with a) stone chapel', alluding, like Whitchurch (q.v.), to the building material by naming its characteristic colour. Stone would have been an unusual choice for small churches in earlier centuries, when there was a plentiful supply of wood. This chapel was also referred to by its dedication; Mattefelon was probably the name of the founder or of a benefactor [*St Mary de Mattefelon* 1282, *New Chapel without Aldgate* 1295, *Whitechapele by Algate* 1340, *Parish of the Blessed Mary Matfelon of White Chapell* 1452: OE *hwīt*, ME *chapel*].

White City W.12, named from the colour of buildings erected when this exhibition centre was established in 1908.

Whitehall S.W.1, thoroughfare named from the former Whitehall Palace, of which only the Banqueting House survives. Previously known as *York Place*, a building on the site had been used as the London residence of the Archbishops of York. Wolsey decided to rebuild on a grandiose scale, but had to surrender the unfinished building to King Henry VIII. The name applied to the Palace was in imitation of that of the meeting-chamber of the Lords in the old Houses of Parliament [*Whytehale al. Yorke Place* 1530: OE *hwīt, hall*, ME *place*].

Whitton (Twic), 'white farm', possibly alluding to stone buildings, but other reasons for the name cannot be ruled out, e.g., light-coloured soil. The name occurs in several other counties, and for some of these the first element may well have been the personal name Hwīta [*Wytton* 1274, *Whitton* 1352, *Whytton* 1357: OE *hwīt, tūn*].

Whyteleafe (Crdn), '(place with) aspen trees', a modern name for a residential district developed since 1855, when a Mr Glover built his house in White Leaf Field in the northern part of Caterham parish. The pseudo-antiquity of the spelling of the name no doubt comes from the whim of developers. A small part of the area is in Greater London, but the two railway stations are in Surrey.

Wickham. See East Wickham, West Wickham.

Willesden N.W.10, 'hill by or with a spring', a meaning somewhat obscured by the modern spelling, introduced c.1840 by the London and Birmingham Railway. The usual form, from the seventeenth century until then, was *Wilsdon* [*Wellesdone* 1086, *Wilesdune* 1185, *Wyllendon* 1274, *Wylsdon* 1563, *Willesdon al. Wilsson* 1658: OE *wiella, dūn*].

Wimbledon S.W.19, 'Wynnman's hill'. The sequence of early spellings presents some difficulties, but the change from -*n*- to -*l*-, due to the Normans, has parallels in other names: *Nicol* was a Norman version of Lincoln, and across the Channel, earlier *Bononia* has become Boulogne. A subsequent change was the introduction of -*b*- as a 'glide consonant' between the -*m*- and the -*l*- [*Wunemannedun* c.950, *Wymendon* 13c., *Wimeldon* 1202, *Wimbledon* 1211: OE *dūn*].

Winchmore Hill N.21, probably 'Wynsige's boundary hill', supported by the fact that the hamlet lay near the boundary of the ancient parish of Edmonton [*Wynsemerhull* 1319, *Wynsmershull* 1395, *Wynsmore Hill* 1543: OE *(ge)mǣre, hyll*].

Winns, The E.17. See Lloyd Park.

Woodcote (Prly), 'cottage in or by a wood' [*Wudecot* 1200, *La Wudecote* 1203, *Wodecote juxta Croydon* 1307: OE *wudu, cot*].

Wood End (Hayes), 'edge of parish by a wood', possibly alluding to part of the woodland for 400 swine referred to in the Domesday Book description of the manor of Hayes [*Wodehende* 1531: OE *wudu, ende*].

Woodford (Rbrg), '(place at a) ford by a wood'. The ford must have been replaced by a bridge at some time before 1238; Woodford Bridge is now used of the part of Woodford east of the Roding. Woodford Green adjoins Epping Forest [*Wodeforda* 1062, *Wdefort* 1086, *Wudeforde* 1225, *Ponte de Woodford* 1285, *Woodfordbrigge* 1429: OE *wudu, ford, brycg*].

Woodgrange Park E.12, 'grange farm by a wood', an outlying property of Stratford Langthorne Abbey [*Woodgraundge* 1557: OE *wudu*, ME *grange*].

Wood Green N.22, 'green place near woodland'. The hamlet was at the edge of Enfield Chase [*Wodegrene* 1502, *Woodegreene* 1611: OE *wudu, grēne*].

Wood Hall (Pinr), 'manor house near a wood' [*Wodehalle* 1271, *Wodhall* 1349: OE *wudu, hall*].

Woodlands (Islw), 'arable strips by a wood' [*Wodelond* 1485: OE *wudu, land*].

Woodridings (Pinr), 'clearing in woodland' [*Woodredynge* c.1530, *Woodreeding* 1733: OE *wudu, *ryding*].

Woodside S.E.25, '(place) beside a

wood', adjoining Norwood (q.v.) [*Le Wode* 1452, *Wodesyde* 1503: OE *wudu*].

Woodside Park N.12, 'park beside a wood'. Finchley Wood was a part of the great woodland area that stretched across Middlesex [*Woodsendfeld* 1548: OE *wudu*].

Woodside Park N.22, 'park beside a wood', an open space in Wood Green (q.v.).

Worcester Park (Kstn), named from Worcester House, residence of the Earl of Worcester, Keeper of the Great Park of Nonsuch in the early seventeenth century.

Wormwood Scrubs W.12, 'brushwood-covered land by Wormholt, i.e., snake-infested wood'. Original *Wormholt* seems to have been misheard as 'Wormwood'; alternatively, the modern name may be merely the contraction of the unnecessarily long 1437 form [*Wormeholte* c.1195, *Wormoltwode* 1437, *Wormewood* 1654, *Wormholt Scrubbs* 1819, *Wormwood Scrubbs* c.1865: OE *wyrm, holt, *scrubb*].

Wrythe, The (Cstn), '(place by) a streamlet'. The name developed in the same way as Peckham Rye (q.v.), but reverted to its original form and was then burdened (in 1867) with an unnecessary initial *W* [*Rithe* 1229, *Le Ryth* 1450, *La Rye* 1484, *The Rye Common* 1847: OE *riδ*].

Wyke Green (Islw), 'green place at

an outlying farm' [*La Wyke* 1238, *Wike* 1243, *Wykeheth* 1557: OE *wīc*, *grēne*].

Y

Yeading (Hayes), 'people or followers of Geddi', a name of a type once considered to be of the earliest period of settlement, but no longer so regarded. However (as M. Gelling expresses it) these names 'preserve for us the flavour of the age of migration' (NTC, 18) [*Geddinges* 757, *Yeddinggs* 1325, *Yeddyng* 1331: OE *-ingas*].

Yeading Brook *riv*, recent name for the upper part of the stream known as the Crane (q.v.).

Yiewsley (Hldn), 'wood or grove settled by Wīfe'. A related form of the personal name is found in Wivenhoe (Essex), 'Wīfa's ridge'. The change from consonantal *-v-* (OE *f*) to vowel *u* sounds brought about the dropping of initial *W-* [*Wiuesleg'* 1235, *Wyvesle* 1406, *Wewesley* 1593, *Yewsley* 1819: OE *lēah*].

Part 2

Street-names
of Greater London

The inclusion of a number of Central London street-names in the Dictionary section may seem to imply that they have an importance or interest well above any such names in the outer suburbs. This would in fact be so if the present urban area had grown outwards from a nucleus without any associated growth of villages and hamlets just beyond its boundaries. As these included some places of considerable antiquity, it must be the case that the names of some of the streets several miles from the ancient City or its neighbour, Westminster, are likely to go back into history as far as those of the central area, better-known though the latter may be.

The oldest street-names

The City of London obviously has a great advantage in that the history of its streets and their names can be found with comparative ease in its abundant and detailed records. The great privileges enjoyed by the citizens were carefully registered in numerous early documents, and the abundant transactions of its ambitious merchants also ensured that voluminous accounts were kept from soon after the Norman Conquest.

It is not surprising, therefore, that some of the oldest names in the City relate to its mercantile life. Eastcheap E.C.3, for instance, is recorded as *Eastceape* about the year 1100, and its spelling took its modern form as early as 1200. It is the 'eastern market', distinguishing it from *Cheap*, now Cheapside E.C.2, which was also known as *Westceap*. *Cheap* means 'market', and the modern form probably alluded at first to houses built beside it. The buying and selling in these street-markets was not a glamorous trade in exotic imports, however, but the more mundane dealing in food and other commodities necessary for the life of the citizens. Eastcheap was a meat market; Cheap was used by dealers in all kinds of merchandise, much as a Saturday

105

market is in a small town today. Poultry E.C.2 retains its medieval sense of 'market for domestic fowls' (ME *pultrie*), whereas, of course, the modern word refers only to the birds. Other specialist markets are commemorated in Milk Street (*Melecstrate* c.1140), Bread Street (*Bredstrate* c.1165), Lime Street, where lime was burnt and sold (*Limstrate* c.1180), and Wood Street, where wood was sold, until it was required that this combustible trade should take place near the river. Wood Street in Barnet was so called for quite another reason, since it led to Barnet Wood, west of the town; but this, too, is quite an early name (*Wodestrete* 1442).

Of the numerous street-names recording the occupations of the men of the City, very few remain. There is still a Hosier Lane E.C.1, but a second has become Bow Lane, so called from its having been built on arches. Another early name for this street was *Cordwainer Street*, from the workers in Cordovan leather who traded there. It was important enough to give its name to one of the wards of the City. High Street E.15 was also formerly known by this name (*Cordewenstrete* 1527).

The outer boroughs cannot compete with the City in the number of early names that can be marshalled, for several reasons. An important one was that for centuries these outlying places were more agricultural than urban, and although there may have been rows of houses leading off the main street of the village (which may well have been a road leading to London), there was little reason to name these clusters of houses, and still less to refer to them in records, where a man's abode might be sufficiently designated by some such formula as 'of this parish'. Occasionally, however, the names of medieval manors have become street-names; Allfarthing Lane S.W.18 is on the site of the manor of *Alferthyng* and perpetuates its name, which means 'half a fourth part', the manor probably having been an eighth portion of an earlier grant of land. The oldest form of the name is *Elverding*, in a document of about 1230. Bonner Hill Road in Kingston bears a name traceable to *Baneworth* 1342, 'Bana's enclosure'; the erosion of *-worth* is similar to that in Baber's Bridge, discussed in the Dictionary section.

The manors of *Lisson* and *Tottenham Court* are also commemorated in street-names; Lisson Grove N.W.1 was part of a lane into the old village from Kilburn, just as Tottenham Court Road led towards the former manor. Basing Court S.E.15 is now the only local reminder of the old Camberwell manor of *Basynges*, which was held by the powerful City of London family who originally came from Basingstoke in Hampshire. Robert de Basynges is recorded as holding land in Camberwell in 1287, by which time the family had produced

106

two Lord Mayors of London. The City Ward of Bassishaw ('Basing's enclosure') takes its name from them, as do Basinghall Street and Avenue E.C.2. Basing Street W.11 alludes to Lord St John de Basing, who was granted the lordship of the manor of Notting Hill in 1549. This was the pliant Sir William Paulet, who was to become first Marquess of Winchester in 1551; Great Winchester Street E.C.2 occupies the site of the house he was granted by Henry VIII—formerly the Augustinian Friary of the City—and the family name is found in Paulet Road S.E.5.

Dowlas Street S.E.5 refers to another Camberwell manor, that of *Dowedale*, as it is called in a document of 1369. The manor in turn took its name from that of the family of John de Uvedale, who was the lord in 1318. In Dulwich, Friern Road S.E.22 preserves the name of the old manor of *Freryn Camerwell*—the Middle English word *frere* doing duty for religious of both sexes, as this land belonged to Holywell Nunnery in Middlesex. Lordship Lane S.E.22 (*Lordstrete* 1488) was the manorial way of this property; with this name may be compared Lordship Park N.16, which continues as Manor Road, traversing the manor of Stoke Newington.

Street-names alluding to direction and topography

Apart from names which indicate the town towards which the road leads (e.g., Hampstead Road, Harrow Road, Edgware Road, and Rochester Way), there are a number which state their direction by means of the points of the compass. These are often main arteries, such as Great West Road W.4 and Great North Road N.6. Western Avenue W.3 was completed in the early nineteen-thirties, more than fifteen years after it was approved.

Many more such names allude to position, rather than direction, and are to be found all over London. Southern Avenue E.4, for instance, is towards the south of a group of roads beside Epping Forest. North Street is located at the appropriate end of Chapel Road, Bexleyheath, and East Street (appropriately placed) meets it at right angles. The westerly and easterly extensions of Wandsworth High Street S.W.18 are West Hill and East Hill respectively. The former *South Street* there is now Garratt Lane; it used to be balanced by *North Street*, now Fairfield Street.

Some of these sets of roads are paradoxically arranged. Northern Road E.13 is parallel to and west of Western Road; Eastern Road, of course, is also parallel to Northern Road, and also west of it. All three meet Southern Road at right angles.

Occasionally, surnames may be the origin. At least two of the *North* names in London allude to Lord North; these are North Mews W.C.1 and North Court W.1. The names of the former railway companies account for others. South Western Road, Twickenham, is near St Margaret's Station, and takes its name from the London and South Western Railway.

Other intrinsic features of a road, apart from direction or relative location, may generate an appropriate name. Hilliness is a characteristic which readily impresses itself on travellers. *Hill* as the specifying element occurs in a great variety of names, the elevation or steepness of which is not guaranteed by this designation. There is a Hill Brow in Bromley and examples of Hill Crest in Barnet, Wimbledon, and Winchmore Hill. Hill Crest Road W.3 is at the top of Acton Hill; Hill Crest Road W.5 is off Hanger Lane, itself a name indicating a steep hill. In the vicinity are Hill Croft, Hillside Road, and Park Hill. There are, of course, many instances of Hill Street and Hill Road. Hill View S.W.20, and the several Hill View Roads, introduce an ambiguity: do they suggest a view from a hill or a view of a hill? Local conditions will obviously answer this. There are a number of examples of Hill Rise, as well as two of Hillrise Road—at Crouch End and Romford. *Rise* itself indicates a slope, and there are numerous examples of The Rise, as well as Battersea Rise and Hornsey Rise.

Some roads in this class bear names indicating position or direction. East Hill and West Hill S.W.18 have already been mentioned, but these names occur in a number of other places, and there is a good selection of streets called North Hill and South Hill as well. Changes of direction are indicated in Corkscrew Hill (West Wickham), with which Zigzag Road (Kenley) may be compared.

An absence of hills may also be marked by a street-name; Wandsworth Plain S.W.18 has a generic element that is not often met elsewhere. Such land might, of course, be boggy, and streets there be designated by such names as Lower Marsh S.E.1, Lower Marsh Lane (Kingston), or Marsh Avenue (Mitcham).

The quality of soil, whether on hill or in the plain, would be noticeable to travellers before roads were paved. Mud Lane W.5 was presumably not favoured in wet weather, and Featherbed Lane (Croydon) would be known for its soft surface. Pudding Lane often has the same significance, but Pudding Lane E.C.3 alludes to the disposal of offal by butchers of the area. Honeypot Lane N.W.9 also bears a name which originated in the stickiness of the soil.

Streets beside rivers and other watercourses are likely to be appropriately named. River Avenue N.13 is beside the New River, and so is River Bank N.21. Embankment S.W.15 is beside the Thames near Putney Bridge; Thames Bank S.W.14 adjoins Chiswick Bridge. West

Ferry Road and East Ferry Road join at Ferry Street E.14, leading to the old Horse Ferry to Greenwich. Horseferry Road S.W.1 has a similar significance; this ferry crossed to Lambeth. Victoria Embankment, Millbank, Chelsea Embankment, and Albert Embankment were necessary river-side works which made possible much nineteenth-century development in London. Sir William Tite played a great part in the design and construction of these defences, and he is duly honoured in Tite Street S.W.3.

The names of tributaries of the Thames, including 'lost rivers', are embodied in the designation of streets. There are six Wandle Roads, Wandle Sides in Croydon and Wallington, Wandle Banks in Wimbledon and Croydon, and Wandle Way in Mitcham. Effra Parade and Effra Road S.W.2 allude to the stream which is now largely underground, but it has not invaded the basin of the Wandle to the extent that Effra Road S.W.19 would suggest. Fleet Road N.W.3 is on the course of the same stream as Fleet Lane and Fleet Street E.C.4. Brixton Water Lane S.W.2 has borrowed an alternative name of the Effra; Neckinger Street S.E.1 bears that of the flamboyantly named stream that enters the Thames at Bermondsey. Brook Street W.1 used to cross (or be crossed by) the Tyburn, which also names Tyburn Lane (Harrow) and Tyburn Way W.2.

The New River is an artificial waterway bringing a supply from Hertfordshire into London. The names of some streets on its course have been mentioned already. To these must be added Myddleton Avenue in Enfield, Myddleton Gardens N.21, Myddleton Park N.20, Myddleton Road N.8, and Myddleton Road N.22. These honour the projector of the enterprise, Sir Hugh Myddleton. The New River Company developed streets near its Clerkenwell headquarters, and these received names often derived from those of officials. Mylne Street E.C.1 commemorates the original surveyor of the estate, William Chadwell Mylne. It is possible that he was not the first of his family to work for the company, as his second name is that of one of the Hertfordshire places from which the river derives its water, alluded to in Chadwell Street E.C.1. Other names honouring officials are Prideaux Place, Garnault Place, Inglebert Street, and Great Percy Street. Myddleton Square and Street are a further reference to Sir Hugh, and River Street E.C.1 alludes to the New River itself.

Boathouse Walk and Canal Head S.E.15 refer to the Surrey Canal. Canal Road E.3 is beside the Grand Union Canal, which skirts the City and begins to go northwards again at Paddington. North Wharf Road W.2 adjoins the wharves here. This was originally the terminal of the Grand Junction Canal, now part of the Grand Union system. Junction Mews W.2 bears the old name.

Ponds and lakes, whether natural or artificial, are also alluded to in street-names. Once again, surnames may be the source of some names that appear to belong to this category. Lake Gardens (Dagenham), for instance, is traceable to *Lakes Farm* 1673; there was a family called Lake in Hornchurch in the reign of John, and Agnes and Richard Lake of Havering are mentioned in a document of 1480. Other ambiguities are possible. Lakeside Road N.13 does indeed lead towards some pools in Broomfield Park. But neighbouring roads are named after English Lakes: Ulleswater Road and Derwent Road. Lake View in Edgware, however, presents no problem, as it adjoins a body of water actually called The Lake, in Canons Park. Pond Square N.6 and Pond Place S.W.3 allude to ponds now filled in; Pond Street N.W.3 commemorates a pool by the source of the River Fleet. This was built over during the nineteenth century. Reservoir Road in Ruislip runs alongside The Lido, or Ruislip Reservoir.

High Streets and High Roads

The principal thoroughfare in many towns, including a number of the constituent places of Greater London, is called High Street. *High* here means 'chief, important', and as such it might be thought that these streets would bear the oldest names in the neighbourhood. In fact, that does not prove to be the case; during many centuries of very slow growth, the streets of a settlement would without doubt be equal in rank. When names became necessary, the various thoroughfares would be designated in accordance with the occupations of the residents, or by reference to local buildings, such as the church, or, as has been seen, by terms alluding to the topography of the area or the muddiness or sandiness of the soil.

As a village grew into a town, a market might be held in its principal street. Cheapside in the City has already been mentioned; not unlike this, the earlier name of High Street, Uxbridge, was *The Markett Place*. Apart from a few recorded instances of occupational street-names (such as that in West Ham, already mentioned) the majority of what later became High Streets had names referring to the towns or villages themselves. High Street, Harrow, was *Harwestrete* ('the street of Harrow') in the fifteenth century; similarly, High Street, Homerton, was *Humberton Street* in 1652. High Holborn must be included here, although it has been suggested that its present name is due to its elevation; however, it was *Holeburne Strate* as long ago as the last quarter of the twelfth century. Borough High Street, first recorded as such in 1799, was earlier *The Borough* or *Long Southwark*.

High Street, Shadwell, was *Upper Shadwell* in 1682, leaving some doubt whether the name refers to importance or topography. There is also an Upper Street in Islington (by contrast with the former *Lower Street*, which is now Essex Road). But there was also (and is still) a High Street in Islington; this was earlier called *The Broad Way* and in the sixteenth century was merely *The Strete*. Broadway is, of course, used in a number of places in Greater London, e.g., Hammersmith and Tooting, as well as a number called merely Broadway or The Broadway. Even Westminster cannot be left out of this list; Broadway S.W.1 may no longer have its former glory, but it does provide an address for the headquarters of London Transport.

When the principal street is part of a main road, that fact may be enshrined in the name. Kilburn High Road, for instance, is a length of Watling Street. It was, however, *Kylborne Streate* in 1535—which may have meant 'Kilburn on the Roman road'. King Street, Hammersmith (first recorded in 1813) was formerly *The Highway*, being in fact part of the Great West Road. King's Road S.W.3 was referred to in 1620 as *The King's High Way from Chelsea to Fulham*; but Charles II took it over and prevented its public use, so that it was still called *The King's Private Road* in 1717.

Although most High Streets have not borne this name for very long, there are a few early examples. Probably the oldest is High Street, Barnet, with was *Le Heyestrate* in 1348, but another medieval example has been known under a different name for more than three centuries. In Edmonton, *Heghestrate* is mentioned in a document of 1342; but by 1650 this road had become *Fore Street*. It is now Lower Fore Street N.9 and Upper Fore Street N.18, the distinction echoing that of the postal districts of Lower and Upper Edmonton respectively. The name is a relatively rare one in the Home Counties, though there is a Fore Street E.C.2, this City example resembling many elsewhere in being 'street in front of a city wall'.

A similar transformation might be thought to have taken place in Barking; a street referred to in 1609 as *Highstreete* is now Heath Street, but the present name is supported by *Hethestrete* 1477. The seventeenth-century form started on a wrong, but quite plausible, tack, since the derivation of the name is from *The Hythe* or landing-place. Possibly because of *-street* suffixed to it, the vowel of the first element undergoes many variations: *Huthstreete* and *Hithstreete* are found alongside *Heathstreate* and *Hethstrete*.

Village streets were being extended, and were even acquiring names, while the settlements were still surrounded by many acres of cultivated land. It is not surprising, therefore, that some street-names should refer to the fields by which (and eventually across which) the developing highways passed.

Field-names and descriptive names

It is interesting to find, even towards the centre of London which appears to the casual observer to have been urban since the dawn of history, that some street-names have all the marks of having been transferred from fields. Yet this is less surprising when it is observed that direct references survive in names such as St Martin-in-the-Fields and St Giles-in-the-Fields.

In the City itself, Smithfield Street offers a well-known instance. The 'smooth field' was used as a meat market; in Holborn, not far away, Jockey's Fields, Hatton Garden, and Saffron Hill convey something of a rural atmosphere. In the outer suburbs, examples are more numerous but also more obvious, since frequently the field-names were deliberately revived, rather than being transferred more or less instinctively, as occurred in the development of medieval or Tudor streets. One such 'instinctive' transfer in fairly recent times, however, has given us Courtfield Gardens S.W.5. The *Courtfield* of Earls Court was cultivated until about a century ago, and this street built there was given the name.

Ryefield Avenue in Hillingdon carries the intelligible name of *Rye Feilds*, recorded in 1682; not quite so clear is Royal Lane, traceable to *Rihille* alluded to in a document of 1484. Similarly, Barnfield Road in Edgware may be compared with *Barnfeld* 1277 and Broadfields Avenue with *Bradfeld* 1281. Bell Lane N.W.4 continues the interesting name *Bell Field*, referred to in a document of 1685. Usually this field-name was given to land the rent for which was used in the maintenance of the church bells. Highfield Avenue N.W.9 has had transferred to it the not uncommon name *High Feld* 1574. Minchenden Crescent N.14 continues the name of *Menechenfeld* c.1275, alluding to land in the parish held by the nuns of Clerkenwell.

Churchfield Road W.3 ran across the Church Field in Acton, having been laid out in its present form as a result of a reapportionment of land in 1860, when the commissioners also ordered the provision of a straight road through the South Field, the thoroughfare being now Southfield Road W.4. In a group of names in North Acton, however, the suffix *-field(s)* alludes not to arable land but to the North Acton Playing Fields, which they surround; Westfields Road, Nothfields Road, and Eastfields Road are on the perimeter, Highfield Road above the other group, and Lowfield Road a little to the south. The road constituting the southern edge of the playing fields was formerly an approach road to Acton aerodrome (which flourished before the first World War). This thoroughfare, Noel Road, commemorates the lieutenant-colonel who was commandant.

Oakfield Road N.14 and Houndsfield Road N.9 preserve field-names going back to the seventeenth century; Highfield Road N.21 has an even longer history. In an Edmonton deed of about 1250, the name *Heghefeld* occurs; this was recorded as *Le Highe Feeld* in 1608. Normand Road W.14 is based on the field-name *Noemansland* 1492, which passed to the residence built on it as *Nomans Land House* 1710 and thence to the road-name. *No Mans Land*, found in field-names in many parts of England, refers to land in disputed ownership, and has developed to *Normans*, etc., in Hertfordshire, Oxfordshire, and other counties.

In Hackney, Mayfield Road E.8 perpetuates *Mayfield* 1557; Shortlands W.6 adopted the field-name without the addition of *Street* or *Road*, but turned a singular into a plural, as the name was *Shortelond* in the early fifteenth century. Ridgway S.W.19 was not arable land, but a path across the fields, at the northern edge of the ploughed ridges. Similar names occur in other parts of London. There are about two dozen instances of Green Lane and five or six of Occupation Road (or Lane); these also look back to open-field agriculture. A green lane or occupation road was a pathway by which villagers could gain access to their own strips in the open fields.

Westmead Road in Sutton utilises a field-name recorded as *Le Westmede* in 1446. Broomfield Road W.13 and Woodfield Road W.5 bear names found in the Ealing Tithe Apportionment. Woodfield Avenue N.W.9 has an even longer history, as it takes its name from a house called Woodfield, built on land known as *Wodefeld* in 1325. Norland Road and Square W.11 preserve the name given to open land on the northern edge of Kensington, *Northlondes* 1423, recorded in a document of 1607 as *Norlands*.

Lammas Avenue in Mitcham, Lammas Grove in S.E.26, and Lammas Road N.9 and E.10, bear a name which refers primarily to a summer festival. The term was frequently applied to land which was made available as pasture after Lammas, the 'Loaf-mass' day on 1st August, a crop having been gathered earlier. In Brentford, The Half Acre goes north from the High Street and continues as Boston Manor Road. Another field-name preserved here is The Ham, across a piece of meadow previously so called. Lots Road S.W.3 crosses land (*Lez Lotte* 1544) parcelled out at an annual drawing of lots; this custom obtained in many places, and survives in a few to this day.

Blacklands Terrace S.W.3 also has for its name that of a former field, and Crabtree Lane S.W.6 is on land that was known in 1449 as *Crabbetrehalfacre*, 'half acre by a crab-apple tree'. Tenter Street E.C.2 and Tenter Street East E.1 allude to land on which cloth was stretched during manufacture; Tenter Ground E.1 is the form in

113

which it frequently occurs as a field-name, though the land here was in fact *The Tenter Yardes* 1589, *Tenter Feild* 1682. Rural industry here is also referred to in Ropemaker Street E.2 and Ropemakers Fields E.14 (*Ropemakers Feild* 1640). Another street connected with this craft, *The Rope Walk* 1746, has now been renamed Northey Street E.14. Not all street-names terminating in *-field* have this origin, of course, but Pitfield Street N.1 can be traced to *Pyttefeld* 1556, though the purpose of the excavation is unknown.

In Colindale, field-names have been used in a concentrated way in roads built on the site of Hendon aerodrome. Branching from Lan Acre are South Acre, White Acre, Further Acre, Hundred Acre, Five Acre, and Near Acre. In the vicinity are Great Field, Longfield, Clayton Field, Field Mead, Corner Mead, Wiggins Mead, Satchell Mead, and Withers Mead. The regularity of the arrangement of the streets (and their names) may seem sufficiently unusual to provoke some scepticism about the authenticity of this group of names. There is no such doubt about Long Acre W.C.2; a reference to *a pasture called Longeacre* occurs in a Patent Roll of 1547. Also in Westminster, Millbank S.W.1 continues the name of *land called the Mill Bank*, referred to in a document dated 1546, alluding to the mills belonging to Westminster Abbey.

To the north-west of Dagenham village, there were some common fields, farmed in strips, earlier known as *Great Busfield* and *Dagenham Butts*, but because at one time the vicar had rented some of the land and then sublet it, it became known as *Glebe*, although it was not technically glebe land. Two road names in Dagenham recall this land—Butfield Close and Glebe Road. The Butts in Brentford, so named in 1664, was land on which archery was practised; Newington Butts S.E.11 had a similar origin, as had also the less obvious Artillery Row S.W.1.

There is something logical about the basing of names of streets on those of fields, since when building takes place it almost always succeeds agriculture in the use of the land. But it will not always be possible or convenient to transfer names from the one to the other; there may be far more streets than fields, or the fields may not have names which are convenient to utilise for the new purpose, or the field-names may not be known. A decision will then have to be made—just as, of course it was necessary to decide to use field-names, if that is what happened. It is the arbitrary way in which names are bestowed upon streets which adds to their difference from other place-names. Intrinsic qualities do not necessitate the use of appropriate names. Because a road is unusually long, it does not have to be called Long Lane—though there are a number of appropriate instances of this; conversely, if the road is called Long Lane we do not really object if it is particularly short. It might be realised that the name had another explanation, such as that it commemorated a man called Long.

DESCRIPTIVE NAMES: TREES AND FLOWERING PLANTS

Street-names often refer to the presence of particular objects nearby. Trees planted along the edge of the roadway may provide the name. Acacia Road is regarded as a 'stock' suburban name. There are, in fact, about a dozen examples, with two each of Acacia Grove and Gardens, two Acacia Closes, and six Acacia Avenues. In some of them, e.g., Acacia Road W.3, there are, or have recently been, some trees of this species in the road. In others, the name may be one of a group, as in Brentford, where Acacia Avenue is accompanied by Almond Grove, Cherry Crescent, Maple Grove, Beech Avenue, Hornbeam Crescent, and Hazel Close.

In groups like this it is interesting to note the variety of second, or generic, names. A *Crescent* is normally expected to comply with a requirement of shape, although not every instance (apart from those just cited) can be said to do so. *Groves* are, strictly, plantations of trees, or small woods, and although the word does not make particularly good sense as a street-name, as a small concession to logical propriety, arrangements are usually made to accompany the term by the name of a variety or species of tree. A *Close* is often a cul-de-sac; occasionally, however, it may be used, like *Croft* or *Mead*, because field-names have been used—or to give that impression. An *Avenue* was originally a tree-lined approach to a house or other building. By ringing the changes on these supposedly attractive designations, building developers can avoid the use of *Street*, *Road*, or *Lane*, which—to the minds of some—lack the rural charm they require for their environment. Additional possibilities will be found in other groups of names. In the neighbourhood of Hillingdon Hospital are clusters of tree and plant names. On the north side of Falling Lane are to be found Apple Tree Avenue, Pear Tree Avenue, Birch Avenue, Peach Terrace, Cherry Tree Avenue, Heather Lane, Heather Close, Gorse Walk, Bramble Close, Violet Avenue, Rosemary Close, Lavender Road, Bryony Close, Campion Close, The Coppice, and The Thicket. Here, *Road* and *Lane* have crept in, but these terms are excluded from the group to the south of Falling Lane: Ash Grove, Elm Grove, Cedar Avenue, Lime Avenue, Willow Avenue, Chestnut Avenue, Whitethorn Avenue, Yew Avenue, Sycamore Close, Laburnum Avenue, Lilac Place.

If there is felt to be any incongruity in Violet Avenue, it at least avoids the hiatus of Viola Avenue S.E.2, which is accompanied by Fuchsia Street and Dahlia Road. Violet Avenue also occurs in Chase Side, Enfield, in the neighbourhood of Woodbine Grove, Myrtle Grove, Hawthorn Grove, Lavender Road, Acacia Road, Rosemary Avenue, and Primrose Avenue. Groups of tree names are to be expected near woodlands or former forest areas, but they are not confined to them. Agave Road N.W.2 is one of the shrub names to be found in Dollis Hill, in the company of Briar Road, Ivy Road, and Olive Road, with a group of conifers—Pine Road, Larch Road, and Cedar Road—and, on the other side of Cricklewood Broadway, Oak Grove, Elm Grove, Yew Grove, and Ash Grove. The only instance of Robinia occurs at Hainault, where a Close of that name adjoins Chestnut Grove, Beech Grove, Cypress Grove, and Lime Grove; Woodman Path, Covert Road, and Inglewood maintain the general spirit of forestry to be found in the group, but less familiar occupation terms appear in Verderers Road and Agister Road.

A *verderer* was a forest official mainly concerned with the timber, but in some forests he had the power of trying minor offences; an *agister* was appointed by the king to settle claims regarding cattle pasture and pigs searching for acorns. The official bow-bearer is not mentioned among these names, but related occupations, etc., are: Arrowsmith Road, Fletcher Road, Crossbow Road. Their prey is not forgotten, some small roads being named Hind Close, Boar Close, Fallow Close, and Hart Crescent. Harbourer Close and Harbourer Road face Regarder Road across New North Road, between which and Forest Road are to be found some more names connected with hunting: Huntsman Road, Falconer Road, Fowler Road, Peregrine Road, and Roebuck Road. A *regarder* was a commission of twelve knights whose duty was to view the state of the forest every three years and to have general oversight of the limits of the forest in order to prevent illegal enclosures or occupation of the waste. The task of the *harbourer* was to trace the deer to its covert or harbour.

Isolated streets named after trees and shrubs occur all over London—though, apart from *elm* and *oak* names, they are scarce in the central area. There is an Elm Street near Mount Pleasant W.C.1, an Elm Court in the Temple, and an Elm Row in Hampstead; it is interesting that these produce two generic names not so far mentioned. *Court* means, primarily, 'an enclosed area, a yard', and from this 'a quadrangle of a college, &c'; in its urban context it was actually defined by Johnson as 'a small opening inclosed with houses and paved with broad stones, distinguished from a street', and in this sense the term went down in the world, as many such places became slums. *Court* also meant 'manor house, great house' (as in Tottenham Court) and so resembled *Place*—another term which has become debased from its use for small rows of poor dwellings. A *Terrace*, *Parade*, or *Row* meant 'a line of houses', which would often receive a separate name in a long road.

Oak Tree Road N.W.8 owes its name immediately to an Oak Tree Field which was formerly worked near the site of the road; it is balanced by Elm Tree Road, and St John's Wood also has Acacia Gardens, Place, and Road, commemorating a tree which formerly stood in the neighbourhood.

The azalea is not much in evidence in street-names; apart from Azalea Close W.7, the only other instance is Azalea Walk in Eastcote. Tamarisk Square W.12 is the only name mentioning that shrub, in a group including Clematis Street, Orchid Street, Lilac Street, Viola Square, Yew Tree Road, Bryony Road, Sundew Avenue, Bramble Gardens, Wallflower Street, Peony Gardens, and Milfoil Street. Sundew, peony, and milfoil are not honoured in this way anywhere else in Greater London.

A unique name of quite a different type occurs in West Wickham, where Corkscrew Hill indicates a sinuous road, rising quite steeply. Nearby are some general names connected with trees, such as Woodland Way, Copse Avenue, The Grove, Wood Lodge Lane, and The Glade. More specific are The Alders, Acacia Gardens, and Rose Walk. Across the Croydon border, Oak Gardens and Ash Road join Oak Avenue, which leads to Myrtle Road, Bracken Avenue, Jasmine Gardens, Erica Gardens, Gorse Road, Larch Tree Way, and Bramble Close, with Briar Lane nearby.

NAMES REFERRING TO BUILDINGS

Possibly because trees are exceptional in towns, they would have been more obvious markers of particular roads than buildings would be, before the introduction of clear labelling of roads. But if the buildings were sufficiently large, or unusual in some other way, they could provide names for the roads in which they were situated. Factories come to mind in the modern context, but while London was still partly agricultural, there were windmills; remains of some are still to be seen in the roads bearing their name, e.g., Windmill Road S.W.18, alluding to the pumping mill, the tower of which survives beside the railway cutting near Spencer Park. Windmill Road S.W.19 leads to the mill on Wimbledon Common, but no trace now remains of those giving names to Windmill Hill N.W.3 or Windmill Street W.1, the latter probably that of the manor of Tottenham Court. Great Windmill Street W.1 alludes to a different mill, perhaps by its very size accounting for the *Great* in the street-name.

117

The only explicit reference to a water-mill occurs in Water Mill Way, near the river Crane at Hanworth. Millstream Road S.E.1 is on the course of the River Neckinger (now covered over), and Millbank, north of the river and a little further upstream, marks the site of the mill at the mouth of the Tyburn, owned by Westminster Abbey.

Specific industries (other than corn milling) are referred to in Iron Mill Lane (Crayford) and Ironmill Road S.W.18. References to coppermills occur in Tooting and Walthamstow, with a Coppermill Lane in each of these places. There is a Factory Lane near Bruce Grove Station N.17 and another in Croydon; near the latter, beyond the gas works are some related names—Commerce Way and Progress Way; curiously, both Progress Way and Commerce *Road* occur at Wood Green, but not as a pair. There is yet another Progress Way near the Martinbridge Trading Estate in Ponders End.

The names of particular firms, or their brand-names, are to be found in the vicinity of their factories. Examples include Nestles Avenue in Harlington, Ruberoid Road at Enfield Highway, Rubastic Road in Southall, and Trojan Road in Croydon. Dragor Road N.W.10 combines the names in the firm of Drake and Gorham Ltd, electrical suppliers, who formerly occupied premises here. Uneeda Drive is not far from Rockware Avenue in Greenford. Standard Road, Sunbeam Road, and Minerva Road N.W.10 all refer to car manufacture; Du Cros Road W.3 is named after a firm of automobile engineers whose premises were formerly nearby. Cowley Road W.3 alludes to Morris cars (made at Cowley, Oxon) distributed by Stewart & Ardern Ltd, established here in the nineteen-twenties. Alliance Road W.3 recalls the Alliance Aeroplane Co, whose works were here.

Aeronautical and railway names

AERONAUTICAL NAMES

Akin to brand-names and the names of manufacturers, those of aircraft types also occur among London street-names; they are often grouped with the names of flying pioneers or other famous aeronauts. A group of such roads occurs in Heston, encircled by Brabazon Road. Cobham Road, Bleriot Road, and Johnson Road are grouped with De Havilland Road, Whittle Road, Sopwith Road, and Wright Road, with Alcock Road leading out of the complex into Armytage Road. De Havilland Road at Burnt Oak adjoins Mollison Way, some distance from Aerodrome Road which adjoined the former Hendon Aerodrome. The third De Havilland Road is in a rather large group of aeronautical names.

The group is in South Beddington, near Croydon. It contains Mollison Drive as its principal street, honouring other aviators in Alcock Close, Brown Close, Barnard Close, Lindbergh Road, Lawford Close, Carter Close, and Cody Close. The informality of Amy Way reflects the mode of public reference to Amy Johnson at the height of her popularity. Though Hinkler was 'Bert' in the press, it is surname treatment only in Hinkler Close, which adjoins Kingsford Avenue and Cane Close. A unique reference occurs in Cayley Close; this alludes to a pioneer indeed, for Sir George Cayley's researches and experiments in the first decades of the nineteenth century made possible the work which led to the construction of the first aeroplanes. It is fitting that Cayley should be remembered on the site of the former Croydon Airport.

Other names are those of aircraft types as well as fliers, such as Gull Close, Heracles Close, Meteor Way, Vulcan Close, Firefly Close, Goliath Close, Avro Way, Brabazon Avenue, Daimler Way, Roe Way, Hermes Way, Hadrian Close, Brancker Close, Shaw Way, and Powell Close. Adjoining Purley Way are Imperial Way, commemorating Imperial Airways, forerunners of British Airways, with Lysander Road and Pegasus Road.

Northolt Aerodrome has also generated some appropriate street-names, remembering particularly the aircraft of the second World War. In one cluster Kittiwake Road is grouped with Convair Walk, Delta Grove, Seasprite Close, Valiant Close, and Mayfly Gardens. Canberra Drive and Merlin Close are nearby. In a second cluster, adjoining Wayfarer Road, are Arrowscout Walk, Chipmunk Grove, Dakota Gardens, Trident Gardens, and about ten others including Montgolfier Walk, the only road-name honouring the balloon pioneer.

RAILWAY NAMES

Long before aircraft shattered the peace of the countryside, the railway made it possible for townsfolk to travel quickly to rural surroundings and for some urban workers even to live beyond the confines of the town. In many respects, of course, the railways were responsible for the growth of Greater London, and it is logical that many road-names should acknowledge the presence of railway stations. A street leading directly into a station is usually Station Approach, but the two dozen or so instances of this are outnumbered by Station Road. St Mary Cray has not only a Station Approach but also a Station Square, compensating by its nearly circular shape for the several square Circuses elsewhere in London. Station Square at

Petts Wood is a trapezium. These seem to be the only attempts ever made to construct a Station Square; it is evidently an architectural paradox. Greenford has a Station View, its immediate neighbour being Belle Vue (also the only instance of this name).

The names of the old railway companies occur in a few street-names. Midland Road N.W.1 adjoins St Pancras Station, terminus of the former Midland Railway; Midland Road E.10 exemplifies a frequent occurrence, in which the road is named after the railway (because of the presence of a station) and the station then takes as its title the name of the road, in this case Leyton, Midland Road.

Great Central Street N.W.1 is the approach road from Marylebone Road to Marylebone Station, terminus of the former (and much mourned) Great Central line. Great Central Avenue runs parallel with the railway from Station Approach at South Ruislip. Termini named after streets obviate the need for such names as Station Road. Broad Street and Liverpool Street Stations are immediate neighbours; the former is part of the medieval street of that name (*Bradestrate* c.1212, *Brodestrete* 1513), meaning 'wide street'; the latter, built early in the nineteenth century, was named after Lord Liverpool, the Prime Minister. Cannon Street, the Southern Region terminus in the City, also bears an ancient name. From such early forms as *Candelwrich-strete* c.1185, *Kandelwrihtestrate* c.1200, the meaning 'street of the candle-makers' can be inferred. It became *Canwyke Strete* about 1430 and was *Canyngesstrete* in 1480, further developing to *Cannon-street* by 1664.

Railway Approach S.E.1 forms, with London Bridge Street, the access way to London Bridge Station; the name occurs also at Twickenham Station and at Wallington. At Harrow-on-the-Hill Station, the traveller reaches the trains from Station Road by way of Railway Approach. Many of the names embodying *Railway* are of roads adjoining the railway, rather than approaches to the station. An exception is Railway Place, by which Fenchurch Street Station is approached.

It is not surprising that buses are not referred to in street names, as by the time they were introduced, roads in which garages or bus termini were located had already been named. There are, however, three names relating to trams—two instances of Tramway Avenue (E.15 and N.9) and Tramway Path, Mitcham.

Places of worship and saints' names

PLACES OF WORSHIP AND RELIGIOUS HOUSES

In many streets, the church is likely to be not only the largest, but also the oldest building, and so it is to be expected that many street-names refer to places of worship. Apart from Musjid Road S.W.11, there do not appear to be any names alluding to non-Christian temples.

Although London is well provided with cathedrals, of the Church of England and of the Roman Catholic and Orthodox Churches, there is only one Cathedral Street, beside St Saviour's Cathedral, Southwark. Of the 30 or so names referring to abbeys, only one—Abbey Orchard Street S.W.1—alludes to Westminster Abbey, being approximately on the site of the monks' orchard. The produce would have been supplemented by their outlying property, now known as Covent Garden.

Of course, an abbey is a monastic house, and not merely the church, and it is as the total institution that it would normally be remembered in street names. Barking, Bermondsey, and Stratford Langthorne Abbeys have given rise to appropriate names in their respective areas. Lesser institutions were sometimes loosely given the title, and Abbey Road N.W.8 is so called because it led to Kilburn Priory.

Less direct references are to be found in some street-names. Off Bermondsey Street, near its junction with Abbey Street, is Cluny Place S.E.1, alluding to the fact that Bermondsey Abbey belonged to the Cluniac congregation, the English superior of which, the Abbot of Lewes, would lodge outside the monastery in Abbots Lane S.E.1. Cluny Mews S.W.5 was in or near the property of the Cluniac abbey of Abingdon.

Other names connected with Bermondsey Abbey are Crucifix Lane and Holy Rood Street S.E.1. The former is near the place where, after the dissolution of the abbey, was set up the crucifix which for several centuries had been revered and was supposed to have been dropped from heaven. Holy Rood Street refers to this cross and adjoins Magdalen Street, where there was a subsidiary chapel of the abbey, dedicated to St Mary Magdalen.

The four main orders of friars were established in London, together with the Friars of the Cross, whose principal house in England was near Tower Hill, and is commemorated by Crutched Friars E.C.3. Austin Friars E.C.2 is alongside the site of the London house of the Augustinian Hermits. The Carmelites, known as White Friars from the colour of the cloak worn over the brown habit, are recalled in the names of Carmelite Street and its continuation Whitefriars Street E.C.4. Another name for this order was Pied Friars, from the original striped habit, and this may be alluded to in Magpie Alley, between Whitefriars Street and Bouverie Street.

The very large priory of the Dominicans extended from the Thames to Ludgate Hill, Blackfriars Southern Region station occupying about half of the site. Blackfriars Lane and Passage E.C.4 cross the former priory area. Greyfriars Passage E.C.1, by the General Post Office, commemorates the Franciscans, who occupied this site for about 300 years until the Dissolution.

The London house of the Carthusian order is recalled in Charter-house Mews, Street, and Square E.C.1, and Carthusian Street E.C.1, all more or less on the perimeter of the site of the monastery.

Mincing Lane E.C.3 refers, like Minchenden Crescent N.14, to a community of nuns. Stow says that the sisters were those of St Helen's Bishopsgate, but the earliest reference to the street under this name is considerably before the foundation date (1212) of St Helen's. It is *Mengenelane* in a twelfth-century document and *Menechinelane* in 1273.

For obvious reasons, the number of street-names alluding to churches was considerable, and attempts have been made at various times to change some of them to avoid confusion. Occasionally, only a slight modification was made. *Church Passage* E.C.3 was changed to Church Cloisters, but more drastic changes were made to some of the other ten Church Passages. One of two in Camberwell was changed to Churchyard Passage, but the other became Camberwell Passage; one of two in Woolwich was changed to Church Hill, the other to St Margaret's Path. At the same time, about half a dozen Church Lanes, about the same number of Church Roads, rather more Church Streets, and a sprinkling of Church Terraces and Church Walks were all renamed. Church Street, Kensington, became Kensington Church Street, but a street of the same name in Kennington became Ashmole Street. Another change produced Old Church Street S.W.3, a logical name, since the church of St Luke (formerly the parish church) has come to be referred to as Chelsea Old Church.

Names alluding to chapels are not quite so numerous, and most of them are not of very long standing. Chapel Street S.W.1 (*Chapeil Streete* 1656) takes its name from the chapel of St Margaret's church burial ground. *Little Chapel Street* in Westminster has been changed in recent times to Caxton Street S.W.1. *Little Chapel Street* in Soho has been renamed Sheraton Street W.1, after the great furniture maker who lived nearby; in Sheraton's time there was a chapel in the street, that of the Huguenots. These French Protestants, whose name is derived from the German *Eidgenoss*, 'confederate', found refuge in England after the revocation of the Edict of Nantes in 1685. Many of them settled in south London; Huguenot Place S.W.18 is beside their cemetery in Wandsworth. A number of Huguenot families attained considerable success, and a few have left their mark on street-names. Minet Road S.W.9 is named after one of these families. The Pleydell-

Bouveries became Earls of Radnor; Bouverie Street E.C.4 and Bouverie Place W.2, Pleydell Court and Street E.C.4, and the Pleydell Estate in Radnor Street E.C.1 are some of the references to this family in central London.

Chantry Road and Place in Harrow, Chantry Close in Kingsbury, Chantry Road in Chessington, and Chantry Street N.1 allude to the endowed chapels established in the Middle Ages, the incumbent of which had the sole duty to pray for the benefactor; the name may sometimes be given arbitrarily, as a quaint, historical-sounding name, but some at least will have some reference to actual chantries. *Hermitage* names may occasionally have been given to streets for purely decorative reasons, but, again, some of those in Greater London allude to the abodes of recluses. Hermitage Road N.15 is traceable to *Le Hermitage* 1465, and there are streets called The Hermitage in Barnes, Richmond, and Uxbridge. Green Lane S.W.16 was *Hermitage Lane* in 1523, and was named from an identifiable site.

Tabernacle Street E.C.2 (*Tabernacle Place* 1799) was so called from the place of worship established in the former *Windmill Hill* by George Whitefield. He built another in Tottenham Court Road, behind which is Whitfield Street W.1. Wesleyan Place N.W.5 and Baptist Gardens N.W.5 allude to chapels of those denominations; Zoar Street S.E.1 refers to Zoar Chapel, built by the Southwark Baptists in the late seventeenth century. Moravian Place S.W.3 takes its name from the burial ground of the Moravian Brethren, some of whom settled here as refugees from central Europe in the eighteenth century.

The former segregation of Jews is evidenced by such names as Old Jewry in the City and by Jews Walk S.E.26. Jews Row S.W.18 is said to be named from the inhabitants of a house in the area.

SAINTS' NAMES

Most streets bearing the names of saints are so called because of the dedication of a church in or near the street, but a few have different origins. Some allude to surnames or titles, e.g., St John's Hill S.W.11, which bears the family name of the Viscounts Bolingbroke, lords of the manor of Battersea. Their title provided the street names Bolingbroke Grove and Bolingbroke Walk S.W.11, and curiously a surname connected with the family displaced that of a saint in the renaming of *St Ann's Road* (off St John's Hill), which is now Marcilly Road S.W.18. This refers to Marie Claire des Champs de Marcilly, Marquise de Villette, the niece of Madame de Maintenant; Marie Claire became the mistress, and then the second wife, of Henry St John, second Viscount Bolingbroke.

St Albans Street S.W.1 and St Loo Avenue S.W.3 both owe their names to titles of nobility. The former alludes to Henry Jermyn, Earl St Albans, who began to develop the area near St James' Palace in the seventeenth century and whose surname is embodied in Jermyn Street S.W.1. St Albans Grove W.8 is named after the Duchess, wife of the ninth Duke of St Albans, who owned property here. St Loo Avenue recalls an earlier noble lady, 'Bess of Hardwick', whose third husband was Sir William St Loe, captain of Queen Elizabeth's guard. She in fact inherited property in Chelsea from her fourth husband, the Earl of Shrewsbury, and this name (given to the street in 1888) does not seem very apt.

Some names of this form are transferred place-names. St Ervan's Road W.10 was one of several streets named after places in Cornwall by their developer, a Cornish clergyman, the Rev. Samuel Walker. He established All Saints' Church in Talbot Road—hence All Saints Road W.11; Cornwall Crescent W.11 also owes its name to this development. St Austell Close in Little Stanmore seems to be arbitrarily named from the place. It is one of a group of West Country names, others being Bideford Avenue and Dawlish Avenue.

St Leonards Road N.W.10 is named from a Buckinghamshire village, near which the owners of the Harlesden land also had property; St Leonard's Square N.W.5 is named from the village near Maidstone, probably for the same reason. A street-name in Chelsea points to yet a third place of this name: St Leonard's Terrace S.W.3 alludes to Upton St Leonard's (Glos), the native village of the builder. St Leonards Road W.13, however, almost certainly refers to St Leonard's on Sea, as it adjoins Hastings Road.

St Helena Street W.C.1 has borrowed its name from a much more distant place. This alludes to the island in the Atlantic where Napoleon was confined until the end of his life, and the street was being built when he died.

Some saints are very well represented in street-names. St Mary's Avenue occurs half a dozen times; St Mary's Road is found in almost every London Borough; and there are a few each of St Mary's Gardens, Square, Walk, Close, and Crescent.

St Peter is named in a fair number of streets, despite some reductions in the past 40 years. The former St Peter's Road in Stepney, for instance, is now Cephas Avenue, using (like the adjacent Cephas Street) the Aramaic form of the saint's name. Great Peter Street S.W.1 was *Peter Street* in the late seventeenth century. Before that it was *St Peter Street*, unambiguously stating the connexion with Westminster Abbey, which is dedicated to St Peter. Peter's Hill E.C.4 commemorates a parish church destroyed in the Great Fire of 1666.

Numerous streets bear the name of St James, some variety being introduced by the use of the apostrophe. There are St James' Avenues in five places, but in Beckenham it is St James's Avenue. Against four instances of St James Road (without an apostrophe) in Lower Edmonton, Purley, Hampton, and Carshalton, may be set two of St James' Road, in Stratford and Mitcham, and one of St James's Road—in Bermondsey. These differences are not significant in matters of interpretation, but are symptomatic of the lack of attention to detail in the spelling of names. A saintly group of names (seemingly arbitrarily applied) in Cowley Peachey includes St David Close, St Paul Close, St Luke Close, and St Lawrence Close. St Nicholas Close is uniform with these, yet St Peter's Road nearby is in the possessive form, and it might be thought that this, therefore, relates to the dedication of a church in the road, but in fact the thoroughfare actually leads to St Lawrence's church.

St Paul names often allude to the extensive ownership of land by the Cathedral, or to Prebends of the Cathedral. This is underlined in the group of names near St Paul Street N.1, which is linked by Canon Street and Rector Street with Prebend Street. St Paul's Road, not far away in Highbury, is named from the church at the corner of Essex Road and was formerly *Hopping Lane*. The old name referred to the cultivation of hops in the area.

One of the St Paul's manors was in Chiswick, where Powell's Walk W.4 is a fairly recent development of *Paul's Walk*. Camden Town abounds with street-names referring to the families who developed it, but it too was a St Paul's prebend and there was a local church dedicated to the apostle, commemorated in St Paul's Crescent N.W.1.

St George Street W.1 is named from its church (usually called St George's, Hanover Square), the dedication being a polite gesture to King George I rather than a spontaneous salute to the patron of England. The parish (established in the early eighteenth century) extended as far as Pimlico, and the dedication accounts for the names of St George's Drive and St George's Square S.W.1. St Philip is represented in a few names: St Philip Square and Street S.W.8, St Philip's Avenue (Worcester Park), and St Philip's Road E.8.

Relatively unfamiliar saints include St Paul's companion, commemorated in St Silas Place N.W.5, from the dedication of a church which stood nearby. St Barnabas, another companion, is somewhat more popular, with six or seven names in the Greater London area; there are St Barnabas Roads in Mitcham, Sutton, Walthamstow, and Woodford Green, and a St Barnabas Street in Pimlico—from the dedication of the church there.

The saint named in St Simon's Avenue S.W.15 is not the apostle associated with Jude, but Simon Stock, the thirteenth-century Englishman who became prior general of the Carmelite order. The Putney street is named from the adjacent Roman Catholic church. St Alphonsus Road S.W.4 alludes to the founder of the Redemptorists, who have a monastery here. A similar reference occurs in St Clare Street E.C.3, off Minories; the latter was the street by the convent of the Minoresses, founded by St Clare, early follower of St Francis of Assisi. St Charles Square W.10 was named after St Charles Borromeo (1538–84); there was formerly a college here dedicated to this saint.

St Thomas Becket is honoured in St Thomas Street S.E.1 and Becket Street S.E.1. By renaming Nightingale Lane E.1, the authorities were able to commemorate another St Thomas—Henry VIII's Chancellor, More—who is named in Thomas More Street. His fellow martyr, the Bishop of Rochester, was also accommodated by a renaming, when *Glass House Street* gave way to John Fisher Street E.1, in 1937.

Other canonised Englishmen include Erconwald (fourth Bishop of London), remembered in St Erkenwald Road, Barking, and Erconwald Street W.12. His sister was first Abbess of Barking Abbey, but has no direct memorial there in street-names, having to make do with inclusion in a group in Harold Wood, where Ethelburga Road is placed alongside Athelstan Road and Archibald Road. Ethelburga Street, off Battersea Bridge Road, is a tribute from south of the river.

In the eleventh century, foreign terrorists kidnapped the Archbishop of Canterbury, who bravely declined to be ransomed by his people and was murdered by his Danish captors. This was Ælfēah, commemorated in St Alfege Passage S.E.10, near the church marking the site of his martyrdom, and St Alfege Road S.E.7, in Charlton, the parish to the east. There is a St Alfege Road also in Edmonton, to which may be added St Alphege Court in Colindale. St Alphage Walk, at Burnt Oak, shows another spelling variation, found also in St Alphage Garden E.C.2, by the ruins of a City church dedicated to him.

St Dunstan, Archbishop of Canterbury half a century before Ælfēah, is commemorated in St Dunstan's Alley E.C.3 because of the church nearby, but in Acton, St Dunstan's Avenue W.3 reminds us that this saint was a skilled worker in metals and the patron of the Goldsmiths' Company, in whose estate this road lies.

Some saints' names are quite rare in this context. St Swithin has a Lane in the City and (as Swithun) a Road in Lewisham. St Ursula has a Grove in Pinner and a Road in Southall. St Wilfrid makes a single appearance, with a Road in Barnet; the same is true of St Joan Road N.9, St Keverne Road S.E.9, St Louis Road S.E.27, St Malo Avenue N.9, and St Maur Road S.W.6.

Dubious and even non-existent saints also appear in street-names. St Kilda Road W.13 and Orpington, and St Kilda's Road N.16 and Harrow testify to the indestructibility of a name that arose from a misreading of a mariners' chart. St Oswulf Street S.W.1 celebrates the canonisation of the (entirely unidentifiable) Saxon leader or land-owner whose stone provided the name of the Ossulstone Hundred, in which Westminster was situated. St Cross may also be included here. Not that St Cross is an impossible dedication (it corresponds to Holy Cross or Holy Rood) but *Saint* in this name was added for con-venience—to reduce the number of roads bearing the name Cross Street, the former designation which quite accurately described this road's location athwart Hatton Garden. There are now only nine examples of this name, but there were formerly more than twice that number.

Some street-names including *St John* allude to ownership by the military order, the Knights of St John of Jerusalem. The headquarters of the 'Language' (or Province) of England were in Clerkenwell—hence St John's Lane and Square E.C.1, and the main road, St John Street, on which the property abutted. The order is also responsible for the district name St John's wood and the street-names based on this.

The position of St Olave's Terrace S.E.1, off Tooley Street, reminds us that the latter name is in fact that of the saint referred to in the former. From early times the final *t* of *Saint* tended to be attached to a name beginning with a vowel; St Osyth was generally pronounced 'Toosy', and St Audrey, 'Tawdry'. In 1598 the name was recorded as *St Olaves Street*, but in 1606 it was *St Tooley's St*, and *Towles Street* two years later.

Place-names, estates of the nobility and gentry

PLACE-NAMES

Place-names may be used for designating streets for a number of reasons. Probably the primary one is the indication of the direction of a main road. Edgware Road, for instance, was named (at its London end) from the place towards which it led the traveller; the road was a part of the ancient Watling Street and was referred to indifferently as *Edgware High Waie* or *London Waie* in the sixteenth and seventeenth centuries. Similarly, Oxford Street will take one part of the way to Oxford, travelling westwards from London. It was earlier called *(The) Oxford Road*, but is referred to by its present name on a stone dated 1718, inscribed *Rathbones Place in Oxford Street*. Many names within the conurbation refer, of course, to places within Greater London or just beyond it, and present no problems of interpretation.

Another large group of names including transferred place-names are those derived from titles of nobility and, dating from quite an early time, the names of dioceses beyond London. As magnates of the kingdom, medieval bishops often maintained establishments in the capital. Ely Place E.C.1 is a good example; this was the palace of the Bishops of Ely, and the enclosed street on the site maintained a strange political independence even after the demolition of the premises. In this name, *Place* originally meant 'dwelling, property', and has now come to mean 'small street'.

Chichester Rents W.C.2 is on the site of the palace of the Bishops of Chichester. The generic term means 'buildings or tenements leased for rent' and occurs elsewhere in central London. The location in Chancery Lane reminds us that the Bishops of Chichester often held the post of Lord Chancellor. Rochester Row S.W.1 is part of the Tothill Fields property of the Dean and Chapter of Westminster Abbey. For some centuries the deans were also Bishops of Rochester.

The abbot of the Sussex monastery of Battle maintained a residence in Bermondsey. Battle Bridge Lane S.E.1 is by the site of a bridge or quay he built at the mouth of a stream here. The Bishops of Winchester had a house near the Priory of St Mary Overy established by St Swithun. Winchester Square S.E.1 is the site of the house, and Park Street S.E.1 a reminder that property owned by the Bishops was known as Winchester Park.

Nearly 30 street-names referring to Winchester are found in Greater London. Some of these allude to the Bishops of Winchester as land-owners. Winchester Walk S.E.1 adjoins Southwark Cathedral, formerly a priory, founded by the Bishop of Winchester. Winchester Road N.9, however, is named after the public school, being grouped with Harrow Drive, Rugby Avenue, Lancing Gardens, Malvern Terrace, Stowe Gardens, and Marlborough Road. A reference to the bishops, but, curiously, in the context of another public school, is found in Winchester Road N.W.3, on an estate belonging to Eton College. The first provost of the college was William of Waynflete, Bishop of Winchester, who is also remembered as the founder of Magdalen College, Oxford; Waynflete Street S.W.18 is near Magdalen Road. Winchester Street W.3 has other Hampshire names nearby—Petersfield Road and Meon Road, the latter reminding us (almost certainly not by design) of the celebrated lawsuit between Waynflete and his tenants in the manor of East Meon in 1461-2.

Winchester Road, Orpington, is also associated with other public-school names; in this complex occur Charterhouse Road, Haileybury

Road, Malvern Road, Stowe Road, Eton Road, and Repton Road. In Cranham, Winchester Avenue is grouped with names referring to other cathedral cities—Peterborough Avenue, Chester Avenue, St Albans Avenue, Canterbury Avenue, Worcester Avenue, and Lichfield Terrace.

The Bishops of Salisbury formerly had a palace in London, the site of which is now Salisbury Square E.C.4. Of the numerous collection of Salisbury Roads in greater London, few occur in groups which might reveal their derivation. Many doubtless allude to the third Marquess of Salisbury, the Prime Minister during the last two decades of Victoria's reign. Salisbury Street W.3 probably refers to him; the fact that the Constitutional Club was here, it has been suggested, may have had some influence in the choice of the name.

Apart from titles, geographical names transferred to streets are abundant and often occur in groups. Brighton Avenue E.17, for instance, adjoins Hove Avenue and connects with Gosport Road, Ringwood Road, Exmouth Road, and Edinburgh Road. But Brighton Road N.2 is unaccompanied by other names of the same class. A group of county-town names occurs near Fortis Green: Hertford Road, Bedford Road, Huntingdon Road, Leicester Road, and Lincoln Road are all connected by Durham Road N.2. A similar group can be found at Snaresbrook, where Rutland Road, Warwick Road, Hereford Road, and Gloucester Road lie between Leicester Road and Buckingham Road E.11. A little further north a group of names, vaguely suggesting wooded countryside perhaps, indicates the proximity of Epping Forest: Charnwood Drive, Sherwood Avenue, Cranbourne Avenue, and Ashbourne Avenue are grouped with Lancaster Avenue, Broxbourne Avenue, Monmouth Avenue, and Hurstwood Avenue. West of the Forest occurs a grand geographical miscellany in Leyton, north of Hainault Road: from Peterborough Road lead Carnarvon Road, Liverpool Road, and Sandringham Road, all of which join, but do not cross, Essex Road, the axis of the system. Parallel with this axis is Epsom Road, from which Matlock Road and Nottingham Road lead across Essex Road to Peterborough Road, and Cheltenham Road and Chesterfield Road go westwards towards Ely Road. In the vicinity are Boscombe Avenue, Cromer Road, Clare Road, and Lyndhurst Drive E.10. It is difficult to detect any pattern in the choice of names; the same cannot be said of a group near Plashet Park, where Chester Road, Derby Road, Dorset Road, Rutland Road and Stafford Road have a unity from being the names of counties (in some instances needing -*shire* to be suffixed), but alongside is Bristol Road—with Colston Road, Clifton Road, and Bath Road on the other side of Shrewsbury Road E.7, so that some homogeneity is established in both group and sub-group.

Ignoring the possibility of surname or other origins, English provincial towns are well represented in Greater London street names. York alone accounts for about forty; many of these allude to various Dukes of York, but some refer to the Archbishops: York Road S.W.11 goes through the manor of Bridge Court, held by the Archbishops of York from 1472, and York Place W.C.2 is the site of a house occupied for only a year or two by the Archbishop in the reign of Mary Tudor. Rochester Walk S.E.1 has a similar origin, from the house there of the Bishops of Rochester; Rochester Row S.W.1 is in the estate of the Dean and Chapter of Westminster Abbey, the Deans having been from 1663 to 1801 also the Bishops of Rochester. The reference in Rochester Road N.W.1 is indirect; George, second Marquess Camden (the owner of the estate), married the daughter of Dr Murray, Bishop of Rochester.

TITLES OF NOBILITY

The most numerous transferred names, apart from those bestowed arbitrarily upon groups of streets, are those of places occurring in titles of nobility, and of country properties of the great land-owners. The titles, of course, really allude to people rather than to places, and often to individual nobles (especially politicians and statesmen) rather than to the entire family.

It is not impossible to discriminate between names alluding to places as such and those which refer to titles. Grouping provides valuable, though not always conclusive, evidence. Aberdeen Road N.18 adjoins Edinburgh Road, Glasgow Road, and Inverness Road, and so may be classified as 'Scottish geographical'; Aberdeen Road N.W.10, however, adjoins a number of other geographical names—Lancaster Road, Fleetwood Road, Dewsbury Road, Kendal Road, and Burnley Road—which do not appear to be a group into which Aberdeen comfortably fits. In fact, this road was actually named after the Earl of Aberdeen, who had an estate on Dollis Hill. The same nobleman is also referred to in Aberdeen Road, Harrow, if other road-names in the vicinity afford any clue; these include Canning Road, Peel Road, and Palmerston Road, indicating that nineteenth-century prime ministers are being honoured here.

Sidmouth Street W.C.1 is a similar instance. It was constructed in the early years of the nineteenth century, when Henry Addington was Prime Minister; he became Viscount Sidmouth in 1805 and was a prominent member of successive cabinets for some years afterwards. By the association of ideas that is sometimes found in groups of names, the streets nearby received names, not of politicians, but of coastal resorts, sugested by Sidmouth's title. The occasion was the renaming of these streets in the eighteen-sixties, by which time, of course, it is possible that the significance of Sidmouth Street was forgotten. The new names were Lancing Street, Lyme Street, and *Rhyl Street*. Cromer Street nearby has, however, a separate (though not necessarily unrelated) history. This was originally *Lucas Street* (from the name of the landowner) but the name was changed because of the ill fame the street acquired in the early decades of the nineteenth century. Other 'seaside' streets are likewise in a separate group; Hastings Street, Thanet Street, and Sandwich Street W.C.1 are part of the endowment of Tonbridge School bequeathed by its founder, Sir Andrew Judde—hence also Judd Street and Tonbridge Street W.C.1. Mabledon Place, Bidborough Street, and Leigh Street all refer to places near Tonbridge.

Many of the dukedoms and earldoms which form part of the London street-nomenclature are those held by members of the royal family. A very large number of such names are of well-known roads in the central area. Cambridge Circus W.C.2, for instance, was named in honour of the Duke of Cambridge, who formally opened this crossroads in 1887. To about the same period belong many of the Avondale Roads scattered throughout London. The Duke of Clarence and Avondale was the eldest son of the then Prince of Wales (later King Edward VII). The duke, who had just become engaged to Princess Mary of Teck, died suddenly in 1892.

An earlier royal duke who has left his mark in this way was the 'grand old Duke of York'. He was the second son of King George III and besides his dukedoms of York and Albany he had also the title of Earl of Ulster, to which was added the bishopric of Osnabrück—a dignity he attained at the age of three. Osnaburgh Street N.W.1 recalls (in the eighteenth-century English spelling of the name) the Duke's connexion with his Westphalian diocese. His other titles occur in Albany Street, York Terrace, and Ulster Terrace N.W.1. Other streets in the vicinity of Regent's Park allude to earldoms and dukedoms held by other sons of George III, whose own kingdom of Hanover is remembered in Hanover Terrace. Hanover Square and Street W.1. are earlier in date and allude to George I, the Elector of Hanover who became King of England on the death of Queen Anne.

Cumberland Place N.W.1, part of the Regent's Park Estate, honours the fifth son of George III. This was Prince Ernest, Duke of Cumberland, who became King of Hanover in 1837. Great Cumberland Place W.1, however, alludes to an earlier duke—William Augustus, son of George II. After his victory at Culloden in 1756 and

131

his campaign which earned him the nickname 'Butcher', *Tyburn Gate* in Hyde Park was renamed Cumberland Gate in his honour, and the street (built some years later) was named from its nearness to the park gate.

Of the numerous Cumberland Roads (etc) in various parts of Greater London, few seem to refer to the last-named Duke. Cumberland Gate, in Kew Gardens, and Cumberland Road, Kew, relate to the son of George III, and Cambridge Road and Kent Road nearby, like Cambridge Terrace and Kent Terrace N.W.1, allude to his brothers Adolphus and Edward. Some other instances of the name merely refer to the county; Cumberland Road, Bromley, for example, is grouped with Durham Road and Westmoreland Road. The association of Cumberland Street S.W.1 with Chichester Street, Gloucester Street, Sussex Street, and Winchester Street, indicates that the reference here is vaguely to the county name as a noble title, but apparently by a random mixing of the titles of many families apart from that of the landowners, the Dukes of Westminster.

Noble landowners, indeed, such as the Grosvenors, the Russells, and the Comptons, provide many of the street-names in central London derived from place-names alluding to their possessions in many parts of the country. The Grosvenor estates in London stretch in a broad and hardly interrupted band from Marble Arch to Pimlico, so that the title of Duke of Westminster had more than a nominal connexion with this territory. In earlier times, their manor of Eye or Ebury was outside the Westminster boundaries.

GROSVENOR AND BEDFORD PROPERTIES

The Grosvenor family began to develop their London property in the early eighteenth century, and in addition to personal names chose as street-names those of places in Cheshire in which they had estates. Waverton Street W.1 and Balderton Street date from the early period of development, as well as Aldford Street W.1. A property in Flint, however, is no longer commemorated, as *Northop Street* is now known as Culross Street W.1. The southern section of the manor was developed in the early nineteenth century, and the name Belgravia began to be applied to the area, from Belgrave Square S.W.1, named after the place in Cheshire.

Halkin Street and West Halkin Street (the latter being west of Belgrave Square) are named after Halkyn Castle in Flintshire. Other Grosvenor properties provide the names for Eaton Square S.W.1 and Eccleston Place and Square. Minera Mews S.W.1 alludes to property in Denbighshire. Other place-names occurring in the Pimlico section of the Grosvenor estate have already been mentioned, and to those may be added Denbigh Street, Aylesford Street, Colchester Street, and Westmoreland Street S.W.1. Alderney Street does not belong to this group, and the reference to the island came about by the accident of similarity. Originally Stanley Street, the thoroughfare underwent a change of name in 1879. Unlike Stanley Road in Fulham, which became (for no obvious reason) Michael Road, and Stanley Road in Erith, which, as it runs towards Railway Pier, became Pier Road, this one became *Alderley Street*, and when Earl Stanley of Alderley protested, a piece of official rapid thinking produced Alderney Street, which was evidently regarded as quite as good.

Bedford Square W.C.1 and Bedfordshire names such as those in Cardington Street, Goldington Street and Crescent N.W.1, and Woburn Square W.C.1, are among the many transferred names deriving from the estates of the Russells. The Duke of Bedford has—or once had—estates in Devon, represented by Taviton Street, Tavistock Square, Endsleigh Gardens, and Endsleigh Street W.C.1 Thornhaugh Street W.C.1 alludes to property in Northamptonshire which came by the marriage of the first Earl of Bedford to Anne Sapcote, who also brought with her the manor of Chenies (Bucks), remembered in Chenies Street W.C.1. In a later generation there was a marriage with a daughter of the Earl of Southampton (honoured in Southampton Row W.C.1), and Southampton Street, Covent Garden, commemorates their life in that area. Connexions by marriage with other great families are recalled in such names as Gordon Square and Huntley Street (alluding to the Dukes of Gordon, who are Marquesses of Huntly) and Torrington Place (from the title of Lord Torrington, father-in-law of the sixth Duke of Bedford). Other properties include Eversholt, Ridgmount, and Houghton Conquest (Bedfordshire); Eversholt Street and Ridgmount Gardens survive, but Houghton Place has disappeared, as has Ampthill Square. Houghton Street W.C.2 alludes to a different place and family. A seventeenth-century member of the Holles family became Baron Houghton, taking his title from the Nottinghamshire village now spelt Haughton, and Earl of Clare; his son set up a great house in the Drury Lane area, and established a market (Clare Market) into which Houghton Street runs at right angles.

COMPTONS AND OTHER GREAT FAMILIES

An institution called the Northampton Polytechnic with an address in Finsbury used to occasion some surprise—and possibly postal confusion—but now that it has become the City University that problem

133

no longer exists. At least, the City is much nearer than Northampton. The explanation, of course, lay in the ownership of land in the area. The manor of Clerkenwell was a possession of the Compton family of Compton Wynyates, the head of which became Marquess of Northampton in the eighteenth century.

Besides Northampton Road and Square, Compton possessions in that county are referred to in Easton Street W.C.1 (from Easton Maudit) and Ashby Street E.C.1 (Castle Ashby). Warwickshire places are alluded to in Wynyatt and Tysoe Streets E.C.1. Yardley Street W.C.1 is named after the first Marquess's birthplace (Yardley Hastings, Northants). Agdon Street E.C.1 bears the name of a farm in the parish of Brailes (Warwickshire), not far from Compton Wynyates.

The names of a number of Somerset and Dorset places occur in the streets on the Portman estate in Marylebone. The original family seat was Orchard Portman, Somerset—whence Orchard Street. There was a connexion by marriage with the Seymours, Dukes of Somerset, both surname and title being entered in the list of street-names on the estate. The family seat was later moved to Bryanston, near Blandford. Hence Bryanston Street and Square, Blandford Street and Square, and Dorset Street and Square. Somerset properties near Taunton are alluded to in Bickenhall Street W.1, Capland Street N.W.8, and Huntsworth Mews N.W.1. Enford Street, Nutford Place, and Melcombe Street bear some of the names from the extensive Dorset properties of the family. Crawford Street is from Tarrant Crawford in Dorset.

Weymouth Street W.1 is not part of the Portland estate, but of the Cavendish property. The third Viscount Weymouth married a Cavendish and took part in the development of the land in Marylebone. Other Dorset place-names occur among the streets of the Holland Park estate. These include Ilchester Place, Abbotsbury Close, and Melbury Road W.14.

ESTATES OF THE LANDED GENTRY

The street-names in the estates of noble landowners are partly transferred place-names and partly personal names of members of the family. The territorial possessions of the lower ranks of the landed gentry, however, seemed to loom larger than the personalities of their relatives, and their estates (usually away from the central area of London) tend to produce street-names consisting almost exclusively of transferred names of places elsewhere.

Streets on the Gunter estates in west London allude to the

Breconshire possessions of the family and to connexions the family had with Yorkshire; the grandson of the founder of the line became M.P. for Knaresborough and Barkston Ash—hence Knaresborough Place and Barkston Gardens S.W.5. The Welsh properties are recalled in Talgarth Road, Gliddon Road, Gilston Road, Gwendwr Road, and Glazbury Road W.14, and Tregunter Road S.W.10. Priory Walk S.W.10 alludes to Abergavenny Priory. Wetherby Gardens S.W.5, Westgate Terrace S.W.10, Bramham Gardens, Collingham Place and Road, Laverton Gardens S.W.5, Slaidburn Street and Wharfedale Street S.W.10 are among the streets bearing transferred names from West Riding places.

Places in Kent associated with the Powell-Cotton family are alluded to in streets built on their estate in West Hampstead. These are Quex Road N.W.6, Garlinge Road, Manstone Road, Ebbsfleet Road, Richborough Road, and Fordwych Road N.W.2. It is interesting to observe that although Cleve Road is virtually continuous with its counterpart east of Priory Road, this eastern thoroughfare has an Essex name—Canfield Gardens N.W.6—derived from the estates of the Maryon-Wilson family. Canfield is the village near which is the farm, Fitzjohns, providing the name for Fitzjohn's Avenue N.W.3. Chesterford Gardens N.W.3 also alludes to Essex property; there was in addition land in Berkshire, referred to in Bracknell Way and Gardens N.W.3. Property in Sussex suggested the names Broadhurst Close and Gardens N.W.6, Daleham Gardens and Mews N.W.3, Fairhazel Gardens N.W.6, Lindfield Gardens N.W.3, Maresfield Gardens, Netherhall Gardens, and Nutley Terrace N.W.3.

Besides their lands in Kent, of which Acol Road and Woodchurch Road N.W.6 are further reminders, the Powell-Cottons owned shooting estates in Abyssinia. Minster Road, meeting Menelik Road N.W.2 to form a continuous, curving thoroughfare, symbolizes this overseas interest. Somali Road and Asmara Road are nearby.

Foreign place-names

Only a small number of streets named after foreign places are likely to allude to shooting estates in which the local landowner is interested. Travel, exploration, trade, and military expeditions account for a good many; one or two allude to a topic that evidently aroused great interest in the 1890s—archaeology. Kashgar Road S.E.19, dating from 1890, commemorates the excavations carried out by Aurel Stein near this ancient town in East Turkestan. Baalbec Road N.5, of about the same date, recalls the excavation of the ancient city of Heliopolis, later Tamburlaine's fort of Baalbek. This road is placed in an exotic

135

setting, having as neighbours Calabria Road, Liberia Road, Corsica Road, and Gallia Road, whose names suggest that they were selected for their sound rather than for geographical or historical significance.

Some foreign place-names allude to service abroad on the part of the owners of estates on which the streets were built. Valetta Road W.3, for instance, on the Essex estate in Acton, refers to the military service in Malta of Lt-Col Cowper-Essex. St Elmo Road W.12 is similarly explained, this martyr having given his name to a fort at the entrance to Valletta Harbour. The officer also served in the war in South Africa, and was stationed for a time in a small town in Cape Province; this place (and not the town in the Netherlands) provided the name Dordrecht Road W.3.

Trafalgar Square and Waterloo Road immediately spring to mind when foreign battlefields are mentioned. Both battles, and many others, are recalled in road names in various parts of London; riverside towns such as Greenwich and Twickenham have their Trafalgar Roads, and Trafalgar Gardens in Merton reminds us of the fact that Nelson lived with Lady Hamilton at her house there. Trafalgar is the only battle named in the group of roads comprising Hamilton Road, Hardy Road, Nelson Road, and Victory Road S.W.19, but another of Nelson's engagements was commemorated in Aboukir Street in Peckham, a side street of Trafalgar Road S.E.15.

Albuhera Close (Enfield) and Corunna Road S.W.8 are two of the rare references in street-names to the Peninsular War. Wellington's own victory at Vimiera receives no mention, but Cintra Park S.E.19 alludes to the convention which followed it, and a battle in the next year is recalled in Almeida Street N.1. Two of Wellington's successes in Spain are commemorated in Salamanca Street S.E.11 and Vittoria Place N.1.

The earlier War of the Spanish Succession is celebrated in a number of street-names. Vigo Street W.1, earlier *Vigo Lane*, dates from the capture of the port in 1719. In 1702 there had been a naval battle just off this place, and no doubt when the name next came into the news it was sufficiently familiar to be used as a street-name. References to Marlborough's victories are limited to Blenheim and Ramillies. Ramillies Roads in Sidcup and Holloway are individual names of this type, but Ramillies Road W.4 is associated not only with Blenheim Road but also with Marlborough Crescent, as well as with a number of others bearing the names of famous men of the period of Queen Anne. Ramillies Street W.1, which connects Great Marlborough Street with Oxford Street, is crossed by Ramillies Place and is about a quarter of a mile east of Blenheim Street. These streets were being built at the time of the campaign.

Blenheim names are fairly numerous. They are often associated with a Marlborough Road (&c) nearby, but are sometimes a seemingly random component in a miscellany of names of all types, as in East Ham, where Blenheim Road E.6, running parallel with Boundary Road E.13, joins Wilson Road with Frinton Road and has Welbeck Road and Hubert Road as neighbours.

NAMES FROM EASTERN EUROPE

A distant victory by an alien monarch is the ultimate explanation of the name of Poland Street W.1. In 1683, John Sobieski defeated the Turks at Vienna; an inn on the south side of Oxford Street was accordingly named *The King of Poland* in his honour, and the street— built a few years after the battle—took its name from that of the hostelry. Eastern Europe's main contribution to London street-names, however, is to be found in the fairly numerous group alluding to the Crimean War.

Alma Road is the Crimean name most frequently occurring, almost all examples being in outer London—no fewer than three in Enfield alone. Alma Street N.W.5 adjoins Inkerman Road, and nearby thoroughfares bear the names of famous commanders in the war. Off Southwark Park Road, Alma Grove S.E.1 is connected by Fort Road with Balaclava Road. One of the Sebastopol forts is referred to in Redan Place W.2, Redan Street W.14, and Redan Terrace S.E.5. There is also a Balaclava Road in Surbiton.

Varna Road S.W.6 alludes to a place to which there was an expedition during the war, although it is not in the Crimean Peninsula; Varna Road in Hampton adjoins Plevna road and is only a few yards from Belgrade Road, indicating an association with the Balkan Wars of the 1870s rather than with the Crimea. In Edmonton, Plevna Road N.9 is connected with Sebastopol Road (by a short length of Felixstowe Road), but the bias is clearly towards the Russo-Turkish War of 1877–8, as the neighbouring road-names show. These are Disraeli Road and Osman Road, the latter commemorating the Turkish general Osman Pasha, who was besieged at Plevna. Batoum Gardens W.6, the name of which was approved in 1878, refers to the fortified town ceded by Turkey to Russia in that year.

Wilna Road S.W.18 dates from 1885; Wilno or Vilna (Lithuania) was intermittently in the news throughout the nineteenth century, but there is no obvious reason why it should have been used as a road-name at this date. Other names from eastern Europe include Danube Street S.W.3; as this was formerly *Little Blenheim Street* it should be grouped with those names. Moscow Road and St Petersburgh Place in

137

Bayswater may both be merely commemorative, recalling a visit by Tsar Alexander I in 1814, but there seems to be an even closer connexion between the area and at least one of the Russian cities, as gravel from the pits nearby is said to have been exported soon afterwards, to be used in the building of roads in St Petersburg. Muscovy Street E.C.3, in an area once occupied by Russian merchants, owes its name to that of a public house, *The Czar of Muscovy's Head*.

ASIAN AND AFRICAN NAMES

A group of streets off Falcon Road S.W.11 bear the names of places in Afghanistan. Dating from about 1879, these names allude to the second Afghan War (1879–80). Afghan Road and Khyber Road run from Falcon Road to Candahar Road, which in turn leads to Cabul Road. Musjid Road, not far away, is not a place-name borrowing. *Musjid* means 'mosque' and as this road is of the same date as the ones just mentioned, the name alludes to the same geographical and cultural context. Maiwand Road E.5 recalls the battle in which the British force under Burrows were defeated by the Afghans on 27 July 1880.

Aliwal Road S.W.11 commemorates a battle in the first Sikh War of 1846; Gwalior Road S.W.15 recalls fighting in India a few years earlier, and Bangalore Street, not far away, looks back to events before the end of the eighteenth century. Benares Road S.E.18 (named in 1890), probably looks back to events during the Mutiny. It is interesting to note that all these roads received their designations 30 or more years after outstanding military events, and it is not impossible that men who had taken part in the various conflicts may have been responsible for the choice of names.

Berber Road S.W.11 alludes to Gordon's famous expedition in 1884, referred to also in two other Battersea names—Soudan Road and Kassala Road. Khartoum Road S.W.17, and identically named roads in Ilford and Plaistow, remind us of the culmination of that disastrous campaign.

Few military exploits in the latter part of the nineteenth century seem to have escaped attention in Battersea, and the arrival of a British force in Ethiopia in 1868 was duly recorded in Abyssinia Road S.W.11. The fortress which was captured and destroyed is named in Magdala Avenue N.19; streets of the same name are found in Isleworth and in South Croydon, where Magdala Road is a short adjunct to Napier Road, commemorating the leader of the British troops.

The South African War of 1899–1902, which loomed much larger on the public consciousness than previous conflicts, owing to developments in communications, also happened to occur at a time which was particularly hungry for military success; it is therefore not to be wondered at that this war, coinciding with the development of the outer parts of the recently constituted County of London, is remembered in numerous street names in the suburbs. Individual names, and groups of various sizes, are found in various parts of London. The Tugela River, for instance, figured early in the war; it is commemorated in Tugela Road in Selhurst and Tugela Street S.E.6. Colenso Road E.5 refers to one of the disastrous battles there; a street bearing the name in Ilford occurs in a group which also includes Ladysmith Avenue, Kimberley Avenue, and Mafeking Avenue.

Pretoria Road S.W.16 is the only instance of this name within the former L.C.C. area, but others occur in Ilford (not far from Natal Road), Romford, and Chingford. Pretoria Road N.17 is associated with Durban Road and *Lorenco Road*—the last being possibly as near as the name-givers could get to the Mozambique name, Lourenço Marques. Pretoria Avenue E.17 is not grouped with other South African names, but Pretoria Road E.16 adjoins Ladysmith Road, Kimberley Road, and Mafeking Road.

Bloemfontein Road W.12, dating from the 1880s, reminds us that events in South Africa brought Bloemfontein into the news frequently during the second half of the nineteenth century. Operations against the Zulus also occupied much attention and when these became outright war in 1879, some streets received appropriate names. Kambala Road S.W.11 refers to Kambula, successfully defended by the British in June 1879, and Ulundi Road S.E.3 commemorates a victory in the following month.

TRANSATLANTIC NAMES

Struggles and suffering of another kind than war brings are remembered in Yukon Road S.W.12, which celebrates the discovery of gold in north-west Canada in 1896. No other names are to be found referring to this event. Indeed, it is remarkable how few Canadian place-names are used for London streets. There is a Quebec Road in Yeading and another in Ilford, where it is grouped with Montreal Road, Toronto Road and some other names redolent of the 'great days of Empire': Aden Road, Dunedin Road, Colombo Road, Christchurch Road, Auckland Road, Adelaide Road, Bathurst Gardens, Melbourne Road, and Brisbane Road. Perth Road connects the group with Eastern Avenue at Gants Hill Cross. Montreal Place

W.C.2 seems to have been named to balance (geographically and alliteratively) Melbourne Place, at the other end of Aldwych, behind Australia House. Toronto Road E.12 lies within a miscellany of geographical names, including Michigan Avenue, Oregon Avenue, Washington Avenue, Worcester Road, and Gloucester Road. Toronto Road E.11 is not grouped with other names of the same type.

In the City, America Square was, before the War of Independence, the resort of merchants engaged in the Transatlantic trade. It is perhaps not surprising that not many streets are named after places in the United States. When the suburbs were being developed, the former colonies were, to say the least, out of favour, and references either antedate the Boston Tea Party or occur in innocuous miscellanies.

In Bethnal Green, Virginia Road was so called before 1746; it was then in open country, and it is likely that the name implied that it was a very remote place. There was a *Virginia Row* slightly to the south, at the edge of the built up area; this has now been renamed Vallance Road, with a similar connotation. Other American names in the neighbourhood—Florida Street and Columbia Road E.2—doubtless owe their existence to the references to Virginia in the older names.

Virginia Street E.1, associated as it is with old Whitechapel street-names such as Ship Alley, almost certainly received its name from the trade with the New World. The same can hardly be said of Nebraska Street in Bermondsey, which dates only from 1892 and has all the marks of an entirely random choice. There are, of course, other considerations. Nebraska was not named as such until 1844 (being until then known as Platte River) and its land-locked position rules it out as an immediate destination for goods from the Pool of London. There is an older street, just off Southwark Street and therefore nearer the river—America Street—which may well be associated with the Transatlantic trade. Jamaica Street E.1 and Jamaica Street S.E.16 date from the 1860s; the former received its name from Jamaica House in the vicinity. Trinidad Street E.14 is situated near West India Dock Road; there is a Grenade Street in the same neighbourhood, possibly alluding to the island of Grenada, but a clearer reference is found in Grenada Road S.E.7, in a small group south of Charlton Park. This complex is named from an assortment of places and rivers in the Empire, other names being Sutlej Road, Indus Road, Kenya Road, Kashmir Road, and Nigeria Road S.E.7.

Maryland Street and Road E.15 are named from a cluster of houses built at a promontory which came to be known as Maryland Point. These cottages were an investment on the part of a merchant who had made a fortune in the colony. Another Maryland Road is found in Thornton Heath, in a group which also includes Virginia Road,

Florida Road, Georgia Road, and Carolina Road.

Personal names in street-names

All over Greater London are to be found streets bearing the personal names of local residents, landowners, builders, developers, or other persons thought worthy of being honoured in this way. Occasionally a Christian name (or other name apart from the surname) is used. Unless it is unusual, such a name is obviously far more difficult than a surname to connect with its origin. A clue, however, may be given by using the family name in an adjacent road. Harold Road N.W.10 and the adjoining Wesley Avenue are named after Harold Wesley, a manufacturing stationer established nearby; Newark Crescent, off Harold Road, refers to Newark, New Jersey, where the firm's American associate company had a factory.

John Webbe Weston owned the so-called Manor of the Maze in Bermondsey in 1812, and Weston Street S.E.1 commemorates this fact; there is an adjoining Webb Street, and formerly a *John Street* as well. Crispe Road and Gascoigne Road in Barking commemorate Sir Crisp Gascoigne, an eighteenth-century landowner; Francis Street S.W.1 perpetuates the Christian name of the owner of property there in the early nineteenth century, Francis Wilcox.

The many streets in Central London commemorating owners and developers of great estates are discussed elsewhere. In the outer boroughs there are numerous instances of names of the same type. Davis Road W.3 commemorates Mr A. S. N. Davis, a trustee of the Cowper-Essex estate in Acton; Beavor Lane W.6 is probably to be associated with the family of Samuel Bever, alluded to in a survey of the mid-eighteenth century. Gamuel Road E.17 refers to Thomas Gamuel, a benefactor of Walthamstow in the seventeenth century.

In the Tithe Apportionment for Wandsworth, G. D. Longstaff is named as one of the occupiers of land, and P. W. Barchard, Abraham Borrodaile, and James Furnage are recorded as owners. These men are remembered in Longstaff Road, Barchard Street, Borrodaile Road, and Furmage Street. Charlwood Road S.W.15 similarly refers to names found in the Putney Tithe Apportionment of 1848: George Charlwood, occupier, and Charles Charlwood, owner. Charlwood Place and Street S.W.1 do not come from this family-name, but from the name of the place in Surrey in which the owner of the land in Pimlico also had property.

Another Surrey place-name which occurs in a number of street-names is Sutton, but Sutton Way W.10 is derived from the surname of William Richard Sutton, one of several Victorian men of substance to interest himself in housing problems. Another was George Peabody, whose name was applied to more than thirty blocks of dwellings in the former London County Council area alone; Peabody Estate is still to be found in several places in Greater London, and Peabody Avenue S.W.1 is one example in the central part.

The great nineteenth-century development of the suburbs of London included the construction of individual streets by a builder who gave his name to the street but is otherwise unknown to history. Brushfield Street E.1 perpetuates the name of Thomas Brushfield, who in fact distinguished himself also in other ways, becoming (for instance) a member of the Metropolitan Board of Works. Herbert Street N.W.5 was built by Vincent Herbert of Hoxton; Whittaker Street S.W.1 was the work of John Whittaker; Whellock Road W.4 commemorates its builder, R. W. Whellock; and Cunnington Street W.4 was named after Thomas Cunnington, a local soap manufacturer, who invested in property in this thoroughfare.

Property-owners would often become members of local councils, and their commemoration in place-names may be due to their distinction in either capacity. One such prominent burgess was the builder, William Atkinson, who was mayor of Acton in 1934–5; his name was modestly excluded from the streets he developed, which were instead called after members of his family. These streets are Wilfred Gardens, Kathleen Avenue, Lucy Crescent, and Allan Way W.3. An earlier Acton councillor, A. C. Crane, is commemorated in Crane Avenue; Councillor Crane was chairman of the then Urban District Council in the coronation year of King George V (1911).

Many surnames are those of men of several hundred years ago. Carterhatch Lane and Phipps Hatch Lane in Enfield look back to Nicholas Carter (1574) and Edward Phipps (1730), the second element indicating that these lanes were approaches to gates of Enfield Chase. Whitmore Road N.1 recalls the association with the locality of Sir George Whitmore, a landowner of the seventeenth century. Chichele Road N.W.2 commemorates Henry Chichele, the fifteenth-century Archbishop of Canterbury, who advised King Henry VI to grant land in Willesden to All Souls College. This prelate is remembered also in Chicheley Street S.E.1, near Lambeth Palace. Dawes Road S.W.6 alludes to William Dawe, mentioned in documents of about 1294, and Sanders Lane N.W.7 is probably to be associated with Richard Saundre (1321).

Names from literature, painting, music and history

Occasionally, famous poets, painters, and composers owned or rented property in the streets now bearing their names. George Cruikshank, for instance, the caricaturist and illustrator, lived in Clerkenwell, where he is honoured in Cruikshank Street W.C.1. An eighteenth-century poet receives his only street-name commemoration in Akenside Road N.W.3, in the neighbourhood where he spent a few years of his life. Keats Grove N.W.3 celebrates a more famous Hampstead poet; Coleridge Gardens N.W.3 recalls a number of visits the writer paid to the area, but it does not claim him as a resident. In an earlier period, however, John Milton and John Dryden did actually live in the vicinity of streets now carrying their names. Milton lived in Bunhill Row, across Chiswell Street from Milton Street, which in his day was called *Grub Street*; this ancient name (*Grubbestrete* in the early thirteenth century) possibly meant 'street infested by maggots', but men with the surname Grub (one of them was a fishmonger) were living in the City in the thirteenth century. In the reign of George IV, the inhabitants, weary of the association of their street with hack-writers, decided to change the name to that of the poet who had written *Paradise Regained* only a short distance away. John Dryden lived in Long Acre for about four years; Dryden Street W.C.2 runs parallel to the road in which he lived.

Chaucer, one of the many poets more talked about than read, has a special connexion with London. His father was a London vintner, he spent much of his working life in London, and he is buried in Westminster Abbey. That he wrote about a pilgrimage to Canterbury which set out from an inn in Southwark is all that many people know of him, and yet no reference to his name in street-names occurs any nearer than Chaucer Road S.E.24. This Herne Hill road is one of a group also including Spenser Road, Milton Road, and Shakespeare Road.

The pilgrimage itself is recalled in Tabard Street, named after the inn at which the company of 'nine and twenty' travellers spent a night before setting out for Canterbury. This is a new name (bestowed in 1877) for the old *Kent* or *Kentish Street* (*Kentstret* 1330, *Kentisshestrete* 1482); the *Tabard* Inn stood a quarter of a mile to the north, on the site of Talbot Yard S.E.1. The pilgrims would have ridden along *Kent Street*, which was then the main road to Canterbury; Pilgrimage Street crosses it, connecting Great Dover Street (the present main road to Kent) with Long Lane (*Le Longlayne* c.1510). Representative members of this fictitious group are named in Manciple Street and Pardoner Street (off Tabard Street), with Prioress Street at the point where Tabard Street merges with Old Kent Road. The choice of these three pilgrims may seem capricious, particularly as none of them was described as being connected with the area in which they are recalled.

Poets and other writers are regularly commemorated in street-names, either individual or grouped, all over London; it is implied that they are great men worthy of immortalising in this special way; the extent to which it is done suggests a knowledge of their work and a respect for their art far greater than the experience of most of us would lead us to acknowledge. Individual names, of course, sometimes occur near the writer's residence. To those mentioned already may be added D'Arblay Street W.1, near which Fanny Burney (later Madame D'Arblay) spent the first few years of her life. Lord Macaulay spent his childhood in a house at The Pavement, Clapham, and Macaulay Road and Square S.W.4 now commemorate the connexion.

Near Little Venice, the name of which he coined, and Warwick Avenue, where he lived after the death of his wife, a distinguished Victorian poet is recalled in Browning Close W.9, flanked on one side by Robert Close and on the other by Elizabeth Close. Elsewhere, Browning is included in large and small literary groups. Near Drayton Green Station, Dryden Avenue runs parallel with Browning Avenue W.7 and adjoins Cowper Road. Shakespeare Road, Milton Road, and Tennyson Road complete this collection. A large literary complex is traversed by Browning Road E.12. Tennyson Avenue and Words-worth Avenue are short roads on the Plashet Park side of East Ham High Street; Byron Avenue and Shelley Avenue extend across the High Street and go through to Shakespeare Crescent. Other roads are Goldsmith Avenue, Ruskin Avenue, Coleridge Avenue, Swinburne Avenue, and Sheridan Road. Tennyson is near the top of the league of poetic popularity, with nearly two dozen street-names. Near Haydons Road station, Tennyson Road S.W.19 is grouped with Caxton Road, Cowper Road, Dryden Road, and Milton Road. Tennyson Road S.E.20 is in royal company, the neighbours being Princes Road, Albert Road, Edward Road, and Victor Road; but Southey Road and Wordsworth Road are comfortably close.

Cowper receives quite frequent street-name recognition, and often suffers the mispronunciation of his name as a consequence. A small group in Wallington consists of Cowper Gardens, Milton Road, and Wordsworth Road; in Bickley there are Cowper Road and Cowper Close, together with Pope Road, Chatterton Road, and Johnson Road, the group being stiffened by allusions to prose writers in Addison Road and Walpole Road. The great essayist has, of course, a residential qualification in Addison Road W.14 (which was further glorified at one time by being the name of the railway station now called Kensington, Olympia). Addison passed the last few years of his life at Holland House nearby, having married the widowed Lady

Holland in 1716. Steele's Road N.W.3 marks the site occupied by Addison's associate.

Daniel Defoe lived in Stoke Newington and is duly remembered in Defoe Road N.16; *Defoe Road* S.W.17, near which the novelist passed some years of his youth, is now part of Garratt Lane. His residence in the area is alluded to in some names just over the Mitcham border: Crusoe Road, Friday Road, and Island Road are grouped, with Pitcairn Road as a make-weight—perhaps by some confusion between Crusoe and the *Bounty* mutineers.

The painter Sir Godfrey Kneller lived in Twickenham, at the Hall which still bears his name. Kneller Road, Twickenham, is one of several commemorating distinguished former residents, among whom was Alexander Pope, recalled in Pope's Road; Walpole Road pays tribute to Horace Walpole, who lived not far away at Strawberry Hill.

Raeburn and Gainsborough are among the painters celebrated in a group in Little Stanmore. Gainsborough Gardens faces Millais Gardens across Cotman Gardens, from which lead also Whistler Gardens and Collier Drive (which in turn faces Rembrandt Road across Constable Gardens). Raeburn Road and Hogarth Road complete the group on this side of the Brent boundary, but just across the border are Landseer Close and Leighton Close. In Hillingdon Heath, Gainsborough, Raeburn, and Hoppner Roads are the three principal components of a small complex of artistic roads; the development is traversed by Romney Road, and subsidiary streets are Lawrence Road and Hayman Crescent. Nearby, Constable Close and Turner Close complete the group. The sculptor John Flaxman is celebrated in Flaxman Terrace. A number of nineteenth-century artists are commemorated together near Bush Hill Park station in Enfield, where Millais Road, Leighton Road, Poynter Road, and Landseer Road adjoin one another. Sir Lawrence Alma Tadema is commemorated in Tadema Road S.W.3, and Anthony Van Dyck in New Malden, where Vandyck Road, connecting Lawrence Avenue with Gainsborough Road, adjoins Reynolds Road and Kneller Road.

Beethoven and Mozart are represented only once each, in street-names in Kensal Town (see below, p. 159). Dr Arne receives two references, in Arne Walk S.E.3 and Arne Street W.C.2, near Covent Garden, where he was born and in the church of which he is buried. Mendelssohn, for all his close connexion with high Victorian London, is not recognised at all, nor, apparently, is Sir Arthur Sullivan. Sir John Stainer, however, is remembered in Bermondsey, where he grew up; Stainer Street S.E.1 joins St Thomas Street with Tooley Street.

Handel's stay with the Duke of Chandos has left its mark on street-names near Canons, but he is also commemorated in the vicinity of the Foundling Hospital, in which he gave organ recitals; Handel Street W.C.1 alludes to his connexion with Coram's charity. Tallis Street E.C.4 and Tallis Grove S.E.7 commemorate Thomas Tallis (1510-85), who died in Greenwich; the City street adjoins the former location of the Guildhall School of Music in John Carpenter Street. The hymnographer Charles Wesley, brother of the founder of Methodism, occupied a house in Marylebone during the last two decades of the eighteenth century; he is commemorated in Wesley Street W.1, near the site of his residence.

FOREIGN WRITERS AND THE CLASSICAL WORLD

European artists are readily accepted in this country, some of them, indeed, receiving a sort of posthumous naturalisation. Holbein Place S.W.1 is an instance of this kind of commemoration. Foreign writers do not usually receive this recognition. Holbein's contemporary Erasmus has, however, been admitted to the canon of London street-names, possibly not only as a crypto-Englishman but also as an honorary Anglican; Erasmus Street S.W.1 is on the Westminster Abbey Tothill Fields estate, and the great Netherlander is honoured beside Edmund Spenser and Dean Farrar (author of *Eric, or Little by Little*), whose spirits preside over Spenser Street and Dean Farrar Street, beyond Victoria Street; Erasmus Street actually adjoins Herrick Street, commemorating the poet Robert Herrick (1591-1674), who passed some happy years nearby, having been ejected from his living at Dean Prior in Devon.

Another great European is honoured in Pascal Street S.W.8, near the New Covent Garden Market at Nine Elms. Pascal's compatriot, Voltaire, is commemorated in Voltaire Road S.W.4, separated by the width of Clapham High Street from Aristotle Road and Cato Road. Other names from the classical world are found not far away; Seneca Road honours the Roman Stoic and tragedian. Solon Road S.W.2, adjoining Seneca Road, commemorates the great Athenian legislator of the 7th-6th centuries B.C. Off Solon Road, Kepler Road S.W.4 bears the name of Johann Kepler (1571-1630), a legislator of another kind. He formulated the laws of planetary motion which led the way to much of Newton's work. From Kepler Road, Plato Road S.W.2 leads to Acre Lane.

Two other classical names occur a little to the south, off Brixton Hill. Endymion Road commemorates the shepherd of Mount Latmus of whom the moon goddess became enamoured; Leander Road, nearby, alludes to the young man of Abydos who nightly swam the Hellespont to join his beloved. The proximity of the River Effra may account for this name.

The Trojan War is commemorated in street-names near Fortune Green. Ulysses Road N.W.6 and Achilles Road connect Ajax Road with Agamemnon Road. There is also an Ajax Avenue N.W.9, adjoining the British Library Newspaper Repository. Achilles Way W.1 connects the two carriageways of Park Lane near the Achilles statue in Hyde Park.

Gods and goddesses are not much favoured in the naming of streets. Jupiter, for instance, does not occur in Greater London; nor does Mars. There is a Mercury Road in Brentford and Mercury Gardens in Romford. Minerva does rather better than this. Minerva Road E.4 is a short road near Walthamstow Stadium. Minerva Road (Kingston) adjoins the Fairfield Recreation Ground; but Minerva Road N.W.10 does not directly allude to the goddess. Like Standard Road and Sunbeam Road N.W.10, this was named after a motor works. Juno Way S.E.14 is the only allusion to that deity.

In any discussion of European literature the name of Dante is likely to be mentioned. Even more than Chaucer, whose great poem took a group of people along a road, Dante deserves celebration in street-names; he introduces the image of a road in the very first line of his masterpiece. However, he is awarded only a single location in London—Dante Road S.E.11. His compatriot Ariosto is not represented at all, but Orlando Road S.W.4 alludes to his character, the paladin Roland. Fontarabia Road S.W.11 is another reference to Roland; it is the place which Milton seems to have confused with Roncesvalles, where Roland's great rearguard action was fought and lost. Scott alludes to it also, and it is probably his work which the name-giver had been reading, as Marmion Road is immediately next to Fontarabia Road. Roland Road adjoins Oliver Road E.17 and these may thus be taken to allude to Charlemagne's peers.

Tasso Road W.6 is the only street-name reference to the poet of *Gerusalemme Liberata*, but his hero Rinaldo occurs to keep him company (though some miles away) in Rinaldo Road, adjoining Lochinvar Road S.W.12; another character receives an incidental mention, as his name is the title of one of Disraeli's novels; Tancred Road N.4 is grouped with other roads bearing names from the titles of those works.

Cervantes, also, receives the tribute of only a single name, and we look in vain for the Don and Sancho Panza (and, indeed, for Rosinante and the Lady Dulcinea). However, near Cervantes Court in Northwood are other names alluding to cultural matters. One refers to an artist, Nicholas Hilliard; Hilliard Road is next to the High Street. Next again is Addison Way, and Waverley Gardens can be found nearby. It is tempting to associate Wieland Road with the German rococo novelist. Not many people, if challenged, could readily name any Spanish writer other than Cervantes, yet no fewer than two names appear to relate to Pedro Calderón de la Barca—Calderon Place W.10 and Calderon Road E.11. The latter is grouped with roads alluding to British artists—Frith Road, Millais Road, and Leslie Road E.11.

Martin Luther is referred to in only one name; Luther Road in Teddington adjoins Latimer Road, the Reformation association confirming the reference. One other German writer may be mentioned, G. E. Lessing, named in Lessing Street S.E.23.

Virgil, who was both a fictitious character (in Dante) and a great epic poet, ought therefore to be a good candidate for enrolment in London street-names. Virgil Street S.E.11 is near Centaur Street. On the Lisson estate, Virgil Place is a pun or associative joke. The adjoining Homer Row was not named after the Greek poet but after the eighteenth-century lessee, Edward Homer; the surname, however, suggested the classical allusions in Virgil Place and Cato Street. A similar naming pun occurred in Acton. Beaumont Road W.4 refers to its developer, Mr Barber Beaumont; but when an adjacent street came to be named, a literary-minded official decided on Fletcher Road, suggesting a connexion with the collaborating dramatists.

CHARACTERS IN LITERATURE

Besides the names of the writers themselves, the titles of their works and the names of characters are used to designate streets. Some of Chaucer's pilgrims have already been mentioned; Shakespearean references might be expected to be more numerous. A small group is to be found off St John's Way N.19. Prospero Road and Miranda Road refer to characters from *The Tempest*; Parolles Road is named after the boastful coward in *All's Well that Ends Well*; Lysander Road alludes to the lover of Hermia in *A Midsummer Night's Dream*; and Cressida Road refers to the heroine of *Troilus and Cressida*. Portia Road E.3, taking its name from that of the character in *The Merchant of Venice*, is not grouped with similar names.

Endymion Road N.4 adjoins the cricket ground in Finsbury Park. Unlike Endymion Road S.W.2, the Harringay Road is one of a group, containing also Coningsby Road, Tancred Road, Venetia Road, and Lothair Road. The group is completed by Alroy Road, alluding to the author's early *Wondrous Tale of Alroy*. The novelist himself, Benjamin Disraeli, receives no mention in this locality. In Ealing, however, to the north of a group consisting of Venetia Road, Lothair Road and Coningsby Road, Beaconsfield Road W.5 takes a small step towards doing justice to the author. Disraeli Road W.5 is further north still, off Lammas Park Road.

Two of George Eliot's works provide names for roads at Knights Hill, where Deronda Road and Romola Road interconnect, off Norwood Road S.E.24. Floss Street S.W.15 may possibly be a further Eliot allusion.

Tributes to Dickens through his characters include Copperfield Avenue and Micawber Avenue at Colham Green; Pickwick Street, Weller Street, Quilp Street, and Little Dorrit Street S.E.1 are in the neighbourhood of Marshalsea, the setting of *Little Dorrit*. Pickwick Road in Dulwich may be a reference to the character. Micawber Road N.1 is an isolated example, and so is Dombey Street W.C.1. Peggoty's Way at Goulds Green is grouped with Dickens Avenue and Thackeray Close.

Waverley Avenue E.4 is confirmed as a Scott reference by the proximity of Marmion Avenue, off which Marmion Approach leads to Marmion Close. Ivanhoe Drive at Wealdstone, Ivanhoe Road S.E.5, and Ivanhoe Road in Hounslow are not accompanied by any other roads alluding to the works of Scott.

Apart from Esmond Court W.8, off Thackeray Street, near which the novelist lived for a time, it is difficult to identify the various Esmond or Pendennis Roads with the works of Thackeray. Esmond Road W.4 is an exception; this is grouped with Ramillies Road and Marlborough Crescent, which allude to the historical background of the novel. Barchester Close (Uxbridge), Barchester Road (Harrow), and Barchester Street E.14 refer to Trollope's fictional cathedral city; these, with Barset Road S.E.15, are probably the only names alluding to the Barsetshire novels.

HISTORICAL NAMES: MONARCHS AND ROYAL FAMILIES

Mention has already been made of transferred place-names being used for the designation of streets, when the former allude to battlefields. Other historical allusions in the names of great generals and statesmen, as well as those of kings and queens, regularly occur on the street map, together with names of royal houses or dynasties to which they belonged.

In Southall, Saxon Road (with Alfred Gardens adjoining) leads to Saxon Gardens and is next to Dane Road, at the end of which are Norman Avenue and Viking Road. Next come Lancaster Road and Tudor Road. Some effort has clearly been made here to arrange the roads in chronological order. Saxon Road, off Roman Road E.6, is quite near Norman Road; in Ilford, Dane Road links Norman Road and Saxon Road with Roman Road. The House of Plantagenet is not forgotten, but it is alluded to in a historical group only in Barnet,

149

between Barnet Vale and Hadley Common. In this complex are to be found Plantagenet Road, Tudor Road, and Bosworth Road. York Road and Lancaster Road lie on either side of the railway at New Barnet Station; they seem to be present, not because of their dynastic references, but as part of another complex consisting of the names of earldoms and dukedoms.

The Tudor period seems to be the most highly favoured for the naming of roads; Henry VIII's wives, after all, are a kind of bulk purchase, and some of the 60 street-names with *Tudor* as their specific component are in large groups alluding to the history and culture of the period. Between Claybury Hospital and Fairlop Station there is a triangular residential estate bounded on the north by Tudor Crescent, with Tower Close, Culpeper Close, and Nonsuch Close nearby. The last name refers to the great house, or palace, begun by Henry VIII and granted by him to the Earl of Arundel. Also in the group are Shakespeare Square, Wolsey Gardens and Cardinal Drive. Between Boleyn Way and Anne Way, Montfort Gardens appears to be an intruder, but across Aragon Drive are Katherine Gardens and Cleeves Walk. Other historical intruders occurring in the complex are Hanover Gardens and Brunswick Gardens, but a final Tudor name comes at the southern point of the triangle, where Marlowe Close leads off Addison Road.

A small Tudor group occurs near Eastcote Station; Cardinal Road spirals into Seymour Gardens, and Cleves Way adjoins. Essex Close and Cranmer Close are part of the complex, and Aragon Drive and Boleyn Drive provide approach roads to it from Field End Road.

The names of monarchs are frequently used in the designation of streets, and some are referred to elsewhere. King Alfred Avenue S.E.6 is the axis of symmetrical roadscape which ingeniously reconciles a triangular outline with a hexagonal centre. At the north end of this avenue, Athelney Street recalls Alfred's base in the Somerset marshes. Elfreda Crescent doubtless alludes to the daughter of King Alfred; she married Baldwin, Count of Flanders. Two sons of the marriage, Arnulf and Adelolf, are commemorated in Arnulf Street and Adolf Street. Near the blunted apex of this triangle is Ghent Street, the presence of which seems to be anomalous. In fact, it is closely connected; the earliest recorded grant of an English estate is Elfreda's gift of Lewisham to the monastery of Blandinium, near Ghent.

Rufus Street N.1 and King John's Court E.C.2 are not far apart; these are among the earliest monarchs alluded to in London street-names after the Alfred references and apart from King Harold's Way, Bexleyheath. King Edward Street E.C.1 alludes to Edward VI, who used the possessions of the London Greyfriars to endow Christ's

Hospital School on the site. A number of other King Edward names refer to Edward VII. With the sole exception of Queen Alexandra Court S.W.19, allusions to the consort of Edward VII are merely Alexandra Road, Street, Avenue, etc. These are very numerous indeed, and a large proportion date from the marriage of the then Prince of Wales to the Danish princess.

Some allusions to queens are less transparent. Mecklenburgh Square W.C.1 alludes to Charlotte of Mecklenburg-Strelitz, wife of George III; Caroline of Brunswick, wife of George IV, is commemorated in Brunswick Square W.C.1. Queen Anne and Queen Victoria, however, dominate street nomenclature in London. Queen Square W.C.1 (despite the statue of Queen Charlotte in the middle) was named after Anne, as was Queen Anne's Gate S.W.1.

A number of London street-names allude to Leopold. There are at least two possibilities: the first was Leopold of Saxe-Coburg, who married Princess Charlotte, the daughter of George IV. He is referred to in Cobourg Street N.W.1 and Cobourg Road S.E.5. Leopold was Queen Victoria's favourite uncle, and she named her third son after him. It is this Prince Leopold who is alluded to in one of the streets lying between Queens Road and Albert Road E.17. This compact royal family group consists of Edinburgh Road (from Prince Alfred, Duke of Edinburgh), Helena Road (named after the third daughter), Lorne Road (alluding to the fourth daughter, who married the Marquess of Lorne), Connaught Road (from the title of the third son), Leopold Road, and Beatrice Road (named after the youngest daughter).

Communications and the world of learning

COMMUNICATIONS

An early method of rapidly conveying information was the lighting of signal fires on hill-tops. This means of communication, especially to provide warning of danger, or to notify a military victory, lasted long enough to be embodied in a few street-names. Beacon Hill N.7 is an instance, and there are other possible examples in Greater London. A more sophisticated system was introduced, entailing the operation of moving parts on a fixed framework. Telegraph Hill N.W.3 was the site of one of these stations.

Some street-name references to telegraphs, of course, are to the electric telegraph, which came into use in the middle of the nineteenth century. Telegraph Street E.C.2 was the location of the offices of some of the private companies responsible for the service, and subsequently of the G.P.O. telegraph station.

As chief post offices are normally in main streets, there are not many road-names referring to them. Post Office Approach E.7 and Postway Mews (Ilford) are therefore worthy of mention. Post Office Court E.C.3 was the site of the postal headquarters from the seventeenth century until 1829. Philatelists may recognise the name of the artist who designed an envelope associated with the introduction of Penny Postage in 1840: Mulready Street, between Salisbury Street and Ashbridge Street, commemorates the man whose name is linked with that recalled in Rowland Hill Street N.W.3 and Rowland Hill Avenue N.17.

The nineteenth-century postal official who invented the pillar-box (and died of laughter while reading Anstey's *Vice Versa*) is better remembered, perhaps, as a novelist: *Trollope Street* S.W.8, the only commemoration of Anthony Trollope in Greater London, has disappeared during the past few years.

References to printing in street-names include Printing House Square E.C.4; although this was the address of *The Times* until its removal to Grays Inn Road, the presence of the newspaper office was not the reason for the street-name. Before the establishment of the newspaper, the street had been the site of the King's Printing House, in which official papers of all kind were produced. A similar name, Printing House Lane, occurs in Hayes. Printer Street E.C.4 was so called because printing was the main occupation in the area, and so differed little (except in age) from other City street-names referring to trades.

Public libraries developed towards the end of the nineteenth century; like post offices, they were sited in or near principal streets, and few names alluding to them can be expected. There is, however, a Library Place E.1; near St George's Circus, Library Street S.E.1 is off Lancaster Street. The immediate vicinity of the library would seem the appropriate place for names alluding to authors, but this is not necessarily so. One public library in a street with a literary name is in Putney, in Disraeli Road S.W.15. Usually, of course, names like Corelli Road S.E.3, Zangwill Road S.E.3, Kipling Street S.E.1 or Kipling Terrace N.9 are likely to be at a considerable distance from the library from which their novels can be borrowed.

THE WORLD OF LEARNING

In a number of other categories are inevitably included street-names referring to men of genius in various fields, but it is interesting to find allusions to several kinds of learned institution as well. University Street W.C.1 is opposite the main entrance of University College in Gower Street, the first institution of higher learning to be established in London in modern times. (The college endowed by Sir Thomas Gresham in the sixteenth century is not forgotten; Gresham Street E.C.2 was named in his honour.) University College owed much to the efforts of Thomas Campbell (the poet), Lord Brougham (honoured in Brougham Road W.3), and Jeremy Bentham. Both the memory and the skeleton of the last-named are cherished at the College, and he is honoured in a group of names at Thamesmead. This complex includes a number of names associated with the University, and particularly the London School of Economics.

Bentham Road S.E.28 is off Carlyle Road and leads, via Titmuss Avenue, to Tawney Way, Saunders Way, and Hammond Way; the last four names refer to social scientists, and Booth Close which adjoins them, refers to Charles Booth, author of the monumental enquiry into poverty in London at the end of the nineteenth century. Octavia Way alludes to Octavia Hill, the foundress of the Charity Organization Society, and Owen Close to Robert Owen.

Not far from Gower Street is the British Museum, directly alluded to in Museum Street W.C.1. A collection of manuscripts in the Museum gave rise to the name Coptic Street, replacing the former designation of *Duke Street*. The nucleus of the Museum's collections was the great accumulation of books and objects formed by Sir Hans Sloane. This great physician became lord of the manor of Chelsea; after his death, the estate was developed and his name is found in Sloane Square and Street and in Hans Crescent, Place, and Street S.W.1 and Hans Road S.W.3.

Collections of books and manuscripts made by a number of prominent men were added to those of Sir Hans Sloane. Some of these men are alluded to in street-names by reason of their connexion with the estates, and not because of their learned interests. The Harleian Library was assembled by Robert and Edward Harley, first and second Earls of Oxford; the Lansdowne MSS were the property of the Marquess of Lansdowne. These noblemen are referred to in Harley Street W.1 and Lansdowne Terrace W.C.1. The ambassador to Constantinople through whose agency the Parthenon marbles were brought to England, the seventh Earl of Elgin, is recalled in Elgin Avenue W.9.

Other institutions and people associated with learned activities are also referred to in street-names. Sir Isaac Newton, for instance, is commemorated in Newton Avenue W.3, built on land formerly owned by the Royal Society; Newton Grove W.4 also commemorates Sir Isaac, this time in the period setting of Bedford Park, where there is also a Vanbrugh Road, celebrating Newton's contemporary, the playwright and architect, Sir John Vanbrugh.

Meridian Road S.E.7 is perhaps a few seconds of arc to the east of the zero line, but it clearly alludes to the work of the Royal Observatory; Flamsteed Road S.E.7 celebrates a great Astronomer Royal. Distinguished cartographers are commemorated in Mercator Road and Saxton Close S.E.13, alluding respectively to Gerhard Kramer (1512–94) and Christopher Saxton, whose great county maps of England were engraved in the 1570s. Kramer, known as Mercator, has of course a wider fame from having introduced his projection and made other cartographic innovations.

Observatory Gardens W.8 refers to the private observatory on the site of which this street is built. It belonged to Sir Henry South, who died in 1867. An astronomer of an earlier period is recalled in Aubert Road N.5, near the home of Alexander Aubert (1730–1804).

Antiquaries and historians are represented in the names of streets. Elias Ashmole (1617–92) founder of the museum in Oxford, lived in Lambeth and is commemorated in Ashmole Street S.W.8. William Stukeley, the eccentric antiquary who was rector of St George's, Bloomsbury, in the mid-eighteenth century, is commemorated in Stukeley Street W.C.2. Edward Gibbon (1737–94) is remembered in Gibbon Walk S.W.15. The author of the *Decline and Fall of the Roman Empire* was born, and spent his childhood in Putney. Gibbon Road in Kingston recalls the two years he spent at school there; they were not particularly happy ones, as he was, he tells us, 'reviled and buffeted for the sins of my Tory ancestors'. Gibbon Road W.3 remembers a different man, Simon Gibbon, who became master of the Goldsmiths' Company in 1629.

SCIENCE AND TECHNOLOGY

Reference is made elsewhere to Michael Faraday's public-spirited interest in education, in which he was associated with Birkbeck. He is also commemorated in street-names not only for this but also as one of the foremost physicists of the century. Curiously, his master Sir Humphrey Davy has not been honoured in this way. Faraday is celebrated in Faraday Road W.10, with Telford Road and Wheatstone Road. Telford was a civil engineer, and Wheatstone made important contributions in electrical theory and technology. *Rendle Street* and *Murchison Road*, formerly nearby, supplemented this commemoration of nineteenth-century scientists. Ronalds Road N.5 celebrates Sir Francis Ronalds, who played a considerable part in the development of the electric telegraph.

Telford is grouped with another civil engineer at Old Oak Common, where Telford Way adjoins Brunel Road W.3. The latter commemorates Isambard Kingdom Brunel, the engineer of the Great Western Railway, but inevitably his father, Sir Marc Isambard Brunel, is also remembered. In Southall, Telford Road and Faraday Road are grouped with Brunel Place, Darwin Drive, and Brindley Way. To these Edison Drive and Swan Road are added, bringing technology into the twentieth century, where Lovell Close, Whittle Close, Marconi Way, and Pannard Place belong, with Fleming Road, alluding to the discoverer of penicillin, and Baird Avenue nearby. A similar group near Welling Station offers a combined celebration of Victorian scientists. Darwin Road, Faraday Road, and Huxley Road enclose Tyndal Road and Maxwell Road; Cavendish Avenue looks back to research of an earlier period—that of Henry Cavendish, who died in 1810 and who is celebrated also in Cavendish Road S.W.12, near the site of his laboratory.

Politicians and generals

Victorian pride in national achievements was not limited to the arts of peace. Politics and statesmanship may perhaps be considered pacific, but war as a possibility and a form of argument must always be remembered in connexion with the prime ministers and other statesmen whose names and titles have made their own contribution to the street gazetteer of London. Gladstone and Palmerston references greatly outnumber those to Disraeli, already mentioned in his literary context.

Gladstone Avenue E.12 is in a complex, mixing literary figures with politicians. Sheridan Road alludes to an eighteenth-century figure from both worlds, and neighbouring roads honour Shelley, Ruskin, Swinburne, and Browning. Gladstone Avenue N.22, adjoining Darwin Road, is grouped with Russell Avenue, Morley Avenue, and Salisbury Road. Williams Grove and Ewart Grove, not far off, lead to Progress Way. Canning Crescent, near Woodside Park, alludes to an earlier politician. Two Victorian generals are celebrated in the area: Wolseley Road N.22 refers to the great Sir Garnet who, as Lord Wolseley, became Commander-in-Chief in 1895. General Buller is recalled in Buller Road and Redvers Road N.22, adjoining Wellesley Road, which probably alludes to Wellington.

From the eighteenth century, Wolfe and his enemy Montcalme are commemorated together in Wolfe Close and Montcalme Close in Yeading, as they are in Wolfe Crescent and Montcalme Road S.E.7. Adjoining the two closes in Yeading is Vancouver Road, which might more happily have been named after Quebec, the scene of their final engagement.

155

Off Palmerston Road E.17, Canning Road and Melbourne Road lead to Wellington Road, summarising the politics of the first half of the nineteenth century. Mansfield Road and Eldon Road E.17, not far away, allude respectively to an eighteenth-century Lord Chief Justice and a nineteenth-century Lord Chancellor. Attlee Terrace here brings the politics well into the twentieth century.

Wolseley Road in Harrow adjoins Wellington, Gordon, and Havelock Roads. This military group balances a political one nearer to Harrow and Wealdstone Station: Canning Road, Peel Road, and Palmerston Road. Havelock, Outram, and Nicholson, who owe much of their fame to the Indian Mutiny, are all represented in street-names. Outram and Havelock Roads near Addiscombe Station are connected by Mulberry Lane. Elgin Road and Canning Road, nearby, allude to Governors-General of India, the latter referring to the holder of the office at the time of the Mutiny. Nicholson Road meets Lower Addiscombe Road opposite its junction with Outram Road.

Of the generals in the Crimean War only Raglan stood high enough in public esteem to be included in groups with other military heroes. In Bickley, Raglan Road is associated with Havelock Road, Marlborough Road, Wellington Road, and Nelson Road; a group in Belvedere consists of Napier Road, Wellington Road, Nelson Road, and Raglan Road. Cardigan Road seems to occur only as an isolated name. The French commander, rather surprisingly, is awarded recognition, in Canrobert St E.2. Woronzow Road N.W.8 does not refer to the Crimea but to Count Simon Woronzow, ambassador to London earlier in the century. He remained in London when his term of office expired.

TWENTIETH-CENTURY NAMES

Just south of Central Park in Dagenham, prominent Labour Party politicians are celebrated in Hardie Road, Macdonald Avenue, and Greenwood Avenue. Another of these early Socialists is recalled in John Burns Drive, near Upney Station, in a group comprising Bevan Avenue, Lansbury Avenue, Keir Hardie Way, Margaret Bondfield Avenue, Ben Tillett Close, and Stafford Close; the last indicates a strange reluctance to use *Cripps* in a street-name. A similar reluctance is shown in Yeading, where he is not mentioned at all, and Sidney and Beatrice Webb have to share a single road: Bondfield Avenue, Keir Hardie Way, Henderson Road, Webbs Road, Bevin Road, Morrison Road, and Owen Road present a selective roll-call of nineteenth- and twentieth-century names.

Snowden Street E.1 was, until 1932, Market Street. The new name commemorates Philip Snowden, created Viscount in 1931. Post-War

Labour politicians are included in the groups already mentioned, and Clement Attlee is also honoured in Attlee Close in Uxbridge as well as in the company of Mansfield and Eldon in Walthamstow. Gaitskell's memory is not so enshrined; Gaitskell Road in Greenwich dates from 1879 and cannot therefore allude to Hugh Gaitskell.

That fairly numerous collections of Labour names should occur but comparable groups of Conservative ones not be found is due partly to the time when these estates were built and partly to the prevailing political allegiance in the local government of the areas concerned. Churchill, naturally, receives some recognition. Churchill Gardens Road S.W.1 is one of a dozen or so street-names in Greater London honouring the wartime Prime Minister. These are supplemented by a few *Winston* names, e.g. Winston Avenue N.W.9. But the Churchill celebrated in Churchill Gardens W.3, on the Great Western Railway housing estate at West Acton, was the first Viscount Churchill, chairman of the company from 1908.

Military leaders of both World Wars are recalled. A compact group from the 1939–45 war occurs off Beckton Road, East Ham: Eisenhower Drive, Tedder Gardens, Mallory Gardens, Maitland Gardens, Bertram Gardens, and Paget Gardens; General Dwight Eisenhower, Freeman of the City though he was, is commemorated only here. Portal Close, Trenchard Avenue, and Tedder Close at Ruislip recall three great names in R.A.F. history. In Sidcup, three army leaders are celebrated in Alexander Close, Wavell Drive and Montgomery Close; in Edgware, Montgomery Road adjoins Churchill Road.

The First World War generals are recalled in small groups such as Haig Road and Allenby Road at Biggin Hill. Kitchener's name was already enshrined in a number of street designations after the Boer War, and probably the relative scarcity of military names of the 1914–18 war is due to the small amount of building development which took place in the years immediately afterwards. A naval leader is paired with a nursing heroine in Tottenham: Jellicoe Road merges with Cavell Road to join Great Cambridge Road just north of Roundway N.17. Beatty Road in Stanmore joins Nelson Road, into which Haig Road runs, a few yards away.

The increasing debt of mankind to impersonal things in both war and peace is reflected in numerous street-names. A military organization is recalled in Shaef Way in Teddington. Future generations may need to be told that this curious word is an acronym: SHAEF was the normal way in which Eisenhower's headquarters were referred to, but 'Supreme Headquarters Allied Expeditionary Force' was the full title.

Credit for success in the air is attributed, in street-names, more to types of aircraft than to heroic aeronauts. It is true that individual valour is sometimes recognised, as in Rainham, where Finucane Gardens, Bader Way, and Malan Square adjoin Eagle Close, Dove Walk, Swallow Walk, Heron Flight Avenue, and Harrier Close. Just over the Hornchurch border, Hilary Close is surrounded by names referring to aircraft types (as in Northolt) and to R.A.F. stations, e.g., Tangmere Crescent.

Numerical and alphabetical names

The movement, or drift, towards impersonality has sometimes affected the naming process itself. Following some foreign examples, and perhaps applying a too ruthless administrative logic, authorities have occasionally used a numerical sequence for the designation of roads.

There are more than a dozen First Avenues, as well as a First Road S.E.18; the last name occurs in a military context, in the Royal Artillery Barracks at Woolwich, where there are also Second and Third Roads. First Way near Wembley Stadium, accompanies Second, Third, and Fourth Ways. Ascending the numerical series, the patient searcher will find only three or four Fifth Avenues; in Romford Road E.12 a sequence ends at Eighth Avenue, but a series in Hayes gets as far as Ninth Avenue.

A numerical scheme in Mitcham originally combined uniformity with variety in an incredibly mechanical way. The first group comprised *First Road* to *Fourth Road*; *Second Road* continued across its artery (Huntingdon Road) as Durham Drive, out of which opened six cul-de-sac developments, named *Fifth Close* to *Tenth Close*, and three on the opposite side, named *Eleventh Close* to *Thirteenth Close*. Durham Drive terminates at South Lodge Avenue, on the opposite side of which are Carisbrooke Road, Tavistock Crescent (which is perfectly straight), and Lancaster Avenue. More numbered roads opened off Lancaster Avenue: *Fourteenth Place* to *Seventeenth Place*. Eighteenth Road connects Yorkshire Road with Tavistock Crescent; Nineteenth Road connects Yorkshire Road with Carisbrooke Road, crossing Tavistock Crescent *en route*.

The past tense used in some of the description of the Mitcham streets suggests that there has been a change in the mode of designating them; most of the names have indeed been changed, but Eighteenth Road and Nineteenth Road survive as reminders of an unlovely arrangement. The other numerals have been replaced by conventional names derived from those of Welsh and English counties.

Numerical sequences are not suitable for most urban layouts in this country; unless the streets are arranged in a grid, the sequence will not be clear, and if Fourth Avenue, for instance, is next to Ninth Avenue and opposite Twelfth Avenue, the stranger visiting the area will be bewildered. Moreover, there is considerably greater scope for irremediable errors in the post. If a correspondent forgetfully writes Fourth Avenue instead of Fourteenth Avenue, the chances of the letter being delivered are obviously not so good as if a slight mistake is made in a name, e.g., writing *Elm Road* instead of *Elm Avenue*.

But numerical systems are not the only means of avoiding names of the ordinary kind. Letters of the alphabet have been used on occasion. The developers of Kensal New Town, the Artizans', Labourers' and General Dwellings Company, originally designated some of the streets by the letters of the alphabet, from A to O. The arteries of the estate were called First Avenue, etc as far as Sixth Avenue.

After a few years, however, the lettered streets were given names, in an alphabetical sequence from Alperton to Oliphant. The significance of some of these names has been lost sight of, but some certainly refer to officials of the company. Droop Street, for instance, refers to one of the directors. Galton Street and Huxley Street are discussed elsewhere. Three streets out of sequence were called Herries Street (from the name of an Improvement Commissioner), Mozart Street, and Beethoven Street. Beginning at Alperton Street (named after the location of the company's brick yard) the series is as follows: Barfett Street, Caird Street, Droop Street, Enbrook Street, Farrant Street, Galton Street, Huxley Street, Ilbert Street, Kilravock Street, Lothrop Street, Marne Street, Nutbourne Street, and Oliphant Street.

A more intelligible alphabetical sequence occurs near Tooting Station. Transferred place-names are used here, from Ascot Road to Jersey Road; the other towns, etc whose names are used are Boscombe, Cromer, Deal, Eastbourne, Frinton, Gunton, Hailsham, and Ipswich. There is an alphabetic bias in this area; some road names are in alliterating pairs: Rural Way and Rustic Avenue S.W.16 occur together, and so do Mantilla Road S.W.17 and Moring Road, and Coteford Street and Cowick Road. There is one group of three: Pendle Road, Pretoria Road, and Penwortham Road S.W.16.

Off Sherwood Park Road, Mitcham, there is an alphabetical sequence. Almond Way begins the series, followed by Beech Grove, Chestnut Grove, Dahlia Gardens, Elm Gardens, and Fern Avenue. The last-named continues across Sherwood Park Road as Greenwood Avenue, and the sequence continues with Holly Way and Ivy Gardens. *Sherwood* is traceable to Sherwood Lodge, named on the Tithe Apportionment of 1840 and perhaps derived from *scīr-wudu*, 'boundary wood'. It is near the Mitcham-Croydon boundary. Other street-names are suggested by the Nottinghamshire Sherwood: Robin Hood Lane and Robin Hood Close.

Memorials to philanthropy

Besides celebrating the possessions of the wealthy, the power of statesmen, and the belligerence of generals, street-names also act as monuments to selfless individuals who have done something (sometimes, indeed, very much) to relieve suffering among their fellow human beings. Coram Street W.C.1 recalls the founder of an orphanage for 'exposed and deserted young children', who bought some fields in Bloomsbury to support his establishment. Development of this land began in the last decade of the eighteenth century, when the streets that were built were named in honour of members of the royal family and of the cabinet. In the second stage of the development, the names used were those of officers of the charity. Bernard Street W.C.1 commemorates Sir Thomas Bernard, vice-president of the foundation. Other governors are named in Marchmont Street, Heathcote Street, and Hunter Street. The last honours the great surgeon, Dr John Hunter (1728–93). Kenton Street W.C.1 remembers a man who bequeathed a fortune to various charities (including the Foundling Hospital); he had exploited his own invention of a method of bottling ale so that it could be exported to the tropics but remain sealed.

Jonas Hanway, the first gentleman to carry an umbrella in London, was a governor of the Foundling Hospital and a tireless worker on its behalf; he is remembered in Hanway Street W.1, built on the site of family property off Oxford Street. Howard Road N.16 commemorates John Howard (1726–90), who lived here for a time. Howard was the prison-reformer who was instrumental in mitigating some of the horrors of eighteenth-century gaols.

Nineteenth-century philanthropy receives due recognition in street-names. In Acton, Brougham Road is grouped with Birkbeck Avenue and Faraday Road W.3, bringing together the names of three men closely associated in the educational work of developing Mechanics' Institutes, the basis of present-day technical education and of Birkbeck College in the University of London. A fourth man, Francis Ravenscroft, is honoured in Ravenscroft Road W.4, near Chiswick Park Station. Birkbeck Road (etc) occurs in several parts of London; these streets were originally developed with the aid of the Birkbeck Bank and Building Society, promoted by Ravenscroft, who gave it the name because of his admiration of George Birkbeck.

Birkbeck and Faraday Roads occur together in South Wimbledon;

Ravenscroft Road runs parallel to Birkbeck Road near the Crystal Palace Cemetery, to visit which it is possible to take a train to Birkbeck Station. At Chase Side, Enfield, Birkbeck Road adjoins Morley Hill, alluding to yet another Victorian educationist. Not far from Ravenscroft Street E.2 is Baroness Road, which, with Burdett Road and Coutts Road E.3, preserves the memory of the valiant Baroness Burdett-Coutts, philanthropist, reformer, and ally of Charles Dickens. Her Christian names are found in Angela and Georgina Gardens E.2.

Games and recreation

Outdoor sports are alluded to in street-names, sometimes in general terms such as Stadium Road S.E.18, Stadium Way, Wembley, or Playgreen Way S.E.6. More specific names include Football Lane, Harrow (leading to Harrow School Playing Fields), Cricketfield Road, West Drayton, Cricket Ground Road, Chislehurst, and Golf Course Drive, Kingston.

Pall Mall S.W.1 is a less obvious example, to be associated with The Mall S.W.1 and (by imitation of the name, but not necessarily of the actual sporting use) of *Mall* used as a street-name elsewhere. These streets preserve the name of the sport pursued in the open space earlier known as *Pall Mall Walk* (1650). It was originally *Spittelstrete* 1222, referring to the Hospital of St James (now St James's Palace). The game of *paille maille* or *pelmel* was first played here in the reign of Charles I.

More specific, even detailed in their reference, are the street-names of the East Acton Estate. This was a local-authority housing project; what was formerly a golf-course became a residential estate, and the subtlety of the nomenclature has achieved an uncanny rightness that makes it, surely, unique. There seems nothing forced or affected in street-names such as The Green (which occurs twenty or so times in Greater London), The Approach (of which there are three others), or Long Drive, and yet when they are seen to be golfing terms their aptness to the history of the area is perceived with pleasure.

Terms relating to the course itself are found in The Approach, The Bye, The Fairway, The Green, and Long Drive; terms referring to play occur in Brassie Avenue, Mashie Road, and The Tee. Transferred place-names alluding to famous courses are used in Carlisle Avenue, Hoylake Road, Kingsdown Avenue, Muirfield, Sunningdale Avenue, and St Andrews Road. Golf champions have provided names for Braid Avenue and Duncan Grove. After the Second World War, Perry Avenue and Taylors Green W.3 were added.

161

Golf Road W.5 (and at Bromley, Ilford, Kenley, and Sutton) and Golf Close, Stanmore, also refer to this game. Bowling Green Close S.W.15 is clear enough in its reference, but some names alluding to the game of bowls are quite old. Bowling Green Lane E.C.1 once had medieval greens, and others in Greater London may be equally old.

Indoor recreations are alluded to in Concert Hall Approach S.E.1 and in Theatre Street S.W.11, adjoining the old Shakespeare Theatre in Lavender Hill, and matching Town Hall Road S.W.11, self-explanatory and only a few yards away. Curtain Road E.C.2 recalls the theatre built in the seventies or early eighties of the sixteenth century. Appropriate though the name may appear to be for a playhouse, it in fact antedates the theatre; the field on which the building was placed was called *Curtain Close* as early as 1544. A more recent theatre name is used in Scala Street W.1, adjoining the site of a building originally used as a concert hall, but used for drama for many years before it was demolished in 1970.

The history of the Old Vic Theatre is summarised in Cons Street S.E.1 and Baylis Road S.E.1; these allude respectively to the Victorian lady who provided a place of respectable entertainment in an area where before there had been no such establishment, and her niece who transformed the Royal Victoria Hall into a theatre of the first rank. Associated with the Old Vic is the Sadler's Wells Theatre in Rosebery Avenue, a thoroughfare built by the London County Council during the chairmanship of the fifth Lord Rosebery. Rosoman Street E.C.1 commemorates an eighteenth-century proprietor of Sadler's Wells.

Whether in the form *Bioscope*, *Biograph*, *Kinema*, or *Cinema*, this mode of entertainment has had little effect on street-names. It may be a power which has changed a way of life, or warped a civilisation, yet its luminaries have not achieved the kind of immortality that a practitioner on the ordinary stage could attain: Betterton, performing in the seventeenth century in the Cockpit Theatre, has a name which is still heard by twentieth century Englishmen when a visitor enquires the way to Betterton Street W.C.2. The only name directly referring to the movies is Cinema Parade W.5. Cinematograph actors and actresses are acknowledged only in the company of those of the stage, as in Northolt: Arliss Way, Bancroft Court, Lynne Way, Compton Crescent, Maurier Close, Lauder Close, Laing Dean, Perry Garth, Irving Avenue, Hawtry Avenue, Thorndike Avenue, Godfrey Avenue, Langtry Road, and Laughton Road. Irving Street W.C.2 is embellished with a statue of the great Sir Henry; this was a renaming, in 1939, of one of half a dozen Green Streets, and served to mark (rather belatedly) the centenary of his birth. Kemble Street honours a whole family of eighteenth-century actors whose chief successes were in the local theatre of Drury Lane, where an earlier ornament was Nell Gwynne, recalled in Gwynne Place W.C.1.

An actor of a much earlier generation—indeed, an almost exact contemporary of Shakespeare—is recalled in Alleyn Crescent, Alleyn Park, and Alleyn Road S.E.21. Edward Alleyn was the principal actor in the Admiral's Men; he made a fortune which enabled him to found and endow Dulwich College, near which these roads are to be found. Not far away, Burbage Road S.E.21 honours another of Shakespeare's acting associates. In East Dulwich, Henslowe Road S.E.22 recalls yet another man of great fame in theatrical history; Philip Henslowe, who became Alleyn's father-in-law, left an account book (usually referred to as his *Diary*) which contains much detailed information about the theatres and companies of players of that time.

David Garrick (1717–79) is commemorated in Garrick Street W.C.2, not far from Drury Lane Theatre, which he managed from 1747. Sarah Siddons (née Kemble) receives some recognition in several road names, for instance in Siddons Road S.E.23, in a group which also includes Kemble Road. Cibber Road, which adjoins Kemble Road, alludes to Colley Cibber (1671–1757), actor, dramatist, and laureate—generally regarded, indeed, as one of the worst poets to hold that office. Vestris Road, in the same group, refers to Eliza Vestris, the early nineteenth-century actress and joint manager (with her husband, Charles James Matthews) of Covent Garden Theatre. Edmund Kean's career was mostly in Drury Lane Theatre, however, and it is fitting that he should be honoured by the naming of a street nearby, Kean Street W.C.2, after him and his son Charles (1811–68).

Apart from Handel's recitals on the organ of the Foundling Hospital, there is little reference to the performance of music in street-names. Cramer Street W.1 is named after Wilhelm Cramer, a German violinist who died in London in 1799. Sporadic musical allusions occur in Lewisham names. Melba Way S.E.13, a small turning off Lewisham Road, commemorates Helen Porter Armstrong (née Mitchell), whose professional name was an adaptation of that of her native Melbourne, and as Nellie Melba was highly regarded throughout a long singing career. Not far away, Lind Street S.E.8 recalls Jenny Lind (1820–87), the 'Swedish nightingale', who was extremely popular in Victorian England.

Ruddigore Road S.E.14 seems to be the only name alluding to the Savoy operas; name-givers have ignored the more euphonious *Iolanthe*, *Pinafore*, *Yeomen*, or *Gondoliers*, and even the majestic *Mikado*. British music, in fact, does not receive much attention among street-names. Balfe Street N.1 honours the Irish-born composer of *The Bohemian Girl*, Michael William Balfe (1808–70), but apart from a possible reference in one of the Elgar Roads, composers were required to be European to be honoured in this way. Some of these are referred to elsewhere, but the titles of some musical works may be noted which are used as street-names.

Zampa Road S.E.16 alludes to the opera by Hérold (1791–1833); the overture continues to be a familiar item of the repertoire of brass bands, like Beethoven's overture to Goethe's play, referred to in Egmont Avenue and Road (Surbiton) and Egmont Street S.E.14. Messaline Avenue W.3 refers to an opera, performed in 1899, by Isadore de Lara (1858–1935), brother of James de Lara Cohen; Cohen, who had acquired Friars Place from Morris Emanuel, began to develop this street in the year of his brother's opera's production in Monte Carlo and Covent Garden. Thirteen years earlier, Wagner's last music drama had been produced; Parsifal Road N.W.6 dates from that year.

Some curiosities

It might be thought that most names have something of the curious about them; to the extent that caprice seems to enter into the application of street-names, that is true enough. But a serious interest in, and study of, place-nomenclature obviously may begin, but hardly end with an admiration of the quaint and strange. Once an explanation is offered, many names cease to be regarded as curious, but there are a few street-names which are sufficiently unusual in their form to be placed on special record.

The first of these is *Of Alley*, now York Place W.C.2, but often referred to and frequently asked about. This is on land formerly occupied by the first Duke of Buckingham, and sold by his almost equally dissolute son. The streets that were built utilised in their names every word of the name and title, George Villiers, Duke of Buckingham. Subsequent renaming incorporated *Duke Street* into John Adam Street, and *Of Alley* received a rather superfluous new label. Other streets, however, retain their old names, and George Court, Villiers Street, and Buckingham Street survive.

The only entry under the twenty-fourth letter of the alphabet in the old L.C.C. *Names of Streets and Places* was XX Place E.1. It derives its name from a sign depicting a barrel on which are inscribed XX followed by ISJS (perhaps the initials of the master and mistress of the house) and the date 1823. There can be little doubt that this was an ale-house sign; the earliest Dictionary quotation, from Hone's *Every-Day Book*, is dated 1827: '. . . best London porter and double XX', the symbol being interpreted as 'ale of medium strength or quality'.

There is more than one curiosity in Woolwich. There is, for instance, John Nash's Rotunda—a polygonal brick shell covered by a concave copper roof—housing a military museum (hence Rotunda Close and Repository Road S.E.18). But, as a name, it is surely Ha Ha Road which arouses most interest. This thoroughfare traverses Woolwich Common and is derived from the landscaper's term for a sunken fence or hedge; the term is supposed to represent the exclamation of surprise of visitors on viewing the apparently vast parklands of their host, not being aware of his sunken garden wall only a few feet away.

Renaming sometimes produces curious results. In an attempt to reduce the number of names using the first letter of the Greek alphabet, *Alpha Place* in Islington became Omega Place. This has now gone, but there is still an Omega Street S.E.14. Oscar Wilde was not favoured as a source of street-names, but when *Gray Street* E.1 was renamed in 1937, it became Dorian Street. The explosively named *Cordite Street* S.E.2 became Myrtledene Road in 1929, and there was a hint of change of taste in painting when *Gainsborough Road* became Orpen Road N.16. Juno Way in Deptford was formerly *Mazawattee Lane*, and Henslowe Passage in Southwark was formerly *Noah's Ark Alley*.

A tiny street in Limehouse, *Robert Street*, was renamed Mandarin Street E.14, so toning in with local colour provided by such other names as Ming Street, Amoy Place, Canton Street, Pekin Street, Nankin Street, and the generalising Oriental Street. A change in allegiance is implied in the change from *Percy Road* to Kingshold Road E.9. *Recovery Street*, adjoining what is now St George's Hospital, was perhaps considered presumptuous, and was therefore discontinued in favour of Effort Street S.W.17.

A selection of names such as this necessarily omits many of interest to some of its readers; but incomplete it must necessarily be, both because of the fragmentary information available and because the naming of streets, in Greater London as elsewhere, is a continuing process. All that can be hoped is that a way of looking at the streets and their names may have been adumbrated, together with some guidance on the different levels of interpretation that may obtain. Detailed local studies are urgently needed; those engaging in them need never fear that they will lack satisfaction and reward.

Glossary of place-name elements

This list includes elements occurring in the place-names discussed in Part 1, together with a selection of those found in some of the older street-names mentioned in Part 2. Names in parentheses are head-words in the Dictionary section under which an older name is discussed, containing the element concerned. Words listed are Old English unless otherwise marked.

āc 'oak tree'   Acton, Knockholt, Little Roke, Noke Hill
æcer 'arable strip'   Long Acre
æsc 'ash tree'   Nash
æwell 'spring, source'   Carshalton
alor 'alder'   Aldersbrook
assis OF 'seat, residence'   Belsize Park
āst 'oast, kiln'   Limehouse
atten ME 'at the' (*masc.*)   Nash, Knockholt, Noke Hill
atter ME 'at the' (*fem.*)   Little Roke
bærnet 'burnt place'   Barnet
bailey ME 'outer court of a castle'   Old Bailey
***balg, *bealg** 'rounded (hill)'   Balham
bān 'bone'   Bunhill Fields
barbican ME 'tower erected over city gate'   Barbican
bearu 'wood, grove'   Barrow Hill
beau, bel OF 'fine, beautiful'   Belsize Park, Beaulieu, Beulah Hill
beofor 'beaver'   Beverley Brook
beonet 'bent-grass'   Bentley
beorg 'hill, mound'   Berrylands, Roxborough
bere-ærn 'barn'   Barnes, West Barnes
bere-tūn 'outlying corn farm, grange'   Norbiton, Surbiton
bere-wīc 'outlying lands of a manor'   Berwick
bigging ME 'building'   Biggin Hill
biscop 'bishop'   Bishopswood
blæc 'black, dark'   Blackfen, Blackheath, Blackwall

166

bōt 'remedy, healing' Botwell

botm 'valley bottom' Locksbottom, Pratt's Bottom, Smitham Bottom

boga 'bow, arch' Bow, Bow Lane

brād 'broad, wide' *Battlebridge*, Broad Street

bræmbel 'bramble, blackberry bush' Bromley

brōc 'stream, brook' Brook Green, Kidbrook, Mayes Brook, Mutton Brook, (Pinn), Snaresbrook, Stamford Brook, Sudbrook Park, Walbrook

brōm 'broom; thorny bush' Brompton, Broomfield Park

brycg 'bridge' Knightsbridge, London Bridge, Phipps Bridge, Priest's Bridge, Queen's Bridge, Redbridge, Uxbridge

būr 'cottage, dwelling' Havering-atte-Bower

burh 'fortified place, manor-house, manor' Barnesbury, Bloomsbury, Borough, Brondesbury, *Canbury*, Canonbury, *Ebury*, Finsbury, Gunnersbury, Highbury, Kingsbury, Newbury Park, Norbury, Ravensbury, Scadbury Park, Sudbury

burna 'stream, brook' (Crane), Holborn, Kilburn, Ravensbourne, St Marylebone, Tyburn, (Wandle), Westbourne Green

byden 'vessel, tub, butt' East Bedfont

*byxe 'box tree' Bexley

cærse 'water-cress' Carshalton

camp 'field, enclosed land' Addiscombe

*candelwyrhta 'candle-maker' Cannon Street

canoun ME 'member of religious order, member of cathedral chapter' *Canbury*, Canonbury, Cannons Hill Park, Canons Park

catt 'cat' Catford

cealc 'chalk, lime, limestone' Chelsea

ceald 'cold' Chadwell Heath, Chalk Farm, Great Coldharbour

cealf 'calf' Chafford Heath

*cēd B 'wood' Penge

*ceg 'stump' Cheam

ceorl 'freeman, peasant, churl' Charlton

ceosol, cisel 'gravel' Chislehurst, Chiswell Street

chapel ME 'chapel' Chapel End, Whitechapel

charteus OF 'Carthusian monastery' Charterhouse

chingel ME 'shingle, pebbles' Chingford

cierring 'turn, bend' Charing Cross

*ciese 'cheese' Chiswick

cirice 'church' Church End, Hornchurch, Whitchurch

clǣg 'clay' Claybury Farm, Clayhall

clerc 'scholar, secretary, cleric' Clerkenwell

167

clif 'steep bank, cliff' Ratcliff
*clop 'lump, hillock' Clapham, Clapton
cniht 'youth, soldier, retainer' Knighton Wood, Knightsbridge
cnoll 'hillock' (Muswell Hill)
cocc 'chief, leader' Cockfosters
col 'charcoal' Colfall Wood
colier ME 'charcoal burner' Collier Row, Colliers Wood
*colün PrW 'water' Colne
contesse ME 'countess' Counters Creek
cot 'cottage, shelter' Eastcote, Woodcote
court ME 'large house, manor' Earls Court, Hampton Court, Tottenham Court
couvent ME 'religious house' Covent Garden
cracche ME 'hurdle, framework' Scratchwood, (Temple Mills)
cran 'crane (poss. also heron)' Cranford
crāwe 'crow' Cranham
*crei OW 'pure, fresh' Cray
creke ME 'inlet, streamlet' Creekmouth
crōh 'saffron' Croydon
cros ME 'cross, wayside crucifix' Charing Cross, Whipp's Cross
crouche ME 'cross, wayside crucifix' Crouch End
cū 'cow' Kilburn
cwēn 'queen' Queen's Bridge
cyning 'king' Kingsbury, *Kingsland*, Kingston
cȳta 'kite' Kidbrook
Dacus MedL 'Dane' (St Clement Danes), (Strand)
dæl 'valley' Marble Hill
dāl 'share, portion' Dawley
Danir ON 'Danes' St Clement Danes
Danskr ON 'Danish' (Strand)
denu 'valley' Croydon, *Dunsford*, Smitham Botton
deop 'deep (valley)' Colindale
dīc 'ditch, trench' Grims Ditch, ?*Parr's Ditch*
dile 'dill' Dulwich
dok ME 'wharf, dock' St Katherine Docks
dræg 'portage, slipway, drag' Drayton Green, West Drayton
dūn 'hill' Brisdown, Cannon Hill Common, Chessington, Coulsdon, *Down*, Downe, Hendon, Horseleydown, Horsenden Hill, Islington, Malden, Morden, Neasden, North Ockendon, Purley Downs, Riddles Down, Rowdown Wood, Selsdon, *Tollington*, Waddington, Waddon, Willesden, Wimbledon
eald 'old' Old Ford, Old Oak Common, Old Street
ēar 'gravel' Erith

ēast 'east, eastern' East Barnet, East Bedfort, Eastcote, East Ham, East Sheen

edisc 'enclosed pasture, park' Sundridge Park

ēg 'island, dry ground amid marshes' Battersea, Bermondsey, *Ebury*, Hackney, Rammey Marsh, *Thorney*, Upney

elm 'elm tree' Barn Elms, Elmstead, Nine Elms

ende 'edge of estate, district' Chapel End, Crouch End, Elmers End, Hill End, Kings End, Mile End, North End, Ponders End, Sands End, Southend, West End, Wood End, (Woodside Park)

eowestre 'sheep-fold' Osterley

faire ME 'a fair' Mayfair

*(ge)feall 'felling of trees, forest clearing' Coldfall Wood

fearn 'fern, bracken' Farleigh, Farnborough

feld 'open country; cultivated land' Enfield, Mansfield Park, Northfields, Southfields, Spitalfields, Suffield Hatch

felte 'mullein' Feltham

fenn 'marsh, fen' Blackfen

feorðung 'fourth part, quarter' Allfarthing Lane, Fairdeans

finc 'finch' Finchley

ford 'river-crossing' *Battle Bridge*, Brentford, Catford, Cranford, Crayford, Greenford, Ilford, Longford, Loxford Park, Old Ford, Romford, Stamford Bridge, Stamford Brook, Stamford Hill, Stratford, Twyford, Woodford

for o 'in front' Fortune Green

frēo 'free' Freelands Wood

frere 'member of monastic or military order; friar' Blackfriars, Crutched Friars, Friern Barnet, Fryant Farm, Whitefriars Street

fūl 'foul, filthy' Fulwell

funta 'spring' East Bedfont

(ge)fyrhð 'woodland, wooded countryside' Frith Manor, (Oak Hill Park), Thrift Wood

fyrs 'gorse, furze' Motspur Park

gara 'triangular piece of land' Kensington Gore, Pyrgo Park

gardin ME 'garden' Covent Garden

garite OF 'watch-tower' *Garratt*

geat 'gap in a wall or fence; gate' Aldgate, Billingsgate, Highgate, Moorgate, Oxgate, Southgate

gōs Gooshays

grāf 'copse, grove' Grove Park, Pratt's Grove

grange ME 'outlying farm or estate' Woodgrange

grēat 'bulky, massive, thick' Gutteridge Wood

grēne (1) 'abounding in plants' Greenford

grēne (2) 'grassy spot, village green' Green Street, Parson's

Green, Rush Green, Slade Green, Stroud Green, Walham Green, Wood Green, Wyke Green

gydig 'foolish, unsteady' Gidea Park

haca 'hook, curved place' Hackbridge, Hacton

hæcc 'half-age, grating, hatch' Colney Hatch, Hatch End, Hoppershatch Shaw, Suffield Hatch

(ge)hæg 'enclosure' Bush Hill Park, Bushy Park, Gooshays, Haringey

hǣð 'tract of waste land, heath' Blackheath, Cambridge Heath, Chadwell Heath, Chafford Heath, Hadley Wood, Hatton, Heath Row, Lessness Heath, Pield Heath, Squirrels Heath, Thornton Heath

halh, healh 'nook of land' Bethnal Green, The Hale, Hale End, Northolt, Padnall Corner, Southall, Tottenham Hale, *Tottenham Court*

halke ME 'corner of parish' Hawk Wood

hall 'large residence, manor house' Clayhall, Haling Park, Vauxhall, Woodhall

hām 'village, manor, homestead' Balham, Cheam, Clapham, Cranham, Crohamhurst, Cudham, Eltham, Hatcham, Higham Hill, Ickenham, Lewisham, Mitcham, Mottingham, Peckham, Rainham, Sydenham

hamm 'pasture, riverside meadow, land within a river-bend' Colham Green, East Ham, Fulham, Ham, Hampton, Petersham, ?Turnham Green, Twickenham, West Ham

hamor 'hammer' Hammersmith

hām-stede 'homestead' Hampstead

hana 'bird, cock' Hanwell

hangra 'wooded slope' Hanger Hill, Pitshanger Park

hēah 'high' Haydon Hall, Hendon, Highbury, Highgate, Higham Hill, Highwood Hill

healf 'half' Allfarthing Lane

hearg 'heathen shrine or temple' Harrow

hecg 'hedge' (Temple Mills)

held 'slope, declivity' Shooters Hill

here 'army' Harefield, Hare Street

hīd 'sufficient land for the support of one free family and its dependants, hide of land' The Hyde, Hyde Park, North Hyde

higna 'household, religious community' Hainault

hlāw 'mount, hill' Hounslow

hlinc 'ridge, bank' Haling Park

hlȳde 'loud' (Wandle)

hlȳpe 'leap, place that can be jumped across' ?Ruislip

hōc 'hook, bend in a river, spit of land in river-bend' Hook
hōh 'spur of land' Cranham, Hew
holh 'valley, depression, hollow' Holborn, Holloway, Holwood Park, Hooley
holt 'thicket, wood' Hainault, Kensal Green, Knockholt, Wormwood Scrubs
horn 'horn' Hornchurch
hors 'horse' *Horseleydown*
hræfn 'raven' Ravensbourne
hrīs 'brushwood' Ricebridge
hrōc rook' Ruxley
hrycg 'long, narrow hill, ridge' Totteridge
hrȳðer 'ox, cattle' Rotherhithe
*humyr OW 'good stream' Northumberland Heath
hwǣte 'wheat' Waddington
hwet-stān 'whetstone' Whetstone
hwīt 'white' Whitchurch, Whitechapel, Whitehall, Whitton
hyll 'elevated piece of ground, hill' Harrow-on-the-Hill, Herne Hill, Higham Hill, Highwood Hill, Holders Hill, Marble Hill, Mill Hill, Muswell Hill, Notting Hill, Northwood Hills
hyrst 'copse, hillock, wooded eminence' Bayhurst Wood, Crohamhurst, Selhurst
hȳð 'landing-place, haven, port' Chelsea, Erith, Lambeth, Putney, Rotherhithe, Stepney
iggoð 'island' Chiswick Eyot, (Eel Pie Island)
-ingas 'people, folk, followers' Ealing, *Ermine Street*, Havering, Mottingham, Rainham, ?Seven Kings, Tooting, Yeading
-ingtūn 'estate associated with . . .' Addington, Alperton, Beddington, Harlington, Kennington, Kensington, Kenton, Oakington, Orpington, Paddington, Wennington
inn 'dwelling, lodging' Grays Inn, Lincolns Inn, Staple Inn
Jewerie ME 'place where Jews were segregated' Old Jewry
kai ME 'wharf, landing-place, quay' Kew
lacu 'stream' Mortlake
lǣs 'pasture, meadow' Lessness
lamb 'lamb' Lambeth, Lampton
land 'tract of land, arable land' *Kingsland*, Norland Road, Northumberland Heath, Woodlands
lang 'long' *Langthorn*, Longford
laning 'lane' Chancery Lane (etc)
lēah 'wood, grove, clearing in a wood' Bentley, Bexley, Bickley, Cowley, Finchley, Hadley Wood, Hooley, Kenley, Lee, Riddles Down, Ruxley, Shirley, Wembley, Yiewsley

171

lieu OF 'place' Beaulieu, Beulah Hill

līm 'lime' Limehouse

(ge)mǣne 'common, communally owned' Mansfield Park

(ge)mǣre 'boundary, border' Mare Street, Winchmore Hill

mearc 'march, boundary' Markfield, Markhouse Road, Marks Gate

mēos 'moss' Muswell Hill

mere 'pool' Marble Hill, Merton, Stanmore

mersc 'marsh' Figges Marsh

micel 'big, great' Mitcham

mīl 'mile' Mile End

minor L 'lesser' Minories

mōr 'waste land, moor' Moorgate, Morden

munuc 'monk' Monken Hadley, Monkhams, (Oak Hill Park)

mūða 'estuary, confluence of streams' Creekmouth

myln 'mill' Mill Hill, Millwall, North Mill Fields

myncen 'nun' Minchendon Drive, Mincing Lane

mynster 'large church, monastery' Upminster, Westminster

nǣss 'headland, promontory' Lessness

nān-man 'nobody' Normand Park, Normanshire Drive

nese ME 'nose' Neasden

nīwe 'new' Newbury Park, Newington, Stoke Newington

norð 'north, northern' Norbiton, Norbury, North Acton, North End, Northfields, North Hyde, North Mill Fields, North Ockendon, Northolt, Northumberland Heath, Northwood, Norton Folgate, Norwood, Norwood Green

ora 'bank' Pinner

oxa 'ox' Oxgate

pale ME 'a paled fence' Palewell Common

park ME 'enclosed tract of land for beasts of the chase' Gidea Park, Osterley Park

*pēac 'knoll, summit, peak' Peckham

pealed MnE 'pared, skinned' Pield Heath

*penno- B 'chief, top' Penge

perie ME 'pear orchard' ?*Parr's Ditch*, Perivale, Perry Hill, Perry Vale

persone ME 'parson, beneficed cleric' Parson's Green

pinn 'pin, peg, brooch' Pinner

pīpe 'conduit, pipe' Phipps Bridge

place 'residence, large house' Ely Place, (Whitehall)

plaissiet OF 'enclosure' Plashet

pleg-stōw 'sport place, communal meeting place' Plaistow

pōl 'deep place in river' The Pool

popler ME 'poplar tree' Poplar
prēost 'priest' Preston, Priests Bridge
primerose ME 'primrose' Primrose Hill
pyrige pear tree' Purley, Pyrgo Park
pyttel 'hawk' Pittshanger Park
rǣw 'row of houses' Collier Row, Heathrow
rēad 'red' Ratcliff
*rippel 'strip of land' Rippleside
riꝺ 'streamlet' Peckham Rye, The Wrythe
roke ME 'rook' Roehampton, Roxborough
rūh 'rough' Rowdown Wood
rūm 'spacious' Romford
(ge)ryd 'cleared (of trees)' Riddles Down
*ryding 'a clearing' Woodridings
*rysc 'a rush' Ruislip
sand 'sand' Sands End, Stamford Bridge, Stamford Hill
sanden 'sandy' Sanderstead
sceacol 'shackle' Shacklewell
sceaga 'copse, small wood' Hoppershatch Shaw
*sceald 'shallow' Shadwell
sceaꝺa 'criminal, thief' Scadbury Park
*scēo 'shelter' East Sheen, (Richmond)
schetere ME 'archer, bowman' Shooters Hill
scīr 'district, division' *Normanshire Farm*
scīr 'bright, gleaming' Shirley
sealh 'willow tree' Selhurst
seaꝺ 'pit, hole' Roxeth
*set-copp 'flat-topped hill' Sidcup
sīde 'side, land alongside' Barkingside, Cheapside, Woodside
slæd 'hollow, valley' Slade Green
smēꝺe 'smooth, level' Smitham Bottom
smiꝺꝺe 'smithy, metal-worker's shop' Hammersmith
sneare 'trap, snare' Snaresbrook
spitel ME 'hospital' Spitalfields
*stǣne 'stony place' The Steyne
stān 'a stone' Brixton, Haggerston, Keston, Leytonstone, Stamford Brook, Stanmore, Wealdstone
stapol 'post, pillar' Staple Inn
stede 'locality, place' Elmstead, Sanderstead, Wanstead
stōw 'place, place of assembly, holy place' Walthamstow
strǣt 'Roman road, place on a Roman road, paved road' *Ermine Street*, Hare Street, Old Street, Stratford, *Stratford-le-Bow*, Stratford Bridge, Streatham, Turkey Street

strand 'bank of a river'   The Strand, Strand on the Green

strōd 'marshy land overgrown with brushwood'   Stroud Green

sundor 'apart, asunder'   Sundridge Park

sūð 'south, southern'   Southall, Southend, Southgate, Southwark, Sudbrook Park, Suffield Hatch, Surbiton, Sutton

tēag 'small enclosure'   Corbets Tey

*tot-hyll 'a look-out hill'   *Tothill*

*trun 'circular, round'   Turnham Green

tūn 'estate, farm village'   Carshalton, Dalston, Drayton Green, Edmonton, Harlesden, Homerton, Hoxton, Leyton, Lisson, Sutton, Thornton Heath, Upton, Wallington

twī 'two'   Twyford

þorn 'thorn-tree, hawthorn'   *Langthorn*,   Thornton Heath

upp 'higher, upper'   Upminster, Upton

vale   ME 'valley'   Perivale, Perry Vale

wād 'woad'   Waddon

wænn 'lump, hillock'   Wanstead

(ge)wæsc 'washing, a flood'   Enfield Wash

walh 'stranger, Celtic-speaking foreigner, serf'   Wallington, Walworth

weald 'woodland, upland wood'   Harrow Weald, Wealdstone

weg 'road, path, way'   Holloway

wella, wiella 'spring, stream, well'   Chadwell, Dormers Wells, Shacklewell, Shadwell, Stockwell, Willesden

wente   ME 'path'   Four Wants

(ge)weorc 'structure, fortification'   Southwark

wer 'river-dam, fishing enclosure in a river, weir'   Edgware

west 'west, western'   West Barnes, Westbourne Green, West Drayton, West End, West Ham, Westminster, West Wickham

wīc 'specialist farm, dairy farm, port'   Aldwych, Chiswick, Hackney Wick, Hampton Wick, (Ravenscourt Park), Wyke Green

wīc-hām 'village established on site of Romano-British settlement'   East Wickham, West Wickham

wisce 'marshy meadow'   Dulwich

worð 'enclosure'   Baber Bridge, Bonner Hill Road, Chafford Heath, Hanworth, Harmondsworth, Isleworth, Tolworth, Walworth, Wandsworth

wro   ME 'nook, secluded spot'   Roe Green

wudu 'wood'   Colliers Wood, Cricklewood, Harold Wood, Highwood Hill, King's Wood, Northwood, Norwood, Norwood Green, Woodlands, Woodridings, Woodside

wyrm 'reptile, snake'   Wormwood Scrubs

Bibliography

Atlases

Bartholomew's Reference Atlas of Greater London, 1968
Geographers' A–Z London Atlas 8th edition, n.d.
JONES, EMRYS AND SINCLAIR, D.J. *Atlas of London and the London Region*, 1968
TREHARNE, R. F. AND FULLARD, H. *Muir's Historical Atlas*, (1938) 1973

E.P.N.S. publications

CAMERON, K. (*ed.*) *Place-Name Evidence for the Anglo-Saxon Invasion and Scandinavian Settlements*, 1975
GOVER, J. E. B. and Others *The Place-Names of Hertfordshire* (EPNS XV), 1938
GOVER, J. E. B. and Others *The Place-Names of Middlesex* (EPNS XVIII), 1942
GOVER, J. E. B. and Others *The Place-Names of Surrey* (EPNS XI), 1934
REANEY, P. H. *The Place-Names of Essex* (EPNS XII), (1935) 1976
SMITH, A.H. *English Place-Name Elements* (EPNS XXV, XXVI), 1956

Other works

ADAMS, I. H. *Agrarian Landscape Terms: A Glossary for Historical Geography*, 1976
BARTON, N. *The Lost Rivers of London*, 1962
BEBBINGTON, G. *London Street Names*, 1972
BRETT-JAMES, N. G. *Middlesex*, 1951
CHURCH, R. *Kent*, 1963
DE SALIS, R. *Hillingdon Through Eleven Centuries*, 1926
DRAPER, W. *Chiswick*, (1923) 1973
EKWALL, E. *The Concise Oxford Dictionary of English Place-Names*, (1936) 1951

175

EKWALL, E. *English River-Names*, (1928) 1968
EKWALL, E. *Street-Names of the City of London*, (1954) 1965
ENSOR, R. C. K. *England, 1870–1914*, 1964
FIELD, J. *English Field Names, a Dictionary*, 1972
FIELD, J. *Place-Names of Dacorum District*, 1977
GLADSTONE, F. M. *Notting Hill in Bygone Days*, 1924
GLOVER, J. *The Place-Names of Kent*, 1976
Greater London Council *Greater London Services*, 1967
HARRIS, C. M. *What's in a Name?*, 1977
HART, J. E. *London Oddities*, n.d.
HAVINS, P. J. S. *The Forests of England*, 1976
KENT, W. (revised by G. Thompson) *An Encyclopaedia of London*, (1937) 1970
ILCHESTER, Earl Of *The Home of the Hollands*, 1956
MARTIN, J. L. (*ed.*) *Names of Streets and Places in the Administrative County of London*, 1955 (with Supplement)
METCALFE, L. AND VINCE, J. *Discovering Canals*, 1968
MORRIS, J. (*ed.*) *Domesday Book: II Middlesex*, 1975
Nelson's Dictionary of Dates, n.d.
NICOLAISEN, W. F. H., GELLING, M. AND RICHARDS, M. *The Names of Towns and Cities in Britain*, 1970
O'LEARY, J. G. *Dagenham Place Names*, 1958
REANEY, P. H. *The Place-Names of Walthamstow*, 1930
ROWLAND, R. N. G. *The Street-Names of Acton*, Middlesex, 1967 (Privately circulated)
SEXBY, J. J. *The Municipal Parks, Gardens, and Open Spaces of London: Their History and Associations*, 1898
SHUTE, N. *London Villages*, 1977
STENTON, F. M. *Anglo-Saxon England*, (1946) 1963
STEVENSON, B. *Middlesex*, 1972
STOW, J. *The Survey of London*, (1912) 1923
TASKER, G. E. *Ilford Past and Present*, n.d. (c.1901)
TERRY, G. *Memories of Old Romford*, 1880
THORNBURY, W. *Haunted London*, 1865
VINCE, J. *Discovering Watermills*, 1970
VINCE, J. *Discovering Windmills*, 1969
WALLENBERG, J. K. *The Place-Names of Kent*, 1934
WILLIAMS, G. R. *London in the Country: the Growth of Suburbia*, 1975
WILLIAMS, GWYN A. *Medieval London: From Commune to Capital*, 1963
WITTICH, J. *Discovering London Street Names*, 1977
WOODWARD, SIR L. *The Age of Reform, 1815–70*, (1962) 1964

INDEX OF STREET-NAMES

Page references in this index may (but do not necessarily) relate to several streets bearing the same name. When the name is combined with a variety of second elements (e.g., Ruskin Avenue, Ruskin Road, Ruskin Street), the symbol &c. is used. Names in italics, as elsewhere in the book, are no longer current. The symbols f or ff are used to indicate the page(s) immediately following the number indexed.

Abbey Rd &c., 121
Abbotsbury Rd, 134
Abbots Lne, 121
Aberdeen Rd, 130
Aboukir St, 136
Abyssinia Rd, 138
Acacia Gdns &c., 115
Achilles Rd &c., 147
Acol Rd, 135
Adam St, 24
Addison Rd &c., 144, 147
Adelaide Rd, 139
Adelphi Tce, 23
Aden Rd, 139
Adolf St, 150
Aerodrome Rd, 118
Agamemnon Rd, 147
Agave Rd, 116
Agdon St, 134
Agister Rd, 116
Ailsa Ave &c., 83
Ajax Ave &c., 147
Akenside Rd, 143
Albany St, 24, 131
Albemarle St, 31
Albert Rd, 144, 151
Albuhera Clse, 131
Alcock Rd, 118, 119
Alderley St, 133
Alderney St, 133
Alders, The, 117
Aldford St, 132
Alexander Clse, 157
Alexandra Ave &c., 150
Alfred Gdns &c., 149
Aliwal Rd, 138
Allan Way, 142
Allenby Rd, 157
Alleyn Csct, 163
Allfarthing Lne, 106
Alliance Rd, 118
All Saints Rd, 124
Alma Plce &c., 137
Almeida St, 136
Almond Gve &c., 115, 159
Alperton St, 159
Alpha Plce, 165
Alroy Rd, 148
Amoy Plce, 165
Ampthill Sq, 133
Amy Way, 119
Angela Gdns, 161
Anne Way &c., 150
Aragon Dve, 150
Archibald Rd, 126
Aristotle Rd, 146
Arliss Way, 162
Armytage Rd, 118
Arne St &c., 145
Arnulf St, 150
Arrowscout Walk, 19
Arrowsmith Rd, 116
Artillery Row, 114

Ascot Rd, 159
Ashbourne Ave, 129
Ashby St, 134
Ashmole St, 122, 154
Asmara Rd, 135
Athelney St, 150
Athelstan Rd, 126
Attlee Clse &c., 156, 157
Aubert Rd, 154
Auckland Rd, 139
Austin Friars, 121
Avondale Ave &c., 131
Avro Way, 119
Aylesford St, 133
Azalea Walk, 117

Baalbec Rd, 135
Bader Way, 158
Baird Ave, 155
Balaclava Rd, 137
Balderton St, 132
Balfe St, 163
Bancroft Ct, 162
Bangalore St, 138
Barchard St, 141
Barchester Clse, 149
Barfett St, 159
Barkston Gdns, 45, 135
Barnard Clse, 119
Barnfield Rd, 112
Baroness Rd, 161
Basinghall St, 107
Basing St &c., 106f
Bath Rd &c., 69, 129
Bathurst Gdns, 139
Batoum Gdns, 137
Battersea Rise, 108
Battle Bridge Lne &c., 27, 128
Bayham Plce, 35
Baylis Rd, 162
Bazalgette Gdns, 95
Beacon Hill, 151
Beaconsfield Rd, 148
Beatrice Rd, 151
Beatty Rd, 157
Beaumont Rd, 148
Beavor Lne, 141
Becket St, 126
Beech Ave &c., 115, 116, 159
Beethoven St, 145, 159
Belgrade Rd, 137
Belgrave Sq, 29, 132
Belle Vue, 120
Bell Lne, 112
Benares Rd, 138
Bentham Rd, 153
Ben Tillett Clse, 156
Berber Rd, 138
Bernard St, 160
Bertram Grdns, 157
Betterton St, 162
Beulah Hill, 27
Bevan Ave, 156

Bevin Rd, 156
Bickenhall St, 134
Bidborough St, 131
Bideford Ave, 124
Birch Ave, 115
Birkbeck Ave &c., 160f
Blacklands Tce, 113
Blandford St, 134
Blenheim Rd &c., 136
Bleriot Rd, 118
Bloemfontein Rd, 139
Boar Clse, 116
Boathouse Walk, 109
Boleyn Dve, 150
Bolingbroke Gve, 123
Bondfield Ave, 156
Bonner (Hill) Rd, 30, 106
Booth Clse, 153
Borrodaile Rd, 141
Boscombe Ave &c., 129, 159
Bosworth Rd, 150
Boundary Rd, 137
Bouverie St, 121, 123
Bow Lne, 106
Bowling Green Clse &c., 162
Brabazon Ave &c., 118, 119
Bracken Ave, 117
Bracknell Gdns &c., 135
Braid Ave, 161
Bramble Clse &c., 115, 117
Bramham Gdns, 45, 135
Brancker Clse &c., 119
Brassie Ave, 161
Bread St, 106
Brecknock Rd, 34
Briar Rd, 116
Brighton Ave, 129
Brindley Way, 155
Brisbane Rd, 139
Bristol Rd, 129
Brixton Water Lne, 109
Broadfields Rd, 112
Broadhurst Clse &c., 135
Broad St, 120
Broadway, 111
Brook St, 69, 109
Broomfield Rd, 113
Brougham Rd, 153, 160
Brown Clse, 119
Browning Ave &c., 144, 155
Broxbourne Ave, 129
Brunel Rd &c., 154f
Brunswick Gdns &c., 150, 151
Brushfield St, 142
Bryanston Sq &c., 134
Bryony Clse, 115, 117
Buckingham Rd &c., 129, 164
Buller Rd, 155
Burbage Rd, 163
Burdett Rd, 161
Burnley Rd, 130
Butfield Clse, 114
Butts, The, 114

Bye, The, 161
Byron Ave, 144

Cabul Rd, 138
Caird St, 159
Calabria Rd, 136
Calderon Plce &c., 148
Camberwell Passage, 122
Cambridge Csct &c., 77, 131
Campion Clse &c., 115
Canal Head &c., 109
Canberra Dve, 119
Candahar Rd, 138
Cane Clse, 119
Canfield Dve &c., 135
Canning Csct, 133, 155, 156
Canon St, 125
Canrobert St, 156
Canterbury Ave, 129
Canton St, 165
Capland St, 134
Cardigan Rd, 156
Cardinal Dve, 150
Cardington St, 133
Carlisle Ave, 161
Carlyle Ave &c., 153
Carmelite St, 121
Carnarvon Rd, 129
Caroline Rd, 141
Carter Clse, 119
Carterhatch Lne, 142
Carthusian St, 122
Cassilis Rd, 83
Cathedral St, 121
Cato Rd &c., 146, 148
Cavell Rd, 157
Cavendish Ave &c., 52, 134, 155
Caxton Rd &c., 122, 144
Cayley Clse, 119
Cedar Ave &c., 115, 116
Centaur St, 148
Cephas Ave &c., 124
Cervantes Ct, 147
Chantry Clse &c., 123
Chapel St &c., 107, 121
Charlwood Plce &c., 141
Charnwood Dve, 129
Charterhouse Rd &c., 37, 122, 128
Chatterton Rd, 144
Chaucer Rd, 143
Cheapside, 105, 110
Chelsea Embankment, 109
Cheltenham Rd, 129
Chenies St, 133
Cherry Csct, 115
Chester Ave &c., 129
Chesterfield Rd, 129
Chesterford Gdns, 135
Chichele Rd, 142
Chicheley St, 142
Chipmunk Dve, 119
Chiswell St, 13, 143
Christchurch Rd, 139
Churchfield Rd, 112
Church Hill &c., 122
Churchill Gdns &c., 157
Cibber Rd, 163
Cinema Pde, 162
Cintra Pk, 129
Clare Rd &c., 129, 133
Clayton Field, 114
Cleeves Walk, 150
Clematis St, 117
Cleve Rd, 135
Cleves Way, 150

Clifton Rd, 129
Cluny Mews &c., 121
Cobham Rd, 118
Cobourg Rd &c., 151
Cody Clse, 119
Colenso Rd, 139
Coleridge Ave &c., 143
Collier Dve, 145
Collingham Plce, 135
Colombo Rd, 139
Colston Rd, 129
Columbia Rd, 140
Commerce Rd &c., 32, 118
Compton Csct, 162
Coningsby Rd, 148
Connaught Rd, 151
Cons St, 162
Constable Gdns &c., 145
Convair Walk, 119
Copperfield Ave, 149
Coppermill Lne, 118
Coptic St, 153
Coram St, 160
Cordite St, 165
Cordwainer St, 106
Corelli Rd, 152
Corkscrew Hill, 108, 117
Corner Mead, 114
Corsica Rd, 136
Corunna Rd &c., 136
Coteford St, 159
Cotman Gdns, 145
Courtfield Gdns, 112
Coutts Rd, 161
Covert Rd, 116
Cowick Rd, 159
Cowley Rd, 118
Cowper Rd, 144
Crabree Lne, 113
Cramer St, 163
Cranbourne Ave, 129
Crane Ave, 142
Cranmer Clse, 150
Crawford St, 134
Cressida Rd, 148
Crispe Rd, 141
Cromer Rd &c., 129, 159
Crossbow Rd, 116
Cross St, 127
Crucifix Lne, 121
Cruikshank St, 143
Crusoe Rd, 145
Crutched Friars, 121
Culpeper Clse, 150
Culrose St, 132
Cumberland Plce, 131, 132
Cunnington St, 142
Curtain Rd, 162

Dahlia Gdns &c., 116, 159
Daimler Way, 119
Dakota Gdns, 119
Daleham Gdns &c., 135
Dane Rd, 149
Dante Rd, 147
Danube St, 137
D'Arblay St, 144
Darwin Dve &c., 155
Davis Rd, 141
Dawes Rd, 142
Dawlish Ave, 124
Deal Rd, 159
Dean Farrar St, 146
Defoe Rd, 145
De Havilland Rd, 118
Delta Gve, 119
Denbigh St, 133

Derby Rd, 129
Deronda Rd, 149
Derwent Rd, 110
Dewsbury Rd, 130
Dickens Ave &c., 149
Disraeli Rd, 137, 148
Dombey St, 149
Dordrecht Rd, 136
Dorian St, 165
Dorset Rd &c., 119, 134
Dover St, 31
Dove Walk, 158
Dowlas St, 107
Dragor Rd, 118
Droop St, 159
Dryden Rd &c., 143, 144
Du Cros Rd, 118
Duke St, 153, 164
Duncan Gve, 161
Dunedin Rd, 139
Durban Rd, 139
Durham House St, 24
Durham Rd, 129, 132
Durnsford Ave, 44

Eagle Clse, 158
Eastbourne Rd, 159
Eastcheap, 105
East End Rd, 45
Eastern Rd &c., 107, 139
East Ferry Rd, 109
Eastfields Rd, 112
East Hill, 107
Easton St, 134
Eaton Plce &c., 132
Ebbsfleet Rd, 135
Eccleston Plce &c., 132
Eden St, 46
Edinburgh Rd, 129, 151
Edison Dve, 155
Edward Rd, 144
Effort St, 165
Effra Pde &c., 47, 109
Egmont Ave &c., 164
Eisenhower Dve, 157
Eldon Rd, 156
Elfreda Csct, 150
Elgar Rd &c., 164
Elgin Ave &c., 153, 156
Elizabeth Clse, 144
Elm Gdns &c., 115, 116, 159
Ely Plce &c., 128, 129
Enbrook St, 159
Endsleigh Gdns &c., 133
Endymion Rd, 146, 148
Enford St, 134
Erasmus St, 146
Erconwald St, 126
Erica Gdns, 117
Esmond Ct, 149
Essex Clse &c., 110, 129, 150
Ethelburga St, 126
Eton Rd, 129
Eversholt St, 133
Ewart Gve, 155
Exmouth Rd, 129

Factory Lne, 118
Fagg's Rd, 48
Fairhazel Gdns, 135
Fairway, The, 161
Falconer Rd, 116
Fallow Clse, 116
Faraday Rd, 154, 155, 160f
Farrant St, 159
Featherbed Lne, 108
Fern Ave, 159

Field Mead, 114
Finucane Gdns, 158
Firefly Clse, 119
First Ave &c., 158, 159
Fitzjohn's Ave, 135
Five Acre, 114
Flamsteed Rd, 154
Flaxman Tce, 145
Fleetwood Rd, 130
Fleming Rd, 155
Fletcher Rd, 116, 148
Florida St &c., 140, 141
Floss St, 149
Fontarabia Rd, 147
Fordwych Rd, 135
Fore St, 111
Forest Rd &c., 49, 116
Fort Rd, 137
Fowler Rd, 116
Francis St, 141
Friday Rd, 145
Friern Rd, 107
Frinton Rd, 137, 159
Frith Lne &c., 10, 148
Fuchsia St, 116
Furmage St, 141
Further Acre, 114

Gainsborough Gdns &c., 145
Gaitskell Rd, 157
Gallia Rd, 136
Galton St, 159
Gamuel Rd, 141
Garlinge Rd, 135
Garnault Plce, 109
Garrick St &c., 163
Gascoigne Rd, 141
George Ct, 164
Georgia Rd, 141
Georgina Gdns, 161
Ghent St, 150
Gibbon Rd &c., 154
Gilston Rd, 135
Glade, The, 117
Gladstone Ave &c., 51, 155
Glazbury Rd, 135
Glebe Rd, 114
Gliddon Rd, 135
Globe Rd, 51
Gloucester Rd, 129, 132, 140
Godfrey Ave, 162
Goldington Csct &c., 133
Goldsmith Ave &c., 144
Goliath Clse, 119
Gordon Rd &c., 133, 156
Gorse Rd &c., 115, 117
Gosport Rd, 129
Gray St, 165
Great Central Ave &c., 120
Great Dover St, 31, 143
Great Field, 144
Great Percy St, 109
Great Peter St, 124
Great Winchester St, 107
Great Windmill St, 117
Green, The, 161
Greenland Rd &c., 35
Green Lne, 113, 123
Greenwood Ave, 156, 159
Grenada Rd, 140
Gresham St, 153
Greyfriars Psge, 122
Grosvenor Rd &c., 46
Grove, The, 117
Grub St, 143
Gull Clse, 117
Gunter Gve, 134

Gunton Rd, 159
Gwalior Rd, 138
Gwendwr Rd, 135
Gwynne Plce, 163

Hadrian Clse, 119
Ha Ha Rd, 165
Haig Rd, 157
Haileybury Ave, 128f
Hailsham Rd, 159
Half Acre, The, 113
Halkin St, 132
Ham, The, 113
Hamilton Rd, 71, 136
Hammond Way, 153
Handel Way &c., 146
Hanger Lne &c., 55, 108
Hanover Sq &c., 131, 150
Hans Csct, 153
Hanway St, 160
Harbourer Clse &c., 116
Hardie Rd, 156
Hardy Rd, 71, 136
Harley St, 153
Harold Rd, 141
Harrier Clse, 158
Harrow Dve &c., 107, 128
Hart Csct, 116
Hastings Tce, 131
Hatton Gdn, 112
Havelock Rd, 156
Hawthorn Gve, 116
Hawtry Dve, 162
Hayman Csct, 145
Hazel Clse, 115
Heathcote St, 160
Heather Clse, 115
Heath St, 111
Helena Rd, 151
Henderson Rd, 156
Henslowe Rd &c., 163
Heracles Clse, 117
Herbert St, 142
Hereford Rd, 129
Hermes Way, 119
Hermitage Rd &c., 123
Heron Flight Ave, 158
Herrick St, 146
Herries St, 159
Hertford Rd, 129
Highfield Ave &c., 112
High Holborn, 59, 110
High St &c., 106, 110
Highwood Hill, 10
Hilary Clse, 158
Hill Brow &c., 108
Hilliard Rd, 147
Hind Clse, 116
Hinkler Clse, 119
Hogarth Rd, 145
Holbein Plce, 146
Holly Way, 159
Holy Rood St, 121
Homer Row, 148
Honeypot Lne, 108
Hopping Lne, 125
Hoppner Rd, 145
Hornbeam Csct &c., 115
Hornsey Rise, 108
Horseferry Rd, 109
Horseleydown Lne, 60
Hosier Lne, 106
Houghton St, 133
Houndsfield Rd, 113
Hove Ave, 129
Howard Rd, 160
Hoylake Rd, 161

Huguenot Plce, 122
Hundred Acre, 114
Hunter St, 160
Huntinhgdon St, 129
Huntley St, 133
Huntsman Rd, 116
Huntsworth Mews, 134
Hurstwood Ave, 129
Huxley Rd &c., 155, 159

Ilbert St, 159
Ilchester Plce, 134
Imperial Way, 119
Indus Rd, 140
Inglebert St, 109
Inglewood, 116
Inkerman Rd, 137
Ipswich Rd, 159
Iron Mill Lne &c., 118
Irving Ave &c., 162
Island Rd, 145
Ivanhoe Dve &c., 149
Ivy Gdns &c., 116, 159

Jamaica Rd &c., 140
James St, 24
Jasmine Gdns, 117
Jellicoe Rd, 157
Jermyn St, 124
Jersey Rd, 159
Jews Row &c., 123
Jockey's Fields, 112
John Adam St, 24
John Burn Dve, 156
John Fisher St, 126
Johnson Rd, 118, 144
John St, 141
Judd St, 131
Junction Mews &c., 109
Juno Way, 147, 165

Kambala Rd, 139
Kashgar Rd, 135
Kashmir Rd, 140
Kassala Rd, 138
Katherine Gdns &c., 150
Kathleen Ave, 142
Kean St, 163
Keats Gve, 143
Keir Hardie Way, 156
Kemble Rd, 162
Kendal Rd, 130
Kent Rd, 132
Kent St, Kentish St, 143
Kenton St, 160
Kenya Rd, 140
Kepler Rd, 146
Khartoum Rd, 138
Khyber Rd, 138
Kilburn High Rd, 111
Kilravock St, 159
Kimberley Ave &c., 139
King Alfred Ave, 150
King Edward St, 150
King Harold's Way, 150
King John's Ct, 150
Kingsdown Ave, 161
Kingsford Ave, 119
Kingshold Rd, 165
King's Rd, 111
Kipling St &c., 152
Kitchener Rd &c., 157
Kittiwake Rd, 117
Knaresborough Plce, 135
Kneller Rd, 145

Laburnum Ave, 115

Ladbroke Gve, 64
Ladysmith Ave, 139
Laing Dean, 162
Lake Gdns &c., 110
Lakeside Rd, 110
Lammas Ave, 113
Lan Acre, 114
Lancaster Ave &c., 129, 130, 149
Lancing Gdns &c., 128, 131
Landseer Clse, 145
Langtry Rd, 162
Lansbury Ave, 156
Lansdowne Tce, 153
Larch Rd &c., 116, 117
Latimer Rd, 148
Lauder Clse, 162
Laughton Rd, 162
Lavender Rd &c., 115
Laverton Plce, 135
Lawford Clse, 119
Lawrence Rd, 145
Leander Rd, 146
Leicester Rd &c., 65, 129
Leigh St, 131
Leighton Clse, 145
Leopold Rd, 151
Leslie Rd, 148
Lessing St, 148
Levehurst Way, 65
Liberia Rd, 136
Library Plce, 152
Lichfield Rd, 129
Lilac Plce &c., 115, 117
Lime Ave &c., 115, 116
Lime St, 106
Lincoln Rd, 129
Lindbergh Rd, 119
Lindfield Gdns, 135
Lind St, 163
Lisson Gve &c., 67
Little Chapel St, 122
Little Dorrit St, 149
Liverpool Rd &c., 66, 120, 129
Lochinvar Rd, 147
Long Acre, 114
Long Dve &c., 114, 161
Longfield 114
Long Lane, 143
Longstaff Rd, 141
Lordship Lne, 107
Lorenco Rd, 139
Lorne Rd, 151
Lothair Rd, 148
Lothrop St, 159
Lots Rd, 113
Lower Fore St, 111
Lower Marsh, 108
Lower St, 111
Lowfield Rd, 112
Lucas St, 131
Lucy Csct, 142
Luther Rd, 148
Lyme St, 131
Lyndhurst Dve &c., 129
Lynne Way, 162
Lysander Rd, 119, 148

Mabledon Plce, 131
Macaulay Rd &c., 144
Macdonald Ave, 156
Mafeking Ave &c., 139
Magdala Ave &c., 138
Magdalen Rd &c., 121, 128
Magpie Alley, 121
Maitland Gdns, 157

Maiwand Rd, 138
Malan Sq, 158
Mall, The, 161
Mallory Gdns, 157
Malvern Rd &c., 128, 129
Manciple St, 143
Manor Rd, 107
Mansfield Rd, 156
Manstone Rd, 135
Mantilla Rd, 159
Marchmont St, 160
Marcilly Rd, 123
Marconi Way, 155
Maresfield Gdns, 135
Margaret Bondfield Ave, 156
Margravine Gdns, 27
Markett Place, The, 110
Markhouse Rd, 172
Marlborough Csct &c., 128, 136, 149, 156
Marlowe Clse, 150
Marmion Approach &c., 147, 149
Marne St, 159
Marsh Ave, 108
Maryland Rd &c., 140
Mashie Rd, 161
Matlock Rd, 129
Maurier Clse, 162
Maxwell Rd, 155
Mayfield Rd, 113
Mayfly Gdns, 119
Mazawattee Lne, 165
Mecklenburgh Sq, 151
Melba Way, 163
Melbourne Plce &c., 139, 156
Melbury Rd, 134
Melcombe Plce &c., 134
Menelik Rd, 135
Meon Rd, 128
Mercator Rd, 154
Mercury Rd, 147
Meridian Rd, 154
Merlin Clse, 119
Messaline Ave, 164
Meteor Way, 119
Micawber Ave, 149
Michael Rd, 133
Michigan Ave, 140
Midland Rd, 120
Milfoil St, 117
Milk St, 106
Millais Rd, 145, 148
Millbank, 109, 114, 118
Millstream Rd, 118
Milton Rd &c., 143, 144
Minchendon Csct, 112, 122
Mincing Lne, 122
Minera Mews, 132
Minerva Rd &c., 118, 147
Minet Rd, 122
Ming St, 165
Minster Rd, 135
Miranda Rd, 148
Mollison Dve &c., 118
Monkhams Ave &c., 70
Monmouth Ave, 129
Montcalme Clse &c., 155
Montgolfier Walk, 119
Montfort Gdns, 150
Montgomery Ave &c., 157
Montreal Plce, 139f
Moravian Plce, 123
Moring Rd, 159
Morley Ave &c., 155, 161
Morrison Rd, 156
Moscow Rd, 137

Mount Pleasant, 71
Mozart St, 159
Mud Lne, 108
Muirfield, 161
Mulready St, 152
Murchison Rd, 154
Muscovy St, 138
Museum St, 153
Musjid Rd, 121, 138
Muswell Hill, 71
Myddleton Ave &c., 72, 109
Mylne St, 109
Myrtle Gve &c., 116

Napier Rd, 138, 156
Natal Rd, 139
Nebraska St, 140
Neckinger St, 71, 109
Nelson Rd, 71, 136, 156
Nestles Ave, 118
Netherhall Gdns, 135
Newark Csct, 141
Newington Butts, 114
Newton Ave &c., 153
Nicholson Rd, 156
Nigeria Rd, 140
Nightingale Lne, 126
Noah's Ark Alley, 165
Noel Rd, 112
Nonsuch Clse &c., 100, 150
Norland Rd &c., 113
Norman Ave &c., 149
Normand Rd, 113
Normanshire Dve, 72
Northampton Rd &c., 134
North End Rd, 72
Northern Rd, 107
Northey St, 113
Northfields Rd, 112
Northop St, 132
North St &c., 107, 108
North Wharf Rd, 109
Northwick Ave &c., 73
Norton Folgate, 73
Nottingham Rd, 129
Nutbourne St, 159
Nutford Plce, 134
Nutley Tce, 135

Oak Ave, 116
Oakfield Rd, 113
Observatory Gdns, 154
Occupation Rd, 113
Octavia Way, 153
Of Alley, 164
Old Church St, 122
Old Jewry, 75, 123
Old Kent Rd, 71
Oliphant St, 159
Olive Rd, 116
Oliver Rd, 147
Omega St, 165
Orchard St, 134
Orchid St, 117
Oregon Ave, 140
Oriental St, 165
Orlando Rd, 147
Orpen Rd, 165
Osman Rd, 137
Osnaburgh St, 131
Outram Rd, 156
Owen Clse &c., 156
Oxford St, 127

Paddenswick Rd, 80
Paget Gdns, 157
Pall Mall, 161

Palmerston Rd, 130, 156
Pannard Plce, 155
Pardoner St, 143
Park Hill &c., 108, 128
Parolles Rd, 148
Parsifal Rd, 164
Pascal St, 146
Paulet Rd, 107
Peabody Ave &c., 142
Peach Tce, 115
Pear Tree Ave, 115
Peel Rd, 130, 156
Pegasus Plce, 119
Peggoty's Way, 149
Pekin St, 165
Pendennis Rd, 149
Pendle Rd, 159
Penwortham Rd, 159
Peony Gdns, 117
Percy Rd, 165
Peregrine Rd, 116
Perry Ave &c., 161, 162
Perth Rd, 139
Peterborough Rd, 129
Petersfield Rd, 128
Peter's Hill, 124
Phipps Bridge Rd, 77
Phipps Hatch Lne, 142
Pickwick St, 149
Pier Rd &c., 133
Pilgrimage St, 143
Pine Rd, 116
Pitcairn Rd, 145
Pitfield St, 114
Plantagenet Rd, 149f
Plato Rd, 146
Playgreen Way, 161
Plevna Rd, 137
Pleydell Ct &c., 123
Poland St, 137
Pond Plce &c., 110
Pope Rd, 144
Pope's Rd, 145
Portal Clse, 157
Portia Rd, 148
Postway Mews, 152
Poultry, 106
Powell Clse, 119
Powells Walk, 125
Poynter Rd, 145
Prebend St, 125
Pretoria Ave &c., 139, 159
Prideaux Plce, 109
Primrose Ave, 116
Princes Rd, 144
Printer St, 152
Printing House Lne &c., 152
Prioress St, 143
Priory Walk, 135
Progress Way, 118, 155
Prospero Rd, 148
Pudding Lne, 108

Quebec Rd, 139
Queen Alexandra Ct, 151
Queen Anne's Gate, 151
Queen Square, 151
Queen Victoria St, 151
Quex Rd, 135
Quilp St, 149

Raeburn Rd, 145
Raglan Rd, 156
Railway Approach &c., 120
Ramillies Plce &c., 136, 140
Rathbone Plce, 127
Ravenscroft Rd &c., 30, 160f

Recovery St, 165
Rector St, 125
Redan St, 137
Redvers Rd, 155
Regarder Rd, 116
Regent St, 76
Rembrandt Rd, 145
Rendle St, 154
Repository Rd, 165
Repton Rd, 129
Reservoir Rd, 110
Reynolds Rd, 145
Rhyl Rd &c., 131
Richborough Rd, 135
Ridgmount Gdns, 133
Ridgway, 113
Rinaldo Rd, 147
Ringwood Rd, 129
River Ave, 108, 109
Robert Clse, 24, 144
Robin Hood Clse &c., 160
Robinia Clse, 116
Rochester Walk &c., 107, 128, 130
Rockware Ave, 118
Roebuck Rd, 116
Roe Way, 119
Roland Rd, 147
Roman Rd, 149
Romola Rd, 149
Romney Rd, 145
Ronalds Rd, 154
Ropemaker St &c., 114
Rosebery Ave, 162
Rosemary Ave &c., 115
Rose Walk, 117
Rosoman St, 162
Rotunda Clse, 165
Rowland Hill St, 152
Royal Lne, 112
Rubastic Rd, 118
Ruberoid Rd, 118
Ruddigore Rd, 163
Rufus St, 150
Rugby Ave, 128
Rural Way, 159
Ruskin Ave &c., 155
Russell Ave, 155
Rustic Ave, 159
Rutland Rd, 129
Ryefield Ave &c., 112

Saffron Hill, 112
St Albans Ave &c., 124, 129
St Alphege Rd, 126
St Alphonsus Rd, 126
St Andrew's Rd &c., 161
St Austell Clse, 124
St Barnabas Rd, 125
St Charles Sq, 126
St Clare St, 126
St Cross St, 127
St David Clse, 124
St Dunstan's Ave &c., 126
St Elmo Rd, 136
St Ervan's Rd, 124
St George's Dve &c., 125
St Helena St, 124
St James Ave &c., 124
St Joan's Rd, 126
St John's Hill &c., 123, 127
St Keverne Rd, 126
St Kilda Rd &c., 127
St Lawrence Clse, 125
St Leonard's Rd, 124
St Loo Ave, 124
St Louis Ave, 126

St Luke Clse, 125
St Malo Ave, 126
St Margaret's Path, 122
St Mary's Ave &c., 124
St Maur Rd, 126
St Nicholas Clse, 124
St Olave's Ct, 127
St Oswulf St, 127
St Paul Clse &c., 125
St Petersburgh Plce, 137
St Peters Rd, 124, 125
St Philip's Ave &c., 125
St Silas Plce, 125
St Simon's Ave, 125f
St Swithin's Lne &c., 126
St Thomas St, 31, 126
St Ursula Gve &c., 126
St Wilfrid's Clse, 126
Salamanca St, 136
Salisbury Rd &c., 129, 155
Sanders Lne, 142
Sandringham Rd, 129
Sandwich St, 131
Satchell Mead, 114
Saunders Way, 153
Saxon Gdns &c., 149
Saxton Rd, 154
Scala St, 162
Seasprite Clse, 117
Sebastopol Rd, 137
Second Rd &c., 158
Seneca Rd, 146
Seymour Gdns &c., 134, 150
Shaef Way, 157
Shakespeare Rd &c., 143, 144, 150
Shaw Way, 119
Shelley Ave &c., 144, 155
Sheraton St, 122
Sheridan Rd, 155
Sherwood (Pk) Ave &c., 129, 159
Ship Alley, 140
Shortlands, 113
Shrewsbury Rd, 129
Siddons Rd, 163
Sidmouth St, 130
Sixth Ave, 159
Slaidburn St, 135
Sloane Sq &c., 153
Smithfield St, 112
Snowden St, 156
Solon Rd, 146
Somali Rd, 135
Somerset St, 134
Sopwith Rd, 118
Soudan St, 138
South Acre, 114
Southampton Row &c., 133
Southern Ave &c., 107
Southey Rd, 144
Southfield Rd, 112
South Western Rd, 108
Spencer Park, 45, 117
Spenser Rd &c., 143, 146
Stadium Rd, 161
Stafford Rd &c., 31, 129, 156
Stainer St, 145
Standard Rd, 118, 147
Stanley Rd &c., 133
Steele's Rd, 145
Steyne, The, 88
Stowe Rd, 128, 129
Strand, 6, 37
Stukeley St, 154
Sunbeam Rd, 118, 148

Sundew Ave, 117
Sunningdale Ave, 161
Sussex St &c., 132
Sutlej Rd, 140
Sutton Way, 141
Swallow Walk, 158
Swan Rd, 155
Swinburne Ave, 155
Sycamore Clse, 115

Tabard St, 143
Tabernacle St, 123
Tadema Rd, 145
Talbot Rd &c., 143
Tallis Gve &c., 146
Tamarisk Sq, 117
Tancred Rd, 147, 148
Tangmere Csct, 158
Tasso Rd, 147
Tavistock St, 133
Taviton St, 133
Tawney Way, 153
Taylor's Grn, 161
Tedder Clse, 157
Tee, The, 161
Telegraph Hill &c., 71, 151
Telford Rd &c., 154, 155
Tennyson Ave &c., 144
Tenter Grd &c., 113
Tenth Clse, 158
Thackeray Clse &c., 149
Thames Bank, 108
Thanet St, 131
Theatre St, 162
Thicket, The, 115
Third Rd &c., 158
Thomas More St, 126
Thorndike Ave, 162
Thornhaugh St, 133
Thriff Wood, 10
Titmuss Ave, 153
Tonbridge St, 131
Tooley St, 127
Toronto Rd, 139, 140
Torrington Plce, 133
Tower Clse, 150
Tramway Ave &c., 120
Tregunter Rd, 135
Trenchard Ave, 157
Trident Gdns, 119
Trinidad St, 140
Trojan Way, 118
Trollope St, 152
Tudor Csct &c., 149, 150
Tugela Rd &c., 139
Tyburn Lne &c., 109
Tyndall Rd, 155
Tysoe St, 134

Victor Rd, 144
Victoria St &c., 151
Victory Rd, 71, 136
Vigo St, 136
Viking Rd, 149
Villiers St, 164
Viola Ave, 116
Virgil Plce &c., 148
Virginia Rd &c., 140
Vittoria Plce, 136
Voltaire Rd, 146
Vulcan Clse, 117

Wallflower St, 117
Walpole Rd, 144, 145
Wandle Bank &c., 96, 109
Wandsworth Plain, 108
Warwick Rd, 129
Washington Ave, 140
Waterloo Rd, 136
Water Mill Way, 118
Watling St, 76, 111, 127
Wavell Dve, 157
Waverley Ave &c., 147, 149
Waverton St, 132
Wayfarer Rd, 119
Waynflete St, 128
Webbs Rd, 156
Webb St, 141
Welbeck Rd, 137
Weller St, 149
Wellesley Rd, 155
Wellington Rd, 156
Wesleyan Plce, 123

Ulleswater Rd, 110
Ulster Tce, 131
Ulundi Rd, 139
Ulysses Rd, 147
Uneeda Dve, 118
University St, 152
Upper Fore St, 111
Upper St, 111

Valetta Rd, 136
Valiant Clse, 119
Vallance Rd, 140
Vanbrugh Rd, 153
Vancouver Rd, 155
Vandyck Rd, 145
Varna Rd, 137
Venetia Rd, 148
Verderers Rd, 116
Vestris Rd, 163

Wesley Ave &c., 140, 146
West Ferry Rd, 108f
Westfields Rd, 112
Westgate Tce, 135
West Halkin St, 132

West Hill &c., 107
Westmead Rd, 113
Westmoreland Rd &c., 132, 133
Weston St, 141
Wetherby Gdns, 135
Weymouth St, 134
Wharfedale St, 135
Wheatstone Rd, 154
Whellock Rd, 142
Whistler Gdns, 145
White Acre, 114
Whitfield St, 123
Whitefriars St, 121
Whitethorn Ave, 115
Whitmore Rd, 142
Whittaker St, 142
Whittle Clse, 118, 155
Wieland Rd, 147f
Wiggins Mead, 114
Wilfred Gdns, 142
Williams Gve, 155
William St, 24
Willow Ave, 115
Wilna Rd, 137
Winchester Rd &c., 128
Windmill Hill &c., 117, 123
Winns Ave &c., 60
Winston Ave, 157
Withers Mead, 114
Woburn Sq, 133
Wolfe Clse &c., 155
Wolseley Rd, 155, 156
Wolsey Gdns &c., 150
Woodbine Gve, 116
Woodfield Rd, 113
Woodchurch Rd, 135
Woodgrange Rd, 49
Woodland Way, 117
Woodman Path, 116
Wood St, 106
Worcester Ave &c., 129, 140
Wordsworth Ave &c., 144
Woronzow Rd, 156
Wright Rd, 118
Wynyatt St, 134

XX Plce, 164

Yardley St, 134
Yew Ave &c., 116
York Rd &c., 130f, 150, 164
Yukon Rd, 139

Zampa Rd, 164
Zangwill Rd, 152
Zigzag Rd, 108
Zoar St, 123

GENERAL INDEX

References in this select Index are to topics not readily accessible by means of the Dictionary section, the Glossary of Elements, or the Index of Street-Names.

abbreviations, 15, 17ff
actors, 162f
admirals, 71, 157
aircraft, 119, 154
ale, bottled, 160
    draught, 164
ambassadors, 7, 41, 153, 156
Anglo-Saxons, 5, 27, 149
antiquaries, 154
apostrophe (in street-names), 125
archery, 85, 114, 116
article, definite, 7
astronomers, 153f
Australia, 31f, 139f
Avenue (in street-names), 115
aviators, 118f, 158

back-formation, 6, 9, 41, 52
badgers, 33
Baptists, 123
Bassishaw Ward, 107
Bath & Wells, Bishop of, 69
Bedfordshire, 133
Berkshire, 135
Boulogne, 99
boundaries, 2, 13, 40, 68f, 85, 99, 137, 166
Bournemouth, 9
Brent, River, 32
Brill, The, 86
Buckinghamshire, 124
builders, 35, 124, 141f
buildings, 117
Burney, Fanny, 144

Canada, 139f, 155
candle-making, 35
Candlewick Ward, 36
canons, 23
Canute, 6, 53
caricaturists, 143
cartographers, 154
cathedrals, 121
causeways, 81
Celtic language, 5, 67, 73, 77
Celts, 5, 11f, 95
chapels, 37, 90, 121ff
charnel-house, 34
charters, 9, 62, 69
Chichester, Bishop of, 66, 128
China, 165
churches, 120ff
Circus (in street-names), 77, 117
Classics, 146ff
Close (in street-names), 115
communications, 151f
composers, 145f, 159, 163f
concert-halls, 24, 162
Conservative Party, 157
Constantine, Arch of, 68
Cornwall, 124
counties, 129, 154
county-towns, 129
Court (in street-names), 116
Cowper-Essex, Lt-Col, 136, 141

Craven, Lady, 27
Crawshay family, 39
Crescent (in street-names), 115
cricket, 68, 75, 161
Cripps, Sir Stafford, 156
Croft (in street-names), 115
crosses, wayside, 37, 42, 198

Danes, 6, 83, 88, 126, 149
Denmark, Anne of, 86
Denmark, George of, 43
Dickens, Charles, 149, 161
districts, administrative, 1
    postal, 15–17, Illus. 9
Domesday Book, 56, 76, 79, Illus. 1
Dorset, 134

Eleanor, Queen, 37
elements, place-name, 3ff, 8ff, 166ff
Elizabeth I, Queen, 60, 79
Empire, British, 139
End (in place-names), 39, 72
engineers, 154f
Eric, or Little by Little, 146
Essex, 6, 135
Ethiopia, 135, 138
Evelyn, John, 85
excavation, archaeological, 135
exhibitions, 43, 75f, 98
explosives, 86, 165

factories, 86, 88, 141, 147
fairs, 48, 69
fields, 47, 83, 112ff
flowers, 115ff
football, 25, 161
fords, 4, 12f, 38, 47, 67, 94
forests, 49, 82, 89, 116, 142
fortifications, 12, 26, 31, 53, 84, 137
French language, 7
friars, 25, 31, 107, 121f, 126

Gelling, M., 101
generals, 155ff
gentry, landed, 134ff
Gilbert and Sullivan, 163
Gloucester, Duke of, 93
    Earl of, 45
gods and goddesses, 146f, 165
goldsmiths, 126, 154
golf, 25, 161f
granges, 11, 72, 90, 100
Grove (in street-names), 115

hack-writers, 143
Hamilton, Lady, 71
hamlets, 1, 12, 53, 89, 93
Hampshire, 91
Henry V, King, 91
Henry VII, King, 81
Henry VIII, King, 61, 99, 126, 150
Hérold, Louis Joseph F., 164

Hertfordshire, 6, 109
Hill, Octavia, 153
hills, 10, 47, 57, 108
historians, 144, 154
hops, 125
hospitals, 28, 83, 87, 146, 161, 163, 165
Huguenots, 122f
Hundreds, 5, 28, 33, 47, 53, 69, 70, 127
hunting, 79, 86, 127

India, 138, 140
inns, 25, 47, 51, 82, 96, 143
Institutes, Mechanics', 160
interpretation, 3, 8, 13, 14, 28, 61
inventors, 154f
Isabella, Queen, 79

Jebb, Sir R., 93
Jerusalem, Knights of St John of, 50, 64, 83, 127
Jews, 37, 75, 123

Kent, 6, 80, 124, 135

Labour Party, 156f
landing-places, 3, 9, 36, 44, 48, 79, 88
Lane (in street-names), 115
Lara, Isadore de, 164
Lea, River, 6, 66, 70
leather-working, 106
lepers, 83
Liberties, 2f, 56, 57
Lithuania, 137
London, Bishop of, 42, 164
lunatics, 28

Malta, 136
manors, 10, 23, 27, 89f, 106f, 132
manuscripts, 153
markets, 58, 105f, 110, 112
Marshalsea Prison, 149
Mead (in street-names), 115
Methodists, 123, 146
Middlesex, 5
mills, 73, 91, 93, 117f
monarchs, 150f
monasteries, 23, 37, 41, 70, 90, 98, 121f
mosques, 121, 138
museums, 153, 165
musicians, 163f

names, derogatory, 51, 61, 71, 88
    field, 34, 40, 58, 61, 71ff, 88, 99, 111–15
    manorial, 7, 36
    personal, 4, 11, 67, 73, 78, 107
    place, 124, 127ff
    street, 13, 115ff
    trade, 118

tribal, 5, 6, 26, 80, 85, 94, 96, 101
Napoleon, 124
nobility, 130, 132ff
Normans, 7, 29, 76, 84, 99
novelists, 143ff, 148f, 152
nuns, 69, 74, 107, 112, 122

orphanages, 35, 160, 163

paganism, 3, 56f
painters, 64, 145, 147
palaces, 34, 81, 99f, 129
paladins, 147
Parade (in street-names), 117
parks, 32, 128, 132
Parthenon, 153
pastures, 26, 70, 97
Paul's Cathedral, St, 33, 74, 125
philanthropists, 30, 160f
philosophers, 146
physicians and surgeons, 93, 153, 160
picnics, 47
pillar-box, 152
pirates, 71
Place (in street-names), 117, 127
playing-fields, 37, 63, 69, 72, 128
playwrights, 146ff
poets, 143f, 147, 153, 155
politicians, 155ff
portages, 97
Powell-Cotton family, 135
prime ministers, 129, 130, 155f
prison-reformers, 160

queens, 32, 61, 80, 150

R.A.F., 157f
railways, 25, 73, 80, 95ff, 99, 157
Redemptorists, 126
Reformation, 28, 148
Rents (in street-names), 128
reservoirs, 96, 110
resorts, coastal, 131
Rise (in street-names), 108

rivers, 6, 9, 27, 41, 47, 52, 84, 108
Road (in street-names), 115
roads, 13, 27, 48, 55, 59, 71, 89, 93, 110ff
Robinson Crusoe, 145
Rochester, Bishop of, 126, 128
Roding, River, 6, 47
Romans, 46, 60, 89, 93, 149
Row (in street-names), 117.

saffron, 42
schools, 65, 128f, 131, 150f
scientists, physical, 154f, 159
social, 153
Scotland, 52, 130
Scott, Sir Walter, 149
sculptors, 98, 145
sequences, alphabetical, 159
numerical, 158f
Serpentine, 97
Shadwell, Thomas, 24
Shakespeare, William, 148
shape, 65, 75, 82
shepherds, 80, 85
shrubs, 116
silk manufacture, 34
snakes, 100
Sobieski, John, 137
soil, 12f, 87f, 108
Somerset, 130, 150
spas, 82, 87
springs, 36, 82, 84, 87, 99
Square (in street-names), 119f
Stein, Sir Aurel, 135
Stow, John, 83
Street (in names), 13, 115
Surrey, 5, 87, 141
Sussex, 91, 135

Tamburlaine, 135
Templars, Knights, 83, 91
temples, 3, 121
Terrace (in street-names), 117
Thackeray, William M., 149
Thames, River, 55, 109
theatres, 82, 162
Thorney, 98
Town (in place-names), 25, 47, 72, 79, 85, 115f
trees, 47, 72, 79, 85, 115f

Trollope, Anthony, 152
tumuli, 60
Tyrol, 93

umbrellas, 160
United States, 140f
universities and colleges, 128, 133, 152

Vice Versa, 152
Victoria, Queen, 80, 95
-ville (in place-names), 7, 77
Villiers, George (Duke of Buckingham), 164

Wagner, Richard, 164
Wales, 95, 132, 135
Walker, Rev. S., 124
Walpole, Horace, 89
Wandle, River, 36, 69, 77, 96
wars and expeditions:
Afghan, 138
American Independence, 140
Crimean, 137
India (Mutiny), 138
Napoleonic, 68, 93, 96, 136
Peninsular, 136
Roses, 98
Russo-Turkish, 137
Sikh, 138
South African, 136, 139
Spanish Succession, 136
Sudan, 138
Trojan, 147
World, I, 157
World, II, 157
Zulu, 139
Warwickshire, 134
Water Board, Metropolitan, 25, 72
water-cress, 36
Watering, St Thomas's, 71
Wellington, Duke of, 96, 155f
Wilde, Oscar, 165
Wolsey, Cardinal, 67, 99, 150
woodlands, 10, 77, 116

York, Archbishop of, 99, 130
York, Duke of, 24, 130f
Yorkshire, 81, 135